Putting Skills into Practice

Aspen Coursebook Series

Putting Skills into Practice

Legal Problem Solving and Writing for New Lawyers

DANIEL L. BARNETT

Professor of Law and
Director of Legal Writing
William S. Richardson School of Law
University of Hawai'i at Mānoa

Wolters Kluwer
Law & Business

Published by Wolters Kluwer Law & Business in New York.

Wolters Kluwer Law & Business serves customers worldwide with CCH, Aspen Publishers, and Kluwer Law International products. (www.wolterskluwerlb.com)

To contact Customer Service, e-mail customer.service@wolterskluwer.com, call 1-8-234-1660, fax 1-8-901-9075, or mail correspondence to:

Wolters Kluwer Law & Business
Attn: Order Department
PO Box 990
Frederick, MD 21705

Printed in the United States of America.

1 2 3 4 5 6 7 8 9 0

ISBN 978-1-4548-1821-2

Library of Congress Cataloging-in-Publication Data

Barnett, Daniel L., author.
Putting skills into practice: legal problem solving and writing for new lawyers / Daniel L. Barnett, Distinguished Professor of Legal Writing, Lewis & Clark Law School.
pages cm.
Includes bibliographical references and index.
ISBN 978-1-4548-1821-2 (alk. paper)
1. Law–United States–Methodology. 2. Legal composition. 3. Law–United States–Language. 4. Legal research–United States. I. Title.

KF250.B375 2014
808.06′634–dc23

2014011491

About Wolters Kluwer Law & Business

Wolters Kluwer Law & Business is a leading global provider of intelligent information and digital solutions for legal and business professionals in key specialty areas, and respected educational resources for professors and law students. Wolters Kluwer Law & Business connects legal and business professionals as well as those in the education market with timely, specialized authoritative content and information-enabled solutions to support success through productivity, accuracy and mobility.

Serving customers worldwide, Wolters Kluwer Law & Business products include those under the Aspen Publishers, CCH, Kluwer Law International, Loislaw, ftwilliam.com and MediRegs family of products.

CCH products have been a trusted resource since 1913, and are highly regarded resources for legal, securities, antitrust and trade regulation, government contracting, banking, pension, payroll, employment and labor, and healthcare reimbursement and compliance professionals.

Aspen Publishers products provide essential information to attorneys, business professionals and law students. Written by preeminent authorities, the product line offers analytical and practical information in a range of specialty practice areas from securities law and intellectual property to mergers and acquisitions and pension/benefits. Aspen's trusted legal education resources provide professors and students with high-quality, up-to-date and effective resources for successful instruction and study in all areas of the law.

Kluwer Law International products provide the global business community with reliable international legal information in English. Legal practitioners, corporate counsel and business executives around the world rely on Kluwer Law journals, looseleafs, books, and electronic products for comprehensive information in many areas of international legal practice.

Loislaw is a comprehensive online legal research product providing legal content to law firm practitioners of various specializations. Loislaw provides attorneys with the ability to quickly and efficiently find the necessary legal information they need, when and where they need it, by facilitating access to primary law as well as state-specific law, records, forms and treatises.

ftwilliam.com offers employee benefits professionals the highest quality plan documents (retirement, welfare and non-qualified) and government forms (5500/PBGC, 1099 and IRS) software at highly competitive prices.

MediRegs products provide integrated health care compliance content and software solutions for professionals in healthcare, higher education and life sciences, including professionals in accounting, law and consulting.

Wolters Kluwer Law & Business, a division of Wolters Kluwer, is headquartered in New York. Wolters Kluwer is a market-leading global information services company focused on professionals.

To Jerry, for being at the beach so early—and everything else;
To Ma, for a lifetime of encouragement;
And to the Janes in my life—Aunt Jane, Jane L., and Jane G.—
for always being there at exactly the right time.

SUMMARY OF CONTENTS

CONTENTS

ACKNOWLEDGMENTS

I owe special thanks to Professor Jane Kent Gionfriddo, Boston College Law School, and Jane Long, Esq., for their invaluable comments to the many drafts of this book. I would also like to thank Jane Long for permission to use the Agreement to Settle Claims and Transfer Property in Appendix 5. I also would like to express my gratitude for the suggestions and hard work from my research assistants, Stacy Du Clos and Elizabeth Blair. In addition, I would like to gratefully acknowledge the financial support of Lewis & Clark Law School and the Boston College Law School Fund. And, of course, I thank my editors and publishers at Wolters Kluwer Law & Business.

PREFACE

As a law professor specializing in legal writing for over 20 years, I have had many opportunities to consult with law firms and governmental agencies about writing—both developing writing training programs and training new lawyers myself. During those consultations, I was often surprised that the new practitioners seemed intimidated by their writing projects. Although they learned the fundamentals of legal writing in law school, many seemed to struggle to effectively use those skills during their first few years in practice.

I think this challenge may be due in part to changes in legal education over the last 20 to 30 years. As practice has become increasingly sophisticated, law schools have responded by adding new courses to teach additional areas of law and practice-oriented competencies. Although much of the first year is still spent on teaching students the basic proficiency to analyze and write about legal issues—both in subject matter courses and the legal writing class—the upper-level curriculum has changed focus. Many of today's advanced law courses are designed to teach students specialized areas of law and sophisticated practice skills through a variety of subjects and clinical experiences.

As a consequence, many of the basic writing skills lawyers use early in their careers are emphasized most in the introductory law school classes. Many students may not have an opportunity to practice them after their first year. These students are then placed in the ever-increasingly fast-paced work environment where the needs of the office dictate the assignments they receive. Rather than having the luxury of assigning new lawyers projects that would allow them to perfect their legal writing competence, senior colleagues are forced to delegate the work that must be completed, even if the projects may require more sophisticated analysis and writing than the new lawyers have encountered. The new practitioners themselves must learn to apply and adapt the basic foundational know-how from law school to complex problems while completing projects under intense time pressures. As a result, many new lawyers feel that their legal education does not immediately prepare them for their first tasks as practicing attorneys.

In an attempt to bridge that gap, many new practitioners turn to sample documents and guides that provide advice on polishing writing. Unfortunately, examples and advice on refining documents do not help them perfect the sophisticated analytical and writing elements necessary to complete complex legal documents. Instead, this type of guidance focuses writers on the form of the document and basic self-editing. But understanding different forms and learning how to edit final drafts—while important—are not sufficient to be a competent legal writer. In fact, when asked to identify the weaknesses of new colleagues' work, senior practitioners rarely identify either the lack of understanding different types of legal documents or the inability to edit final writing as the main problem. The criticism is much more fundamental: New practitioners' work does not provide a clear analysis of the problem because the writer has either ignored the questions assigned or the ideas are so hard to follow that the writing is not helpful.

Most often, the same deficiency is at the core of both problems: The writer has not fully figured out the underlying analysis. When writers do not have a full understanding of the foundational ideas, they often write around the precise topic, handling tangential questions that they do understand, rather than tackling the issue that they were asked to answer. Similarly, while their writing may not be grammatically or technically wrong, because they are unclear about the underlying analysis, their writing is confusing and hard to follow. To avoid these problems and effectively complete their writing projects, new practitioners need to develop the techniques necessary to fully analyze legal issues and clearly present those analyses in writing.

This book is designed to help law students and new practitioners develop those techniques by providing tangible and specific guidance on how to use the substantive knowledge and skills they acquired in law school to confidently complete their assignments early in practice. I think the best way to use this book is to quickly work through it chronologically, even though much of the information—especially in the earlier chapters—may seem like a review. Thinking about the fundamental tasks and analytical skills in the way that I describe them should help readers complete their initial projects efficiently and confidently. All readers should, of course, take the information that I provide and tailor it to develop the techniques that work best for them. But if readers spend time thinking about these ideas through the lens that I have set out, I think they will be able to use their analytical skills and substantive knowledge more proficiently and creatively as they work on their first projects in practice.

INTRODUCTION

The Lawyer as Writer: Applying Legal Writing Theory to Law Practice

Lawyers write. A lot. Although law practice involves many tasks, most of them require some type of legal writing. At the core of that writing is legal analysis. While the form of the documents may vary—from internal office memos or client letters to court briefs to transactional documents—all legal writing must be guided by the writer's understanding of the relevant law. Consequently, the essence of good legal writing is good legal analysis presented effectively.

To hone the skills to successfully develop and present legal analysis, new practitioners should recognize that legal writing—like all writing—is a process. In the mid-twentieth century, English composition scholars demonstrated that writing is much more than an end in itself. Instead, the very process of composing the final writing necessarily informs the ideas that are being expressed. Most writers go through several steps as part of the progression from generating an idea to the final expression of that concept. The legal writing academy has demonstrated that composition theory explains the way legal writers work through their writing as well.

Composition theory establishes that people process ideas differently. In legal writing, that idea simply means that each lawyer will develop a unique method when writing about the law. However, most lawyers generally go through the same basic stages when writing about legal analysis: the idea generation or brainstorming phase, the preliminary drafting step, and the presentation stage. For most legal writers, the line between the different stages is hard to delineate because the writing process is recursive: Most writers must move back and forth between the different phases. Often, as authors attempt to finalize the writing, they realize that they have not fully worked out some ideas and must move back to the earlier stages. Furthermore, most legal writers move from one phase to the other intuitively and may not be aware of the different stages of their own process.

Although the precise nature of the stages varies with each legal writer, understanding the general traits of the different steps should help most new lawyers recognize the progression necessary to examine and write about a legal issue. In the earlier phase of the process, most lawyers use writing to generate ideas as they brainstorm and evaluate different concepts that could be relevant in the analysis. Using the writing process to discover and determine relevant ideas is particularly important in legal writing where the author is trying to establish an accurate description of the law that governs the situation. The more the writer uses this stage of the writing process, the clearer those concepts usually become. During this early phase, the main focus of the writing is the writer him- or herself. The purpose of the writing is to help the writer come to a full understanding of the legal analysis rather than trying to explain that analysis to a reader.

Once the major ideas have been identified, most writers move to a drafting stage to shift the focus of the writing from the first stage—where the author uses the writing to develop an understanding of the analysis—to the second phase—where the focus of the writing is presenting the analysis clearly to the reader. This is the time when most writers begin to give form to the writing that will become the final document, although the initial drafts may not seem very presentable. Eventually, writers move to the final writing stage when most writers polish their writing, using self-editing and incorporating feedback on their writing from colleagues and others.

In this book, each of these phases of the legal writing process is explored in detail. Part I explains the idea-generation phase, where the lawyer must discover and evaluate the ideas necessary to handle the legal question. Part II focuses on the preliminary drafting stage, where the author moves from figuring out the necessary legal concepts to writing about them in whichever form the assignment requires. In this part of the book, the basic types of legal writing are discussed in detail, including internal office memoranda and other predictive documents, court briefs and other persuasive writing, and agreement drafting. Finally, in Part III, the final writing step is explored, including suggestions on clear writing, self-editing, and dealing with feedback from senior colleagues.

Putting Skills into Practice

PART I

ANALYSIS DEVELOPMENT

Generating and Evaluating Legal Ideas

CHAPTER 1

Analyzing Legal Questions

Most writers begin by brainstorming about the ideas they will explore in the writing. For legal writers, this step starts as soon as they hear about a client's situation. At that point, they immediately identify potential legal issues and possible avenues to resolve those issues. The process continues as they research the issues to locate the relevant law and begin to analyze what they find to evaluate the situation.

During this brainstorming stage, new practitioners often feel slightly overwhelmed: The more they learn about a question, the more issues they often uncover. And for each new issue, lawyers may identify several new avenues of exploration. Since almost any area of law is relatively unknown to most new practitioners, they may feel intimidated with all of the ideas they encounter during the brainstorming stage. Fortunately, this step does not last very long. Once the research leads lawyers to the relevant law, they begin to shift from brainstorming about possible questions to evaluating which of the issues should be dismissed and which ideas need more exploration based on the applicable law.

During these initial stages on their first projects, new practitioners need to review a few basics about handling legal writing projects for guidance. First, they should examine their note-taking methods to record their progression. They should also be sure that they fully understand the hierarchy of the relevant legal authority that governs the question. Finally, they should assess their basic research skills and consider the different analytical challenges they may encounter.

A. DEVELOPING EFFECTIVE NOTE-TAKING TECHNIQUES

During the initial writing stages, legal writers need a method to document the ideas they have considered and eliminated. These notes can take many forms, including rough outlines; quick summaries of the different sources of law they have considered; and charts or diagrams of what the law means and how the different pieces of the analysis fit together. As writers prepare these notes, they evaluate the different possibilities about what the authority adds to the relevant analysis. As they work from specific pieces of authority to the written observations, their understanding of the analysis is constantly tested and refined. Although the process may feel somewhat unwieldy at points, writers refine the analysis by sifting through all the brainstormed ideas to find the relevant concepts.

The form of these observations varies for each lawyer, so new practitioners must find a method that works best for them. Ideas and advice from others will help, but new lawyers must determine their own efficient approach to documenting progress on their projects. When considering the best method, while the main priority should be to find a technique that assists them in developing the relevant concepts, new legal writers must consider that their notes will have other uses as well.

For example, in most problems, lawyers probably will explore ideas from their research and analysis that lead nowhere, and they will need to retrace their steps to find more productive lines of inquiry. Thus, their notes should be detailed enough to give them a rough road map of their research path and preliminary analysis so they can retrace their steps quickly if necessary.

In addition, projects in law practice are often interrupted—sometimes for long periods. Detailed preliminary notes can help facilitate restarting projects so that the writers may avoid repeating large segments of their work. Similarly, new attorneys often encounter situations where they must pass their research notes to another lawyer who will finish the assignment. A thorough summary of the research path along with explanations about the ideas they have considered and rejected would be a head start for the lawyer taking over the project.

B. UNDERSTANDING WHAT LAW APPLIES: THE BASICS MATTER

As a legal writer begins to generate ideas about a legal question, the writer must understand what sources of law govern the issue. While this task of understanding the hierarchy of relevant law is quite basic, it is critical to determine the overall analytical framework of the question. Law students study this important step during the beginning of the first year, but it may not be emphasized again unless students enroll in an advanced legal writing or research class, or a clinical course.

But when completing projects in practice, understanding the hierarchy of authority is essential because lawyers must begin by determining what law applies. Often, when new lawyers feel stumped by a project, they can begin to unravel the problem by reconsidering this very basic question. Their first impression about the hierarchy of the relevant law may be incorrect or vague. As a result, they may not look for the correct authority, or they may not understand how the different types of authority relate to each other. Once they have an accurate understanding of the relationship of the different types of relevant law, they are able to use that accurate analytical framework to begin to work through the problem.

C. UNCOVERING THE ANALYTICAL FRAMEWORK: A REVIEW OF THE SOURCES OF LAW

Every time lawyers encounter a new legal issue, they must determine the different sources of law that apply and why. Those are basic ideas, but their understanding guides everything else the lawyers must do to answer the questions. Therefore, new practitioners must take the time to determine the law that applies to their particular situations and remind themselves where the relevant law fits in the hierarchical scheme of legal authority.

Thus, fundamental legal process concepts lead the lawyer's first steps. Given the federal nature of our legal system, the first determination is whether the issue is a federal or state question. Once that answer is established, the lawyer must find the relevant law of the jurisdiction. The federal constitution is the highest authority in the country, and each state constitution is the highest law for the respective state. If the question does not involve a constitutional issue, the next level of authority is statutory law, including relevant regulations, executive orders, and administrative rules and decisions related to the statute. Under state law, municipal ordinances may also apply. Finally, when statutory law does not govern the question, judicially created common law may apply.

While these basic principles often provide the relevant analytical framework, in many problems these concepts become more complex because a variety of different sources of law may apply. For example, a problem may involve both federal and state law. Additionally, a problem could include a statute with attendant regulations that answers part of the question. However, a provision of the statute may have been declared unconstitutional, leaving prior common law in place. In this situation, the lawyer would have to piece together constitutional, statutory, regulatory, municipal, and common law to understand the analytical structure of the problem. Similarly, in practice, the role of administrative law is more prominent than many new lawyers appreciate from law school. In many problems, regulations provide much of the relevant law. Therefore, new lawyers must fully understand the regulatory scheme, if any, relevant to their problems so they can find and use the necessary administrative law that applies.

1. Relevant Court and Regulatory Systems

Whatever the source of law that provides the analytical foundation of the problem—constitutional, statutory, regulatory, municipal, or judicially created common law—often the lawyer must reconcile different judicial or regulatory interpretations of the law to fully grasp its meaning. To reconcile those decisions, the lawyer must fully understand the relevant court system and regulatory scheme.

a. Review of the Court System

When dealing with judicial opinions, lawyers must be familiar with the structure of the different courts of the jurisdiction to understand the weight of authority of the cases. Most often, determining the level of authority of opinions is fairly simple because the basic hierarchy of the court system is the same in all jurisdictions. Decisions from the highest appellate court are binding on all lower courts in the jurisdiction. Intermediate appellate court decisions are binding on any lower courts over which the court has jurisdiction. On the federal level, the intermediate appellate courts—the United States Courts of Appeals—are organized geographically and have jurisdiction over the lower courts in their geographical "circuits." Some states organize their intermediate appellate courts in a similar manner, and decisions from the intermediate appellate court of the specific geographical area are only binding on the lower courts in that area. In other states, however, all intermediate appellate court opinions are binding on any lower courts in the state. The decisions of a court without authority over the lower court may be influential as persuasive authority, but they are not binding.

While the basic structure of the court system is simple to remember, how decisions from different courts affect a question can vary in complexity depending on the particular legal issue and area of law. For example, although federal cases dealing with state law questions may only be persuasive authority, some federal interpretations of state law may be very influential on the courts of the state. Furthermore, the court system itself may be more complex depending on the area of law. If a lawyer is dealing with a bankruptcy question for the first time, for example, the lawyer must understand the relationship between bankruptcy courts and other federal courts. Similar examples of these authority questions exist on the state level, as well.

b. Administrative Law

To fully grasp the authority of administrative decisions, the lawyer must understand the applicable regulatory scheme. While the details of those schemes vary, administrative agencies have two basic roles: rulemaking and adjudication. The rulemaking duty gives agencies the power to enact relevant rules and regulations, pursuant to statutory authority. The adjudicatory responsibility requires agencies to resolve disputes and sometimes to provide guidance regarding the legality of proposed actions. To fulfill these adjudicatory functions, agencies must interpret statutes, rules, and regulations.

The level of influence of regulatory interpretations depends on the agency and the area of law. Some decisions are binding on the future actions of the agency. Other interpretations are only advisory and—while not binding on future actions of the agency—provide important insights on the agency's view of the particular legal questions. In addition, some problems include judicial opinions and decisions from regulatory agencies interpreting the same source of law.

The level of authority of administrative interpretations and the relationship between the agency decision and judicial opinions can have an important impact on the ultimate meaning of statutes, rules, and regulations. For example, when handling federal tax issues, lawyers must understand how to find and use relevant Internal Revenue Code regulations, administrative decisions, and other written guidance from the Internal Revenue Service and the Treasury Department. They must also appreciate the role of cases from the United States Tax Court and decisions from other federal courts on tax matters. Many law students leave law school without studying federal tax regulations or other federal or state regulatory interpretations. Therefore, lawyers must be sure to become familiar with any relevant regulatory scheme when approaching the particular issue.

D. FINDING THE LAW: A QUICK REVIEW OF THE RESEARCH PROCESS

While a complete review of research techniques is beyond the scope of this book, a reminder of the basic steps should help new practitioners develop skills to research even the most complicated legal questions. To begin, when faced with a new problem, lawyers should use their own experience and knowledge to help brainstorm about the relevant research paths. In addition, asking senior attorneys how they would begin the project if they were doing the research may be a good resource, especially when dealing with a new area of law.

Using their own experience and advice from others, new practitioners should consider beginning with secondary sources that provide a short introduction to the area of law. If lucky, they may even locate a resource that provides a good summary of the analysis for their particular question. Although determining the best secondary source depends on the specific problem and jurisdiction, if lawyers find sources that deal specifically with the subject matter of the problem, they should probably use them before examining more general sources, such as a legal encyclopedia. Similarly, using a source that concentrates on the law of a particular jurisdiction may be more efficient than sources that are more general.

No matter where new practitioners begin the research, they must remember that they are responsible for finding and analyzing the law on their own.

Therefore, they need to be careful not to allow their preconceived notions or the information they have learned from senior colleagues overly influence their evaluation of the analysis. Similarly, they need to be careful not to excessively rely on secondary sources to sway their analysis. They must research and independently analyze all relevant primary authority.

As lawyers find the law through their research, they read and analyze the authority to determine if the law is relevant and complete. Therefore, the research process continues until they complete their projects. As their understanding of the question develops through the writing process, they may discover new ideas that they must research. However, they will likely find that the part of the process where they are uncovering new authority ends fairly early in the writing progression, and they will shift from focusing on finding the law to spending more time analyzing it. At this point, they need to use a citatory service—like Shepards or KeyCite—to verify that the authority is still good law and has not been superseded or overruled so that they do not waste time analyzing law that is no longer applicable. As a final step in the writing process, they need to repeat this step to verify that all of the authority they have relied on in the document is good law before they submit it.

E. USING THE LAW: WHAT TO EXPECT

As research uncovers the relevant authorities, the hard work of determining the meaning of the law begins. While the type of assignment will eventually affect how the lawyer uses the law—because supporting arguments requires lawyers to employ legal ideas differently than using the law to produce a predictive memorandum or drafting a transactional document—the first step in any project is to develop a solid, unbiased understanding of the legal concepts. Strategic choices about how to best use those concepts should only happen once the lawyer has a good, neutral grasp of the ideas. Therefore, lawyers should begin determining an objective analysis of the problem.

Most often, developing an objective understanding of the law requires the lawyer to reconcile many different pieces of authority. While the authority provides the parameters that control the question, those parameters are rarely explained in any one place. Thus, the analysis that governs the situation often is amorphous and may only be fully understood by reconciling ideas from a variety of legal authority.

The task of determining the meaning of the law varies in complexity depending on the legal problem. Generally, the more straightforward problems are state common law questions where the legal authority includes only a few cases from the state courts interpreting the common law issue, although some state common law questions can involve dozens of disparate cases, if not more, which are difficult to analyze and reconcile. Very complex problems will often include judicial and administrative interpretations of relevant statutes, administrative rules, and regulations. For example, a lawyer may be asked to analyze a federal securities law question that involves a federal statute and Securities and Exchange Commission rules and regulations. The lawyer may find federal appellate and trial court interpretations of those statutes and the rules and regulations, as well as interpretations by the Securities and Exchange Commission in administrative decisions and advisory letters. In all of these situations, the lawyer must find the meaning of the law by reconciling the group of interpretations.

As lawyers begin to confront their first projects in practice, having a sense of the types of analytical challenges that they may encounter when reconciling a variety of interpretations should help them handle different assignments. Some projects involve legal questions that are fairly well settled and therefore do not require much analytical work. Other assignments may involve questions of first impression that will require the lawyer to rely on persuasive authority to analyze the question. Most often, however, new lawyers deal with legal issues that are governed by binding primary authority with many interpretations and therefore require that they reconcile those interpretations to answer the question.

1. Problems Involving Clearly Decided Questions of Law

New practitioners will likely encounter problems where the law is clearly decided and thus reporting the answer will be fairly straightforward. Some questions involve an area of law where the primary binding authority fully explains the relevant ideas and the application of those concepts suggests a direct answer. For example, lawyers may find an applicable statute that fully defines the relevant terms necessary to answer the question. Similarly, they might find a statute that has ambiguous terms, but the relevant judicial decisions clarify the ambiguity.

While new lawyers may encounter problems with clear answers, such problems are typically easy to handle because the answer is so apparent. Often, they find a secondary source that answers the question. Other times, the primary authority itself is so clear that determining the analysis happens quickly. Similarly, while they may be asked to draft a memo documenting the analysis, the memo probably would be short and quick to prepare. Furthermore, these situations do not usually lead to litigation or protracted negotiations. Thus, while these types of problems are satisfying because the answer is so concrete, they typically do not take up the bulk of new lawyers' time.

2. Questions of First Impression

On the other end of the spectrum are questions of first impression. New lawyers may encounter newly enacted statutes or regulations without any clarifying interpretations or—although less common—new state common law questions.

To answer these types of problems, lawyers rely on canons of statutory construction and persuasive authority, including secondary sources and authority from other jurisdictions. Therefore, lawyers must understand the jurisdiction's rules on statutory construction, including the use of legislative intent and history, and have a sense of which persuasive authority might have more weight on the specific question.

Analyzing questions of first impression can be challenging and often involves judgments about what persuasive authority to use, which requires experience and a thorough understanding of the area of law. Thus, when new lawyers face this type of assignment, they should seek guidance from the senior colleague who assigned the project before proceeding very far. Before seeking that advice, however, junior lawyers must verify that the question actually is one of first impression. This process can be intimidating, especially when the question seems like one that should have more authority than the research process is uncovering. For example, there might be a statute that is several years old, but the lawyer's research does not find any cases interpreting it. However, the secondary sources indicate that courts in other jurisdictions with similar statutes have published many opinions interpreting those provisions. In such a situation, junior lawyers should methodically take all necessary steps to double check the research process. Once they are certain that the courts or regulatory agencies of the relevant jurisdiction have not dealt with the statute, they should ask the senior colleague for guidance before spending time analyzing persuasive authority.

Often, when senior lawyers understand that the issue involves a question of first impression, they will decide not to spend the client's money or the office's resources on an analysis of persuasive authority. Evaluation of persuasive authority in these situations may not help the lawyers provide specific advice to the client beyond explaining that the question is open in the jurisdiction.

However, if the matter is moving toward litigation, questions of first impression may be a critical part of the case. At that point, senior lawyers may ask for a full analysis of the issue based on statutory construction and persuasive authority. In those situations, the senior colleagues often have guidance about the best persuasive authority to use. They may feel that a particular commentator or the law of certain jurisdictions is most influential.

While new practitioners may not spend a lot of time handling these types of projects—unless they work in a specialized practice focused on appellate work—such assignments often are challenging and enjoyable. They usually require the lawyers to creatively use cases and other primary authority along with persuasive sources to develop and support their ideas.

3. Legal Issues Requiring Cross-Decision Interpretive Analysis

While new lawyers may occasionally encounter problems where the law is settled or questions of first impression, most projects that new practitioners receive early in practice involve questions with binding primary authority with several unclear judicial or regulatory interpretations. Therefore, new lawyers often spend the bulk of their time on projects that require the time-consuming tasks of finding and reconciling all relevant judicial and regulatory agency decisions to analyze the question. Sometimes the projects require reading and reconciling just a few decisions, but other times the assignment may involve many long and complicated decisions. In fact, the very reason these assignments are usually given to the junior lawyers is the time required to reconcile large groups of decisions. Although this is a complex skill, using the least expensive lawyers for the task is most efficient.

Because new lawyers spend so much time using interpretive analysis of cases and administrative decisions, the next chapter provides a thorough review of this process.

SUMMARY

New practitioners need to develop strategies to efficiently get started on their projects. To begin, lawyers must determine the relevant issues, research the relevant law, and develop the analysis that controls the situation. To work through this phase efficiently, new practitioners should take several concrete steps:

- Take good notes on brainstorming and research.
- Identify possible applicable law:
  - Understand different sources of law; and
  - Review applicable court and regulatory systems.
- Research the law.
- Use the law to handle different types of problems:
  - Clearly decided questions;
  - Questions of first impression; and
  - Issues requiring cross-decision interpretive analysis.

CHAPTER 2

Cross-Decision Interpretive Analysis

Mastering the skill of reconciling groups of judicial and regulatory decisions is critical for lawyers because it is required to analyze most legal issues. Even when statutes or regulations control a situation, courts and regulatory agencies often interpret those provisions. For a complete legal analysis, lawyers must examine the statutory and regulatory language as well as the decisions interpreting them. When common law controls, they must understand the full meaning of the relevant opinions as a group. Therefore, most legal questions require lawyers to reconcile relevant judicial or administrative decisions, or both. The term that I use to describe this reconciliation process is "cross-decision interpretive analysis," because it requires an analysis of all relevant interpretations by courts, administrative agencies, or other decision makers to find the true meaning of the law.[1]

Law students are introduced to cross-decision interpretive analysis early in law school, mainly focusing on common law during the first year as they study judicial interpretations. However, in practice, the problems that lawyers encounter are often more complex than the situations law students study in their foundational courses. Therefore, this chapter begins with a quick comparison of the types of problems used in law teaching and situations typically encountered in practice. The chapter then explores methods to help new practitioners hone the interpretive analysis skills necessary to handle complex legal questions.

1. I have expanded the term "cross-case reasoning" used by Professor Evensen and her colleagues to describe the skill that lawyers use to determine the meaning of unstated legal analysis from a group of cases. Dorothy H. Evensen et al., Developing an Assessment of First-Year Law Students' Critical Case Reading and Reasoning Ability: Phase 2 (Law School Admissions Council Grants Report 08-02, Mar. 2008) (available at http://www.lsac.org/docs/default-source/research-(lsac-resources)/gr-08-02.pdf?sfvrsn=2).

A. CROSS-DECISION INTERPRETIVE ANALYSIS IN LAW SCHOOL

In law school, the goal of most courses is to teach key legal principles rather than the interpretive process that decision makers use to develop those concepts. Therefore, casebooks often include judicial opinions because they provide a complete and explicit explanation of the court's process of reconciling precedent to decide the question. The students are challenged to understand what the explanation means by applying the explicit ideas to new situations through in-class hypothetical and exam questions, but the students usually are not required to read the precedent cases the court used to develop its explicit interpretation of the analysis. Even when students read a case and some of the earlier opinions the court relied upon to come to its decision, the casebook authors often select those precedent cases because they demonstrate a linear evolution of the analysis or demonstrate how the change of societal concerns affects the evolution of the law.

Therefore, law school casebooks may give students an incomplete sense of the law. Students sometimes finish the first year of law school thinking that judicial opinions are the principal source of law that governs most legal questions. Furthermore, students may believe that those opinions generally provide full and explicit explanations of the issues they analyze and that those analyses evolve through a linear progression. The reality is more complicated: Both courts and regulatory agencies interpret the primary authority that governs most day-to-day legal issues, and the thoroughness and development of the explanations in those interpretations varies. The interpretations may explicitly articulate a thorough explanation of the relevant analysis, and occasionally the analysis evolves in a clear, almost linear way. However, in practice, the variety of opinions and types of analyses that new lawyers encounter makes analyzing those decisions more complex.

B. CROSS-DECISION INTERPRETIVE ANALYSIS IN LAW PRACTICE

In practice, lawyers encounter problems that require cross-decision interpretive analysis of cases or regulatory decision, and sometimes both. Therefore, new practitioners must recognize the differences and similarities between judicial and administrative decisions, and understand the types of analytical challenges that arise when reconciling those decisions.

1. Comparing Judicial and Administrative Decisions

The exact differences between judicial opinions and administrative decisions depend on the jurisdiction and the area of law. In all jurisdictions, courts have the authority to interpret and apply the law. The concept of *stare decisis* governs, and the hierarchy of the jurisdiction's judicial system determines the precedential value of judicial opinions. The role of administrative decisions, on the other hand, is more nuanced. Depending on a variety of factors, agencies may not be bound by *stare decisis*. Therefore, regulatory decisions have different precedential weight than judicial decisions, both on administrative agencies and on courts. Furthermore, procedural rules are often less rigid in an administrative process than in court proceedings, and the decisions are generally less formal.

Therefore, when new lawyers face a question in an unfamiliar area of law that includes administrative decisions, they must invest the time to fully understand the value of the relevant administrative law to effectively use all applicable decisions. While administrative decisions may not have the same precedential weight as court decisions, lawyers generally use all judicial and administrative opinions related to a particular issue as guidance regarding the meaning of the relevant law. Although certain administrative decisions may not be technically binding or include formal explanations of their reasoning, their interpretations are often a good indication of how a future administrative body or court will interpret the same question.

2. Challenges of Cross-Decision Interpretive Analysis

Although judicial opinions and regulatory decisions have different influence on certain questions and may take a slightly different form, the analytical challenges for the lawyers reconciling both types of decisions are similar. Sometimes the analysis is comparable to the kinds of problems law students tend to see in law school courses—in which the law develops in a linear or rational manner, and they find language that explicitly explains the analysis. Thus, lawyers should always examine decisions to determine if the relevant opinions include explicit and complete explanations of the relevant analysis, similar to the types of cases they studied in law school. In addition, they must be prepared to encounter decisions that can only be understood through implicit ideas since many legal analyses do not evolve in a linear fashion, and many decisions do not fully explain the relevant analysis.

a. Explicit Analysis

In some situations, lawyers encounter legal problems with opinions that include an accurate explicit explanation of the relevant analysis. In these situations, the decisions explain the issue and articulate the legal principles to answer the question. The decisions apply those principles to the facts to support the result. Upon verifying that the articulated explanation of the legal principles accurately explains the results of the relevant decisions, the lawyers may then rely on the explicit language.

b. Implicit Analysis

The complete analysis in the majority of legal problems requires an understanding of what the decisions stand for implicitly because the applicable decisions do not completely and accurately explain the relevant analysis. The reason that many problems cannot be answered with explicit analysis is related to the way courts and regulatory agencies are required to resolve disputes. Most courts and agencies are not able to choose the problems they decide, and therefore the law develops according to the facts of the cases that happen to come before them. These problems often involve a handful of disparate fact patterns that the court or agency struggles to reconcile. In using the concept of *stare decisis*, the courts or agencies may have difficulty deciding which facts make cases similar and different. Furthermore, the questions that come before the court or agency may not be the best vehicles for a fully rational development of the law because the facts may be unique, or the cases may be very different. Accordingly, the law for most issues develops in fits and starts. Given this messy evolutionary process, it often takes a long period of time and many decisions before the law related to a particular issue develops in a complete, clear, and explicit way. Thus, lawyers faced with most problems must make sense of the group of decisions before any one opinion has fully clarified the issue. They can find the true analysis only through an understanding of what the decisions stand for implicitly. Although implicit analyses vary, there are general characterizations of the approaches that lawyers encounter.

1. Consistent Implicit Approach

In many situations, the opinions implicitly support a consistent approach for the issue, even though they do not provide explicit language regarding the question or only provide part of the explanation explicitly, in one or several decisions. Although lawyers must use ideas that can be found only by reading between the lines of the opinions, they are relatively confident of the implicit analysis because the pattern of the decisions confirms the unarticulated explanation. For example, lawyers could encounter a problem in which the courts find a requirement satisfied every time certain facts are present, but the decisions do not specifically say which facts are necessary. However, each time the facts are absent, the court finds the requirement unsatisfied. Even though no decision explicitly says that the facts are required, the lawyers would be comfortable explaining that the facts are necessary to satisfy the requirement. In this situation, even though the analysis may be implicit, the analysis is relatively clear. Therefore, the lawyers may need to determine a more full explanation than can be found in any one opinion, but the explanation will be fairly simple to develop and support because the pattern of cases consistently supports the explanation.

2. Inconsistent Implicit Approach

Lawyers also face problems that require implicit reasoning to explain the relevant analysis because the group of decisions includes opinions that seem to contradict each other. In some situations, lawyers may have to infer the reasoning to reconcile a group of decisions that includes opinions with contradictory explicit explanations. For example, a problem could include a set of decisions that explicitly state that certain facts are required to satisfy a particular requirement. However, another set of opinions may explicitly provide that different conditions are necessary to fulfill the requirement without explicitly rejecting the other decisions' approach or explaining the difference.

Similarly, some problems include decisions with inconsistent analyses that are completely implicit. For example, lawyers may encounter a problem where some decisions implicitly suggest that a particular set of facts is required to satisfy a requirement, while other decisions implicitly suggest that different facts are necessary.

These types of inconsistent analyses may indicate that the law is evolving, even though the case or agency decision does not clearly explain that the newer analysis has replaced an earlier approach. Courts and regulatory agencies may add or remove requirements or considerations in an analysis that were important in earlier decisions without stating that they are making such a modification or without explaining why the alteration is necessary. The evolution may be due to changes in the policy that initially supported one approach. As society changes, courts or agencies may find that the policy rationale for the initial approach is no longer relevant and thus they must modify the analysis. Alternatively, a policy shift may not be the cause of the change, but instead the courts or agencies may be refining their analysis. Often, as courts and agencies handle the same topic over time, they perfect their approach, even though the underlying policy concerns remain the same. Other times, a group of decisions may include opinions with explicit or implicit contradictory standards that cannot be explained by policy changes or chronological development of the analysis.

While an analysis that includes contradictory ideas may be an indication that a higher court or administrative body should intervene and answer the question, lawyers addressing these types of questions usually do not have the luxury of asking for such clarity. Therefore, they must make a judgment and infer the standard they think is likely to be the one that a future court or agency would use to answer the question. When making this judgment, they should choose the approach they would use if they were the person responsible for deciding the question. As a judge or agency would do, the lawyers would be required to apply the precedent to influence their final decision about an explanation of the topic. Thus, they would need to use the policy and, if possible, the pattern or chronology of the decisions to help make a final determination of the relevant analysis.

Despite their best efforts, making a final determination from contradictory decisions can be difficult. Therefore, lawyers should keep track of the different approaches because the differences may influence the final form of their analysis of the issue. If they are preparing an internal office memo or some other type of predictive document, they may need to include predictions and counter predictions because of the different possible analyses. If they are writing a court brief or other persuasive document, they may be able to develop creative arguments based on the different approaches.

3. Unique and Wrongly Decided Decisions

Lawyers sometimes must infer reasoning to explain why a group of decisions includes an opinion or opinions that appears contrary to the other decisions. Sometimes lawyers encounter an opinion that, at first, seems to suggest a different approach for the issue. However, upon a more careful evaluation of the decision, they determine that the opinion does not support a different analysis. Although the language of the opinion might seem to be a different or contradictory approach, the inconsistency may be because the case has a unique set of facts, even though the opinion does not explicitly explain that the unique facts made a difference in its analysis. The distinctive facts may require a different approach to the issue even though the decision is not rejecting the previous analysis. Thus, lawyers may infer that the opinion does not mean that the court or agency is rejecting the approach that the other decisions support, except in cases with the unique facts. Therefore, the opinion may simply indicate a maturing of the analysis to help deal with unique situations.

In addition, lawyers sometimes must conclude from the weight of the decisions as a group that one or more of the opinions is wrongly decided. For example, a group of opinions could implicitly support the idea that the court uses certain facts in a balancing test. However, a couple of opinions might explicitly reject the idea that these facts are important. Nonetheless, later decisions seem to continue to use the facts when evaluating the balance. Furthermore, the lawyers would find that the use of the facts in the evaluation appears justified given the stated policy goals in using a balancing test. Thus, they could infer that the weight of the authority strongly suggests that the decisions rejecting the use of the facts in the balancing examination are wrongly decided. In this situation, they would discount those cases when making a final determination about the relevant analysis.

Once lawyers understand the types of challenges they may face with cross-decision interpretive analysis, they must develop a technique to work their way through a group of opinions to accurately and efficiently determine that analysis.

C. A METHOD FOR CROSS-DECISION INTERPRETIVE ANALYSIS

Law school introduces students to cross-decision interpretive analysis in a variety of ways, although some new lawyers may not be able to identify the specific process they learned. Many students acquire the process by osmosis because law school courses may not methodically outline the techniques. In fact, absorbing such analytical skills is the point of many of the teaching tools used in law school, including the so-called Socratic Method. Rather than describing a methodical approach to work with cases, students read a variety of opinions, and then their professors challenge them to "reason" their way through new hypothetical questions. Even though students are learning how to reason like a lawyer, they may not be able to explain a method behind the reasoning process in a way that allows them to identify and rely on all the steps they are taking each time they analyze a group of cases. Identifying those steps will help lawyers reconcile any group of decisions relevant to a legal question.

To begin, lawyers must understand that the process of reconciling a group of decisions often requires them to uncover several layers of analysis. Therefore, the method of putting together the relevant analysis is something like completing a jigsaw puzzle of concepts. The best way to approach this process depends on the problem itself and the personality of the individual lawyer. Generally, however, lawyers approach these problems like jigsaw-puzzle enthusiasts approach their puzzles. Some like to begin randomly with whichever two pieces fit together and complete the puzzle from that point. Others systematically find each edge piece of the puzzle and have the entire border completed before attempting to work on the rest of the puzzle. Most, however, use a combination approach. They begin by finding as much of the border as possible, but if a few pieces happen to fit together outside the border, they work on that part of the puzzle for a while. When they are stuck, they go back to completing the border.

This combination strategy is probably the best way for most new lawyers to approach their first assignments. They should begin with the "border" of the legal question by determining the relevant sources of law that govern the question and the basic analytical framework of the analysis. Once they have a fairly good understanding of these steps, they need to develop the different pieces of the analysis, while keeping in mind that they may need to reevaluate the overall analytical framework as their understanding of each part develops.

For example, a problem might involve a statute with a one-word element that must be satisfied, but the statute or relevant regulations do not define the term. In this situation, the courts of the jurisdiction have interpreted the term. In their interpretation, the courts determine that there are several requirements for the one-word statutory element to be satisfied. To answer the question, lawyers would have to identify the term from the statute and then, using all of the relevant interpretations, establish that the court is using a three-step test for the element and determine the meaning from each of the three steps.

Thus, when lawyers begins to reconcile a group of decisions, they should most often begin by sorting the decisions by level of authority. Then, they should work through the opinions with the goal of determining the overall approach. Once they have a fair understanding of the overall structure of the analysis, they must go back through the decisions to figure out the different pieces of the analysis.

Appendix 1 illustrates the process of reconciling a group of decisions by applying the methodology discussed in this part to a specific legal question.

1. Sort Decisions by Level of Authority

Once lawyers are ready to work through the decisions as a group, if the problem involves decisions with different levels of authority, they should consider organizing the decisions based on those levels of influence to help determine the weight of each opinion in the reconciling process. Although lawyers do not always work through the cases based on the level of authority, developing a technique that easily reminds them about source of the different opinions often helps make the process more efficient and accurate. If the problem includes only judicial opinions, they should keep track of the cases by court and date, though they may analyze the cases together, moving back and forth between lower and higher court opinions.

If the problem includes judicial and administrative decisions, they should consider separating the judicial opinions from the regulatory decisions. Often, when working on problems with both judicial and administrative decisions, analyzing the decisions by category will help to quickly uncover differences between them that may be significant in evaluating and making judgments about the final analysis.

2. Determine the Overall Structure of the Analysis

The first step in reconciling a group of decisions is to determine the overall analytical framework. Lawyers must identify what the different subparts of the analysis are and the role each piece plays. Is there a checklist of requirements? Or a threshold requirement with several attendant considerations? Or does the analysis balance a variety of considerations together or on a sliding scale of some kind?

When trying to establish the overall analytical approach, lawyers must anticipate possible changes as the analysis matures in the decisions over time. Because the law evolves in this way, they should have a good sense of the overall analysis before delving into the different pieces of the analysis.

Otherwise, they might spend time on a piece of the analysis, only to determine later that the issue is no longer relevant or not being used in the same way.

The best way to find the overall structure is to quickly read all of the decisions together to determine the different steps of the analysis and the overall policy that drives it. Lawyers should consider using a flow chart, diagram, or some kind of written outline to keep track of the ideas found when working through the decisions to find the overall structure.

a. Choose the First Opinion to Read

When reading the decisions to establish the overall approach, deciding which opinion to read first is often a hard call. One tactic would be to read the most recent decision that has the highest level of authority. For example, if the decisions include cases, lawyers could begin with the highest appellate court of the jurisdiction. However, the most recent decision—even a decision with the highest level of authority—may not provide the most complete picture of the overall analysis. Therefore, beginning with the decision that seems most central to the analysis is usually best. Often, lawyers will have a sense from the research process—either from a relevant secondary source or skimming the decisions—that a couple of cases or particular administrative decisions seem central to the analysis. If so, reading those decisions first may be more efficient.

Whatever decision lawyers choose, they should keep in mind that it is only one decision of a group. As just the first piece of the puzzle, the framework it suggests may be inaccurate. Thus, they must not become convinced of the overall approach suggested in the first opinion until they have verified it on the decisions as a group.

b. Verify the Overall Analysis on the Group of Decisions

After reading the first decision, lawyers should check the overall approach from that decision against the other opinions. At this point, they are trying to identify any shifts in the structure of the analysis. Jumping directly to the most recent decision—no matter what the type of decision or level of authority—is often a good method to quickly uncover changes in the overall analysis. If the decisions have modified the overall structure, contrasting an older central decision with the most recent one should help them uncover the change, even if it is subtle.

After comparing the major decisions with the most recent ones, lawyers should work through all of the decisions in either chronological or reverse chronological order, possibly by type of decision and level of authority, to verify that overall framework. If the decisions change the approach, reading the decisions in chronological order should help them quickly identify that modification and understand the reasons for it.

Even when the overall approach seems clear, lawyers should not be fully convinced of the overall structure of the analysis. In many problems, they will only be able to complete an understanding of the different pieces of the analysis and how they relate to each other by fully developing an analysis of all of the components. Thus, they should verify a basic understanding of the overall structure, but be open to changes as they work on each subpart.

3. Analyze Components of the Analysis

Once lawyers have a basic sense of the overall structure of the analysis, they must determine the analysis of each subpart. To accomplish this task, they must go back through the opinions and focus on how the various decisions handle the different components. They must decide how each subpart is used and why. These determinations are important because the lawyers must ultimately develop an explicit or implicit explanation from the group of decisions for each component and determine the reasoning or policy that supports each part of the analysis. Therefore, they should consider using a chart or some kind of note taking for each part of the analysis. Using those notes, they will be able to find and verify explicit explanations of the subpart from the opinions, develop an implicit analysis regarding the question from the decisions, if necessary, or deal with opinions that handle the issue inconsistently.

a. Isolate Relevant Portions of the Decisions

For each component of the analysis, lawyers should consider using a chart to help reconcile the ideas from the opinions relevant to the topic. Another technique is to make margin notes in the decisions themselves to identify the portions of the opinion relevant to different parts of the analysis. Whichever method is chosen, the technique must allow the lawyers to isolate the relevant portions of the decisions for each topic and quickly refer back to those sections. Furthermore, the technique must help them restart work on the analysis after possibly long hiatuses because work on projects is often interrupted in practice settings.

Lawyers should divide the topic-specific chart or notes by decisions grouped together by level of authority in chronological order, or reverse chronological order, to help keep track of the different decisions. The decision name, court or agency, citation and date should be included for each decision. In addition, they should add to the chart the facts for the specific issue. Isolating the facts for the topic that were included in the decision will help them reconcile the meaning of the different opinions.

The chart also should include the result of the specific issue in the decision. If the issue is a requirement, was it satisfied? If it was a consideration, did the decision use the consideration and rely on it? Determining the result may not always be clear because sometimes decisions do not specifically state or explain the result on each issue. Nevertheless, listing the result in the chart is important when using the chart to develop an understanding of the analysis for the topic, even if the result is not completely certain.

Finally, the chart should include all the explicit language in the decision, if any, relevant to the topic. This step requires lawyers to work through each opinion and isolate any relevant explicit language. When adding that language to the chart, they should use quotations and relevant page number or other location references as a reminder that the language comes directly from the opinion. The range of what they may find in each decision is very broad: They may find no explicit language or may find complete paragraphs.

Once lawyers have developed a chart of all the decisions regarding a topic, they are ready to begin the process of reconciling the decisions to figure out the analysis. The chart will help to determine if the decisions have provided an accurate explanation for the issue explicitly. If not, the chart will help them develop the implicit analyses or identify inconsistent and wrongly decided cases.

b. Identify Explicit Analysis

As discussed in Part B of this chapter, decisions sometimes explicitly explain the analysis for a particular issue. If lawyers find accurate explicit analysis, they should rely on that language when dealing with the question. To determine if the opinions include an accurate explicit analysis, they should identify explicit language and verify if the language is an accurate expression of the analysis by testing that the decisions as a group support the explicit explanation.

1. Locate Explicit Explanations

If lawyers have completed a chart of the decisions for the relevant component of the analysis, finding explicit explanations is usually straightforward. They simply review the chart to see if language from any opinions seems to explain how the court or agency handled the issue. If so, they should verify those explanations on the decisions as a group to determine their accuracy.

2. Verify Explicit Explanations

To verify an explicit explanation on the group of decisions, lawyers must be convinced that the language explains the result for the topic in each decision. Sometimes this task is not difficult because the decisions include the same, or somewhat similar, explicit language in each opinion to explain the resolution of the issue. If most of the decisions use similar language to explain the issue and the language seems to justify the results in the opinions, they should be confident that the decisions as a group verify the explicit language as an accurate explanation.

Other times, the verification process will be more challenging. Although one or more decisions may include explicit language, other opinions may not use that language to explain the result. In this situation, the lawyers' task is to take the explicit language found in one or a few of the decisions and test it on the opinions that do not have a clear explanation to see if the explicit language explains the result of the decisions without an articulated explanation. If the explicit language from some opinions explains the result on the issue in decisions with no explicit explanation, they should be relatively confident that the decisions as a group support the explicit explanation.

Similarly, if different opinions use different language to explain the result, lawyers need to check if the different explanations are simply different expressions of the same idea by testing the variations of the explanation on the decisions as a group. If the group of decisions verifies more than one of the explicit explanations as accurate, they should choose the explanation that seems to express the idea most clearly.

Sometimes the verification process will suggest that the explicit language does not seem to work as an explanation. Different opinions may include contradictory language or inconsistent explanations of the same issue. Different explanations may be an indication that the analysis is changing, even though the decisions may not fully indicate such a modification. Similarly, the verification process may show that the explicit language from the opinions does not seem to explain the result in many of the decisions with no explicit explanation, so lawyers would have a sense that the analysis includes something that is not articulated explicitly in any of the opinions. In both of these situations, lawyers will have to use the decisions as a group to infer the true analysis.

c. Determine Implicit Analysis

If the decisions do not explicitly provide an accurate and complete explanation of the issue, lawyers must infer the explanation from the decisions as a group. To develop an implicit analysis, they must use their own words that are reasonably supported by the decisions. Often, they must infer the complete explanation from the opinions because they do not include any relevant language at all. Other times, they may need to infer only part of the explanation because the decisions may include some helpful language. In both situations, the lawyers will only be able to determine the full and correct analysis by reading between the lines of the decisions and inferring the relevant analysis from the decisions together. To develop such an implicit analysis, they must come up with potential explanations and verify them on the decisions as a group.

1. Brainstorm Possible Implicit Explanations

The first step to infer a reasonable explanation is to brainstorm ideas about possible explanations. To guide this process, lawyers must use the relevant facts and results and any explicit reasoning in the decisions. To begin brainstorming, they should study the chart or notes from the decisions for ideas from the patterns and policy. For example, they may see that a certain set of facts seems to be present when a court finds a requirement satisfied, but absent in the cases where the court decides that the requirement has not been satisfied. Similarly, they may see that certain facts are present when the court decides that a particular consideration influences its analysis. Lawyers should use these patterns to brainstorm possible explanations. In addition, the policy that the court has articulated may help them hypothesize possible explanations for a specific issue.

2. Verify and Refine Possible Explanations

Once lawyers have determined a possible explanation, they must check it on the decisions as a group, just as when decisions explicitly articulate an analysis as explained in Part C.3.b.2 above. To verify the potential implicit explanation, they should determine if the proposed explanation explains the results of the decisions in the relevant group of opinions. Therefore, they must take the hypothesized explanation and determine if it appears to provide the missing explanation in the decisions.

When developing an implicit explanation, lawyers should consider beginning the verification process by first testing the proposed explanation on the decisions where the court determined that the topic was satisfied or, if the analysis includes some type of balancing analysis, the decisions where the consideration positively influenced the outcome. As lawyers test the proposed explanation on these decisions, they will often realize that they need to revise the initial brainstormed explanation to successfully explain the results of all of the decisions.

As lawyers revise the explanation and begin to feel that the amended proposed explanation seems to be working, they should move from these positive decisions to the opinions where the requirement was not satisfied or had a negative effect on the determination. Moving from decisions that came to a positive result on the topic to decisions with a negative result often helps them see more clearly the changes that need to be made to the proposed explanation so that it works on the decisions as a group.

When developing implicit explanations lawyers will rarely find a "bull's-eye" answer or just one explanation that works, since no decision has articulated the explanation itself. Rather, they will likely determine that the decisions taken as a group support a range of reasonable explanations. The number of different explanations will vary from problem to problem. The range of reasonable explanations often becomes more limited as the number of relevant decisions increases because the fact patterns that support the different explanations will likely be more restrictive. On the other hand, in problems with just a handful of relevant opinions, the smaller group of decisions may support a broader range of reasonable explanations. While the range may be somewhat broad, all problems include explanations that are clearly wrong and outside the range of reasonable explanations.

d. Working with Contradictory Opinions

In most situations, the verification process will uncover either an explicit explanation or an implicit explanation that tests back on the group of decisions as a reasonable analysis. However, as explained in Part B of this chapter, lawyers should be prepared to face situations where the verification process reveals that one or more decisions are unique or are decided incorrectly.

At times, the verification process may uncover a decision that does not confirm the lawyers' understanding of the explicit or implicit explanation. However, they decide that the outlier opinion does not change what the explanation should be. For example, they may decide that the decision has such unique facts that it would not alter the analysis supported by the other decisions.

In other situations, the lawyers' process may uncover a decision that the court or agency seemed to have decided incorrectly. If they find that most of the opinions seem to use a consistent approach, but another decision or two uses a different analysis, they may decide that the weight of authority confirms the approach used by most of the decisions. Similarly, sometimes the overall policy may confirm that a decision falling outside the lawyers' understanding of the analysis is wrongly decided.

In these situations, lawyers will have to make a judgment about how to use the decision because the answer may not be completely clear. Often, they will need to discount the unique or wrongly decided decision when using the opinions to determine the final analysis, either explicit or implicit.

D. HANDLING LEGAL AMBIGUITIES

During the idea-generation stage, legal writers must move from brainstorming and evaluating ideas relevant to the analysis to finding the most effective use of those ideas, utilizing their neutral understanding of the underlying analysis and the predictive, transactional, or persuasive purpose of the document as a guide. Because most writing assignments given to junior colleagues involve legal analysis that requires them to analyze a group of decisions—judicial or administrative or both—that interpret the legal question, new lawyers need to reflect on how to handle the analytical challenges typically found in these types of problems in different types of documents.

In particular, new lawyers must be prepared to handle legal ambiguity because most analyses require interpretive analysis of decisions with unclear or inconsistent ideas. The specific type of document will principally control how they ultimately explain those ambiguous ideas. The different types of legal writing will be discussed in detail in later chapters. However, understanding the different possibilities in various types of documents should assist new legal writers to quickly develop techniques to refine their understanding of analytical concepts, no matter what the form of their first assignments.

When preparing a predictive memo or drafting an agreement, new lawyers often can only fully appreciate the underlying analysis if they evaluate the strengths and weaknesses of potential arguments. Understanding how the underlying analysis would support arguments often uncovers subtle nuances that they did not first consider when determining their neutral analysis. Similarly, to effectively draft arguments, new lawyers should fully understand the analysis they would include in a predictive memo so they will be able to identify and fully support the best arguments based on the underlying law.

Therefore, when assigned their first projects, new legal writers should spend time considering how they might handle various issues in different types of documents. Although they will not take all the necessary steps to finalize those different documents, spending time considering how they would use the analysis in another type of document will often help them refine their understanding of the ideas and more successfully explain those concepts in their assignment.

Appendix 2 illustrates how lawyers could handle the analytical challenges of a legal question requiring cross-decision interpretive analysis in different types of projects.

SUMMARY

Many assignments that new lawyers handle early in practice require them to use cross-decision interpretive analysis. They should take several concrete steps to analyze such problems quickly and efficiently so they will be ready to use the preliminary drafting phase to use that analysis as the foundation for the specific document they have been assigned:

- Appreciate the nature of cross-decision interpretive analysis in law practice.
  - Consider different types of decisions: judicial or administrative.
  - Understand explicit versus implicit analysis.
- Use techniques to work through problems requiring interpretive analysis.
  - Sort decisions by level of authority and date.
  - Determine the overall structure of the analysis.
  - Analyze each component of analysis.
- Think about how various analytical challenges affect different types of projects.

PART II

THE DRAFTING STAGE

Moving from Generating Ideas to Presenting Them

CHAPTER 3

Using the Preliminary Drafting Stage: Understanding the Writing Process

Once legal writers have completed the initial steps to develop the underlying analytical concepts, they are ready to begin drafting their documents. During this preliminary drafting stage, writers generally use the writing process to perfect their grasp of the ideas so they can accurately explain the legal analysis ideas to the reader. To attain this goal, lawyers use their writing to move from a basic understanding of the concepts to the sophisticated analysis necessary to analyze most legal problems.

Legal writers generally begin this phase by moving from preparing rough notes—charts, diagrams, or other written observations—to writing the analysis in descriptive form, allowing idea development to be the concentration of the writing process. As their understanding advances, the focus of their writing shifts from developing ideas to expressing them clearly.

During this phase, the presentation of the document should not overtake refinement of the analysis. If writers concentrate on stylistic and format changes too early, that focus may hinder their ability to develop a complete understanding of the ideas. Often, as legal writers refine their ideas, they realize that they had not fully grasped all relevant analytical nuances, and they need to shift back to developing the concepts, possibly undertaking more research or brainstorming about the analysis. After reworking the ideas, they can move back to perfecting the presentation. To nimbly make these shifts, most legal writers should wait to put the final polishing touches on a document until they are confident about their understanding of the analysis.

While experienced legal writers have developed effective drafting-stage strategies, new lawyers generally need to find their own methods to use the phase efficiently. To develop useful techniques, they should begin by considering their own individual learning style. Using that information, they will be able to develop approaches to deal with writer's block and learn to collaborate with colleagues who have different learning styles and writing techniques.

A. DIFFERENT TYPES OF WRITERS

Researchers have documented the differences between visual and auditory learners and how left- or right-brain dominance affects the thinking process. Similarly, they have shown variations between sequential and intuitive thinkers. There is a variety of other differences about how people work with ideas. In writing, these variations often manifest themselves on a fairly basic level: Some people need to outline before they can begin the drafting stage, while others prefer to begin writing even if their ideas are not completely developed, allowing their ideas to flow spontaneously through the writing itself. Most writers use a combination of outlining and spontaneous writing to begin drafting their documents.

1. Outline-Reliant Writers

Writers who tend to begin the drafting stage with an outline generally need a complete understanding of how all of the ideas fit together before they feel comfortable writing the document. Therefore, much of the difficult work of determining how concepts relate takes place mentally as they translate their rough notes into an outline. Once they work through the different ideas and their relationships, the outline provides a fairly thorough plan for the document, which may allow them to complete the actual writing fairly quickly. However, legal writers who favor outlines face a couple of challenges when moving from generating ideas to writing about them: They can get stumped if they do not have a complete understanding of the relevant analysis from their notes, and they may be less willing to use their writing to revise and perfect their understanding of the relevant ideas. Therefore, outliners need to learn to develop different approaches to handle these challenges.

If outline-reliant writers find themselves spending a lot of time reworking the rough notes or outlines instead of writing the actual document, they probably are struggling to understand the relevant ideas or their relationship to each other. To help move beyond this block, they may need to use a method to force themselves to use their writing to help develop ideas. The outline and notes may be too succinct to allow the flexibility to experiment with different formulations of the concepts to fully understand the analysis. Using writing to help work through ideas may feel foreign to outline-dependent writers, but the technique can often help overcome analytical roadblocks.

One technique is to annotate the outline by adding quick narrative explanations of relevant ideas in rough paragraph form. By using annotations in their outlines, writers are frequently able to revise and expand the outline to the point they feel comfortable to begin drafting the document. In fact, as they begin writing, they may find that full paragraphs of the annotated outline will fit into the final document.

The technique is most effective if writers do not force themselves to work through the outline in chronological order. Rather, they should add annotations to the ideas they understand best, wherever they fall in the outline. Developing these concepts first will often help clarify their relationships to the other ideas on the outline. Those connections frequently improve the understanding of all the pieces of the analysis, including the ideas that were most elusive. Furthermore, these insights may show writers that they should organize the outline differently. As they move ideas around, the analysis may become clearer to them.

Another challenge for outliners is to be flexible once they begin writing. Sometimes they struggle to develop ideas not included on their original outline, even if the writing process suggests that those ideas are relevant. An approach that can assist outliners handle these situations is to keep track of the new ideas separately, rather than trying to fit them into the document itself. As these new ideas arise, writers should add them to a list to be revisited. The key is that writers should not feel that reconciling the idea or its relationship to the rest of the document is necessary at the time the item is added to the list of unclear concepts. Rather, they should plan to reconsider all the undeveloped ideas after working through the document pursuant to the original plan. Simply adding the concepts to the list will help ensure that the idea is not lost and will allow them to come back and continue to work on the concept before finalizing the document.

When adding ideas to that list, writers should try to include a quick narrative—more than just outline-type notes—about what the ideas seems to suggest and where they might fit in the overall analysis. By including these short descriptions separately from the document—but at the time the writing process uncovers them—writers may begin to expand the ideas, without the constraints of the document or the outline.

Writers should refer back to the unclear ideas after preparing an initial draft of the document. Frequently, they will decide that an idea is not ultimately relevant or that they addressed the issue somewhere else in the document. Other times, they may realize that some of these additional ideas are critical to the analysis and must be more fully developed and incorporated into the final document.

2. Spontaneous Writers

Writers who generally write more spontaneously are inclined to use writing itself to find the framework of the ideas and develop their meanings. Rather than outlining a plan before drafting a document, they tend to let the ideas to flow onto the page however they come because they use the writing itself to determine the best organization. They understand, however, that they often need to perfect the organization and expression of ideas as they move through the drafting stage. Just like outline-reliant writers, spontaneous writers have some challenges they need to understand to use their writing process effectively.

The main challenge for spontaneous writers is ensuring that they do not submit their writing as final until they have adequately edited their work to verify that the ideas are clearly expressed to the reader. This step is particularly important when faced with the time pressures of law practice. Spontaneous writing can sometimes give authors a false sense of security that they have fully explained all the necessary ideas because the document itself appears to be finished. However, since such writers use their writing to process through organization and different concepts, the writing may not be complete, even though the document looks like a final product. If possible, spontaneous writers should schedule time after they think the writing is final to review it before submission. After this hiatus, they will be better able to check their work to be sure the ideas are expressed clearly to the reader in the most organized fashion.

During this review, spontaneous writers need to carefully verify that they have expressed the ideas clearly and in a logical progression for the reader. Often, spontaneous writers work their way to the best articulation of an idea as they write about it. The earlier drafts frequently require editing because that working-out process may not be the best way to present the ideas to the reader. Often, the clearest expression may be buried in the end of a section when the reader would benefit from that explanation much earlier in the writing.

Similarly, earlier drafts may not have good introductory sections or connections between ideas. Spontaneous writers may be unsure how the different ideas relate as they flow into the writing. When writers do not fully understand the relationship of the overall concepts as they begin drafting, connections and transitions may appear at the place where they figure them out, rather than the location that would be best for the reader.

To help ensure that they have presented a logical progression of ideas with introductory sections and transitions between the key concepts, spontaneous writers often benefit from outlining their own writing. A good tool is to prepare an outline by simply using the introductory sections and key topic sentences as verification that these important elements are clear to the reader. When taking this step, writers should rely only on the writing itself—just as their readers will have to do—so they do not imply the ideas from their own understanding of the problem. By depending solely on the writing to develop a quick outline, writers may quickly uncover problems with organization or lack of introductions and transitions.

Taking this outlining step can help spontaneous writers revise their work by moving key concepts to the beginning of sections and adding the necessary introductions and transitional ideas as they move from one concept to the next. In many situations, they will have already worked out these connections so that all they need to do is some quick editing to be sure the connections are highlighted in the best place for the reader. At other times, they may discover that they have not fully explained—or figured out—what those connections are and need to continue to work on developing some of the ideas so the connections are clear to them and eventually their readers.

Another challenge for spontaneous writers is keeping track of ideas that need further exploration. Often, writing about one part of the analysis will inspire ideas that relate to a different part of the document. Practitioners need an efficient and reliable reminder system to keep track of these new ideas because they rarely have the luxury of completing an assignment in one sitting.

The system could be as simple as keeping a list at the end of the document of new ideas that the writing process generated and a quick road map of ideas when they are interrupted to jog memory of the ideas they were planning to discuss. In addition, writers can bracket or highlight areas that need further attention. Whatever method writers choose, they must be disciplined about using it so the ideas that the writing process generates are not lost.

3. Combination Writers

Most legal writers use a combination of outlining and spontaneous composing to complete their projects. These combination writers intuitively move back and forth from outline to descriptive writing, using both techniques to develop and organize the ideas. But even these writers could benefit from a review of the strategies for outliners and spontaneous writers because they may tend to favor one technique over the other. Furthermore, they may need assistance when faced with a complex problem that challenges their own writing method. If writers have experimented with a variety of approaches before they are tested by such a challenge, they should have strategies that will help them work through the obstacle.

In addition, although combination writers are usually comfortable using their writing to work through ideas even if they do not have a complete outline of their writing plan, as they move to the finishing stages of their writing, they may have difficulty allowing themselves to develop new ideas that their writing generates. They may resist expanding a new line of inquiry when it upsets the final appearance of their document. At this point, these writers should consider using other documents in addition to the final work product to help use their writing to work through these new ideas. By using separate documents that are not constrained by the final presentation, they may feel more liberated to use writing to develop ideas, no matter how inelegant the writing might be. Then, they can pick and choose the helpful parts of the process writing and incorporate those pieces to develop and finalize the presentational document.

B. WRITER'S BLOCK IN LEGAL WRITING

Generally, writer's block is understood to apply to creative writers who struggle to find inspiration to create and develop their ideas. In legal writing, writers are not describing original ideas, but rather using concepts from legal authorities to explain the law or make arguments. However, most legal writers will eventually face a legal issue with ideas that puzzle them so much they are unable to find a path out of the analytical morass no matter how much they study the underlying authority. Although the source of this problem may not be lack of creative inspiration, it causes the same result: The writer is unable to complete the writing. Fortunately, many of the same techniques that help creative writers overcome writer's block often help legal writers when they feel stymied by a problem.

1. Free Writing Exercises

One effective technique is to use free writing to explore the ideas causing the obstruction. Although the goal of free writing is to allow ideas to flow through writing unconstrained, writers need a structured environment to allow the process to work. Usually, writers should place themselves somewhere where they will be completely undisturbed for a predetermined period. They do not need to begin with a long free writing session: Even ten to fifteen minutes can be beneficial.

During this period, writers should use a new document that is separate from the work product. Once the time begins, they should write without stopping during the predetermined period. Writers should not be concerned about any presentational-writing matters. Therefore, sentence structure, word choice, correct punctuation, and any other presentational issue should be set aside to allow the ideas themselves to flow on the page—whatever those ideas are.

To begin, writers may attempt to explain where they seem stuck in the analysis. Once they have articulated the obstruction, they should simply put any other ideas on the page that come to mind. After an initial free writing period or two, they may need to use free writing with more specific goals to help begin to focus the ideas. For example, writers can begin a free writing session by using smaller ideas to check their understanding of the global issues. They can begin by writing about some very specific idea in the analysis that they understand and then move from that idea to larger concepts to see if they can identify how ideas relate to each other. By free writing about the relationships between concepts, the writing may uncover new ideas about the analysis or more clearly identify the source of the confusion.

Similarly, writers may try free writing from large organizational concepts that seem clear and write about how the larger concepts lead to the smaller analytical pieces. Again, being forced to write about the different ideas from this perspective may help identify the deficiencies in their understanding of the analysis. While simply understanding the flaw will not solve the problem, recognizing where the problem is can often help provide a new approach for working on the issue.

Other times, writers may need to broaden their perspective beyond the specific legal issues by writing about how their questions affect larger policy issues or relate to other areas of the law. Writing about how specific issues relate to broader legal concepts may help writers perceive those issues differently, which may help provide new tactics for handling the problems.

2. Experiment with Different Writing Techniques

Using different writing techniques than a writer uses naturally is another helpful technique. Spontaneous writers might try outlining to see if an outline uncovers connections that their spontaneous writing had clouded. During this outlining session, they should outline by putting the ideas they understand in a sequence and move things around to test how they relate to each other. Then, they might force themselves to summarize major ideas in a sentence or two on the outline. This labeling process can sometimes help writers see clearly that several different ideas are actually the same. They can then start reducing the number of ideas on the outline, which helps clarify the analysis.

Similarly, writers who do not use charts or other visual notes may consider drafting a flow chart or some other graphic representation of the analysis. For writers who do not naturally use visual aids when analyzing a problem, trying to do so may help clarify a deficiency in their understanding of the problem that is not the struggle they thought they were having. If they are unable to connect different parts of the analysis on a chart, they may realize that they have not fully understood the overall framework of the problem. Understanding those analytical connections may be key to solving the block.

3. Take a Break from Writing

In some situations, writers may need to simply stop writing because it has become unproductive. During this break, writers might consider talking through the analysis with someone. Explaining an analysis to a trusted colleague sometimes helps identify analytical deficiencies that the writer did not understand from the writing itself.

Another technique is to use a recording device to talk through the ideas. Orally expressing the ideas and then listening to them may uncover the root of the problem. Much like the free writing techniques, when talking through problems in this manner, writers may need to start with small ideas, working their way to the larger issues. Other times, doing the opposite may be more helpful. Writers also may find that simply asking questions and then trying to answer those questions helps clarify the analysis.

C. WORKING WITH COLLEAGUES WITH DIFFERENT WRITING TECHNIQUES

Understanding and experimenting with different writing methods improves new legal writers' own writing and allows them to work more effectively with colleagues. In practice, lawyers often complete documents as a team, with different lawyers drafting different parts of the final text. The team supervisor may not have the same writing method as the other members. Some supervising colleagues recognize that lawyers have different writing processes and learning styles, but others may expect their team members to complete assignments using the same techniques that they use. This expectation can create particular challenges for new practitioners.

Supervising lawyers who are outline-reliant writers may require junior attorneys to submit preliminary outlines of their portion of the document, even if they would not typically complete an outline. Similarly, if senior lawyers are spontaneous writers, junior colleagues' need for some type of outline plan before beginning to draft the text may create tension. The senior lawyers may not recognize the contribution of an outline because the junior colleagues have not written out large portions of text. Adapting to the needs of supervising lawyers will often allow new practitioners to work more effectively with their colleagues. Therefore, the more writers experiment with different writing techniques when working alone on projects, the more they can prepare themselves for situations where they may be forced to utilize methods that they might not use naturally in their writing process.

SUMMARY

New practitioners need to learn to use the preliminary drafting stage to perfect their understanding and expression of the relevant legal analysis. During this beginning phase, legal writers should use writing to sharpen their command of the concepts so they can eventually shift the focus from developing ideas to expressing them clearly. To use this stage effectively, new practitioners should consider a few concrete steps:

- Determine personal writing type:
    - Outline reliant?
    - Spontaneous?
    - Combination?
- Consider strategies for writer's block:
    - Free writing techniques
    - Experimenting with different writing techniques
    - Taking a break or talking to a colleague
- Develop approach to work with colleagues with different writing techniques.

CHAPTER 4

Predictive Writing

Many of the first assignments new lawyers are given in practice require a neutral prediction of how the law governs the client's situation. They may report such predictions to colleagues in complete formal internal office memoranda, quick emails, or shorthand memos. Other times, they may prepare drafts of client letters explaining advice based on their evaluation of the situation. Occasionally, senior colleagues may only request copies of the relevant authority with a very short written summary of the analysis. Or they may ask junior lawyers to simply present the analysis verbally in a meeting or during informal discussions.

Whatever the final form of the project, the main task is for writers to make a neutral prediction about the likely outcome. To make such a prediction, the challenge is to determine the legal analysis that applies to the situation. Therefore, new practitioners must recognize that no matter what the form of the answer, senior lawyers need a complete and accurate analysis of the question. If writers provide answers without undertaking all necessary analytical steps, they are likely to analyze the question with a false or incomplete understanding of the relevant law. Even if senior colleagues request "quick" answers, they expect an accurate and thorough reply to the questions.

Accordingly, new legal writers should develop strategies to use the drafting process to develop a thorough neutral prediction and present such analyses in different types of documents, including memos, informal communications with colleagues, and client letters. Most legal writers use initial drafts to work out many of the analytical subtleties necessary to accurately make these predictions. Thus, early drafts help them improve the predictions and supporting analyses, using the drafting process to develop and refine the different ideas. As the analyses progress, they eventually shift the focus of their writing from figuring out the correct predictions to presenting them effectively to the reader.

When writing complete memos, moving from developing ideas to effectively presenting them occurs naturally for many writers. However, even when completing less formal assignments, writers must develop strategies to take these same steps, even if they do not have the time to draft a formal memo. To help new legal writers develop these strategies, this chapter first explores the analytical foundation for all types of predictive writing. Then, the chapter explains how to present those ideas in formal internal office memos, less formal written and oral communications with colleagues, and client letters.

A. USING THE WRITING PROCESS TO PERFECT AN OBJECTIVE ANALYSIS

To help new lawyers use their own writing process to effectively prepare objective assignments, a full understanding of the purpose of predictive writing is needed, as well as an understanding of the different analytical steps necessary to make neutral predictions in most types of legal writing. In addition, new lawyers should consider organizational options for complex questions and develop techniques to use the writing process to verify the accuracy of their analyses.

1. Remember the Objective Purpose

Lawyers prepare objective assignments to provide a neutral assessment of the situation. When new lawyers are given such assignments in practice, they should contrast the point of the assignment with many of their law school experiences. In law school, working on exam questions and other projects, students often are asked to analyze and support many sides of an issue without necessarily using that analysis to predict the most likely result. In practice, however, senior lawyers need a bottom-line answer to the question and a complete analysis supporting the reason for that answer. Even when the answer may not be completely clear, senior colleagues expect junior lawyers to make judgments based on their understanding of the law to provide the most accurate prediction possible.

When making such judgments, new lawyers should analyze the situation as they would if they were the judge or administrative agency determining the final result. Making a prediction from this point of view helps ensure that prediction is based on the result the writer believes is most likely given the law and the facts of the situation rather than the result that would be best for the client. Once junior attorneys have determined the neutral prediction of the situation, senior lawyers may benefit from alternative outcomes based on creative legal arguments that might help the client. But any such novel arguments should be presented as such and not supplant a neutral prediction based on the law and facts.

2. Develop the Analysis to Support Predictions

Generally, the goal of providing a neutral prediction means that writers should fully explain the legal analysis for a specific issue before applying it to the relevant facts. Writers are less likely to be influenced by favorable results for their clients if they develop the analysis for an issue and then apply it to the situation separately. Similarly, explaining the analysis before applying it allows readers to fully understand the law before being influenced by the facts of the situation. Thus, readers have an easier time grasping the analysis and understanding why that analysis dictates a certain result, even if it is not the best answer for the client.

To help separate the analysis of the legal issues from the application, writers need to determine the overall structure of the analysis and use that organization to guide their reasoning process. Once they have worked through all of the different questions based on that initial structure, they may need to reconsider different organizational options to better understand and explain the analysis.

a. Determine the Overall Structure

The first step in developing a complete analysis is to determine how the ideas are divided and organized. Typically, the underlying authority provides an inherent logic that should guide this process. If that logic suggests that the analysis has several components and those parts relate in a particular order, writers should arrange the analysis following that specified order, rather than trying to tailor the organization to favor the client's position. Other analyses, however, may provide several organizational options that writers could use to provide a neutral prediction of the client's situation.

For example, some analyses may include threshold issues that must be determined before other considerations are relevant. Writers would need to fully explain the threshold issue—and possibly apply the analysis of that question to the facts—before being able to move to the other questions. Another analysis, however, might include several considerations that are balanced together. In that situation, writers would need to explain each consideration and how the balancing evaluation would affect the outcome before being able to apply the ideas to the facts of the situation.

b. Discussion of Law for a Specific Issue

Once legal writers have determined the overall organization, they should develop the analysis for each component. To provide a complete analysis, legal writers should carefully introduce each specific question and then provide a full explanation of its analysis and support. Once they have introduced and laid out an explanation, they usually should provide examples from decisions to illustrate their ideas.[1]

1. Introduction

The explanation of an analysis should begin with a clear statement introducing the idea. Although this step often takes many attempts, eventually writers should boil the statement down to a precise topic sentence. Developing clear topic sentences helps writers determine each precise issue and its relationship to the other ideas. Therefore, a topic sentence must articulate the issue, clearly identify the role the issue plays in the analysis, and remind the reader where the issue fits in the overall framework. For example, if the issue is the second of several requirements, the topic sentence should clearly identify the issue as a requirement and that it is only one among others. If the question is a consideration, though not determinative, that difference must be clear.

The step of precisely stating the topic and its role often verifies the accuracy of the analysis. Writers who are unable to clearly articulate these ideas in a topic sentence often quickly realize that they have not fully figured out some basic ideas about the analysis. Thus, this basic writing step will uncover some gaps in their understanding of the analysis and send the writers back to the underlying authority to work through these questions.

For an example of a topic sentence introducing an issue, see annotation 8 to Appendix 3A.

2. Explanation

After introducing the idea, writers need to explain the analysis. To help develop a full explanation, they should move from broad to more specific ideas. Thus, the general principles that they have extrapolated from working through the authority to develop the analysis should be laid out early in the discussion of the issue because they are the key information the reader needs to understand the analysis. After laying out the general principles, writers should support those explanations by demonstrating how the relevant policy supports the writer's explanation. Showing how the spirit behind the law supports the explanation is critical to help the reader understand the writer's explanation. In addition to the reasoning, depending on the type of writing, writers provide additional support with citation for their ideas.

For an example of an explanation of an issue, see annotation 9 to Appendix 3A.

---

1. Many law students learn some form of IRAC to help organize a presentation of legal analysis, particularly for exam writing. While an IRAC formulation can help organize many legal problems, it can sometimes create confusion when applied to complex analyses. Therefore, many legal writers are more successful at explaining the different analytical components without attempting to use such a formula.

3. Illustrations

After the explanation, legal writers may provide examples from the decisions to illustrate how the opinions support the explanation and reasoning. Writers should not use illustrations, however, to fill in gaps in their analysis. The examples should illustrate ideas that have already been fully explained. Thus, illustrations rarely come early in the discussion of a particular issue. With issues that are simple to explain, writers should generally include at least a sentence or two before illustrations begin. In more complicated analyses, the illustrations may not be included for several paragraphs or even pages.

Furthermore, writers should be able to group illustrations together. They should not explain anything more about the analysis between illustrations, other than quick transitions that move the reader from one example to the next. If writers find that some further explanation of the analysis is necessary, they probably need to go back and revise the earlier explanation to make it more complete.

The number of illustrations varies with the different type of predictive writing. Generally, writers do not need to illustrate all possible decisions, but only provide a few examples. Unlike a judge or other skeptical audience, the readers trust that the law supports the writer's analysis. They do not expect writers to prove that analysis by explaining the details of all of the decisions that might support it. Thus, writers generally only include examples of decisions to quickly illustrate their analysis, but in complex analyses, they may need many examples to illustrate all of the ideas included in the explanation of the analysis.

To effectively describe each illustration, writers must apply their explanation to the facts to show how it explains the result of the decision. This step demonstrates to the reader that the writer's explanation is accurate and complete because it should fully explain how the explanation supports how the court or administrative agency reasoned to the result in the decision.

For examples of illustrations of decisions, see annotation 10 to Appendix 3A.

c. Application

After fully explaining and supporting the analysis, writers should apply those ideas to the facts of the situation. Since they already should have fully explained the law, this application should be fairly straightforward. They simply take the ideas from the discussion of the law and apply them to the relevant facts to state and support the prediction. In addition, writers may need to include counter predictions if the analysis does not support a clear prediction.

In situations where writers are not able to take these application steps fairly quickly, they probably did not completely explain and support the law for the question. They may need to rework to determine more fully the relevant explanation before they will be able to easily apply that analysis to make the necessary predictions. This back and forth process varies from writer to writer and problem to problem, but writers should learn to embrace it and use it to their advantage to develop the best analysis possible.

1. State and Support the Prediction

To begin an application, writers should use a topic sentence that clearly states the likely result so that the reader understands the prediction right up front. If writers are unclear about the result, they should explain that the answer is not clear, but then state a prediction that they believe is most likely. Once that prediction is fully supported, they should state and support relevant counter predictions.

To support the prediction, writers should apply their explanation of law for the issue to the relevant facts. As further support, they should compare the client's facts to the facts of some of the decisions that were used to illustrate the explanation. The comparisons should demonstrate why the client's facts are similar or different to the decisions. For each comparison, writers should lay out the relevant facts from the client's situation and the relevant facts from the decision they are using for the comparison. They must then explain why the facts are similar or different using the explanation from the discussion of law.

Generally, readers follow comparisons more easily when writers begin by comparing the client's facts to decisions that have the same result as the writers' prediction and then contrasting the client's facts to decisions with a different result than the prediction. For example, if writers have predicted that the client's facts will not satisfy a particular requirement, they should first compare the client's facts to decisions where the requirement was not satisfied. Then, they should contrast the client's facts to decisions where the requirement was met.

For examples of comparisons supporting a prediction, see annotation 12 to Appendix 3A.

2. Counter Predictions

The amount of detail to include in counter predictions depends primarily on the specific document. However, in most objective assignments, writers should explain what they believe the likely result would be if a trial court or administrative agency decided the question. The reader is relying on the writer's expertise from analyzing the situation to make such a prediction. Readers understand that the predictions are not completely certain because the writers base them on their best understanding of the law and the law rarely provides guaranteed answers. Thus, the job of writers is to state and support their best prediction. However, sometimes writers are unable to predict what the likely result would be because the law does not provide a clear answer to the client's situation. Similarly, predictions are often difficult in situations with contested facts because the result could vary depending on which facts the decision maker accepts. In these situations, writers may need to include predictions and counter predictions.

When making the judgment about when to include counter predictions, writers should not simply include any possible arguments in an application section. They should only use a counter prediction when the likely result is a close call—either because the law is unclear or important facts are in dispute. Accordingly, when adding a counter prediction, writers must fully explain both the prediction and counter prediction to demonstrate to the reader the difficulty of predicting. They should fully support the prediction first and then separately include a fully supported counter prediction, using all the analytical steps discussed above for a prediction.

For an example of a counter prediction, see annotation 15 to Appendix 3A.

d. Illustration of Basic Objective Presentation

The chart below illustrates the analytical components necessary to support a prediction for a specific issue—as discussed in this part of the chapter.

Objective Presentation: Basic Outline of Analytical Components

- Description of law
  - Introduction of topic
  - Explanation of legal principle
  - Policy behind legal principle
  - Examples from decisions to illustrate legal principle and policy
- Prediction: Application to facts
  - Prediction on client's facts
  - Application of legal principle to facts to support prediction
  - Application of policy to support prediction
  - Comparisons of examples from decisions to client's facts to support prediction
- Counter Prediction: Application to facts
  - Counter prediction on client's facts
  - Application of legal principle to facts to support counter prediction
  - Application of policy to support counter prediction
  - Comparisons of examples from decisions to client's facts to support counter prediction

3. Refine the Analysis Through the Presentation of Predictive Writing

As writers become certain about their predictions through earlier drafts, they need to begin to shift the focus of their writing from developing and applying the ideas to presenting them to the reader. As they focus the writing on the reader, writers should review their work, starting with a careful reevaluation of the overall organization. They also should refine the writing by simplifying illustrations, checking predictions and counter predictions, and using consistent language.

a. Reevaluate Overall Organization

While the basic outline of a predictive discussion should guide early drafts, writers may need to vary this format when faced with complex analyses to tailor the overall organization to the specific analysis. Specifically, writers may need to reconsider placement of the various predictions.

If an analysis includes more than one distinct and independent issue, writers generally have a couple of organizational options for the applications. They could provide an introduction of the different issues, explain the law for the first issue, and then apply that law to the facts for that question. Then, they would move to the next independent question and do the same thing. Another organizational option after the introduction would be to provide the different descriptions of the law for all of the separate issues and then, in the same order, apply the explanations to the relevant facts for the various issues.

For example, when analyzing a question with an analysis that had two independent requirements, writers would have two options. After introducing the two requirements, they could provide a discussion of the law for the first requirement and then, immediately apply that analysis to the facts relevant to that question to make and support a prediction for the first requirement. Then, they could move to the second requirement, explain the law and then apply the law for that requirement to the relevant facts.

Another option would be to explain the law for the first requirement and then move to the explanation of the law for the second requirement. After fully, but separately, explaining both requirements, they could provide an application for the first requirement and then an application for the second issue.

However, if an analysis involves some type of test in which the different parts are interrelated, writers should explain the law for all of the different issues before trying to apply any of the legal ideas to the client's facts. For example, when using a sliding scale test in which the evaluation of one factor affects how much of another factor is necessary, writers probably would have only one option. Because the analysis of one idea affects the analysis of another, they should explain the entire sliding scale analysis—including the different factors completely—before applying any of the ideas to the facts of the situation.

Other types of analyses require legal writers to consider additional organizational variations. Generally, when making these determinations, they should choose the option that provides the clearest and most efficient presentation for the reader, without allowing strategic evaluations of their client's position to influence their decision. Often, writers can more confidently make these choices after completing a working draft of the analysis. Understanding how the different variations can aid the presentation of the ideas is usually clearer after experimenting with different options in writing.

b. Edit Illustrations of Decisions

Legal writers often discuss the details of many decisions in early drafts, where they lay out and explain different approaches from various opinions. Although providing detailed descriptions of many decisions is not the best way to present the concepts to the reader, it sometimes is an effective way for new practitioners to translate ideas from their rough notes into a description of the relevant analysis. Therefore, new legal writers should not be concerned that their initial drafts include passages that concentrate too heavily on descriptions of opinions because they will be able to edit their writing to provide a better presentation as their understanding of the analysis progresses.

As they move through that progression and shift the focus to the reader, writers should edit their work to ensure that they are not using details of decisions in place of a complete explanation of the analysis for the reader. If they illustrate decisions instead of providing a full explanation of the issue, the reader must do the hard work of extrapolating the relevant analysis from the decisions, which is the writer's job. Similarly, if writers wait to provide a full explanation only after laying out several illustrations of decisions, they burden the reader with the task of reading and working through those examples without the benefit of the writer's explanation of the analysis. Trying to read illustrations of decisions without a clear explanation makes the reader's work much harder and longer.

c. Replace Possible Arguments with Predictions and Counter Predictions

Providing a neutral prediction is difficult when the underlying law does not provide a clear answer, which is often the problem that new lawyers encounter when drafting objective assignments. To help in this situation, writers may need to explore different sides of the issue in early drafts to help determine an accurate prediction. Some legal writers write out possible arguments, relevant responses, and counter arguments to determine the most accurate prediction. Similarly, others explore all strengths and weaknesses of potential outcomes to develop their analysis.

Accordingly, early drafts of predictive writings often include give and take discussions where writers bounce back and forth between supporting positions and countering them. While this kind of internal debate helps the writers, these passages are often long and would be hard for a reader to absorb quickly. Thus, writers need to edit this type of process writing as they become more certain about their predictions. However, they should not short-cut the process if they need to use their writing to convince themselves of the analysis and how it should be applied to the situation, realizing that the writing can be edited as their ideas develop.

To help edit this type of process writing, writers should recognize that readers do not benefit from the back and forth discussion. Readers only need the prediction and its support. If writers feel that a counter prediction is necessary, they should state and support that counter prediction in the same way as the prediction. By verifying the predictions to ensure that application discussions move from fully supported predictions to complete counter predictions, rather than jumping back and forth between strengths and weaknesses of possible arguments, they will ensure that their predictions are accurate, complete, and easy to understand.

d. Verify Consistency of Language

As writers fully analyze an issue, they should be able to use similar language when discussing the question. Using consistent language in this way allows them to verify the accuracy and clarity of the analysis. Even small variations in word choice can make ideas vague for the reader. Therefore, as writers finalize their understanding of an analysis, they should verify that they are expressing their ideas consistently throughout the discussion of each issue. To take this step, they should check for uniformity of language when explaining the analysis, illustrating the ideas with examples, and applying the analysis to the particular facts of the situation.

For example, if a writer explained that the "subject matter" of an agreement had to be limited in some way, but later stated that the "scope" of the agreement needed certain limitations, the reader would have to determine if "subject matter" and "scope" referred to the same idea. Similarly, if a writer stated that something had to be "secured" but later referred to that idea as "locked," the reader would wonder if "secured" and "locked" were the same idea. "Locked" could be a means of securing something, but would it be the only acceptable method? Similarly, shifting verb choices from "require" to "consider" or other variations can change the meaning of the analysis dramatically.

The first place to check for use of consistent language is to compare the language in the explanation of an issue with any examples of decisions to illustrate that explanation. If writers have accurately described the analysis in the explanation, they should be able to use that same language to show how the decisions illustrate that explanation. Furthermore, to make the presentation clear and efficient for the reader, illustrations should be easy for the reader to follow since the relevant law should have been fully explained before moving to the examples. If writers are unable to explain the decisions with the same language used in the explanation of the issue, they probably have not fully developed the relevant analysis. Even slight variations in language can be an indication of deeper analytical flaws. Thus, writers may need to refine the explanation until the language chosen to articulate the analysis generally can be used to explain the decisions that they select to illustrate that analysis.

Similarly, checking for consistent language in the explanation and prediction for an issue is another verification that the analysis is complete and accurate. If writers have fully and accurately explained the relevant issues in the discussion of law, they should be able to use that same language in the application. Additionally, using consistent language ensures that the presentation of the application is easy for the reader to follow since writers should have explained the relevant law that supports the prediction in the discussion of law for the issue. Therefore, they should apply the ideas from the discussion of law for the issue using the same language.

However, in earlier drafts of application sections, writers may use a different articulation of the analysis in the application than they used in the discussion of law for the issue. If so, they must determine which articulation is most accurate and effective in explaining the ideas. Then, they should take the new different language back to the discussion of law and see if they can incorporate it there. If the revised language works in the discussion of law, and they believe it is a clearer and more precise explanation, then they should also use it in both the discussion of law and application. However, if the revised language does not seem to work in the discussion of law, the writers should realize that the law probably does not support the revisions and therefore they should not use it in the application.

B. FORMAL INTERNAL OFFICE MEMORANDA

Senior colleagues ask new lawyers to prepare formal memos to help them in a variety of situations—from advising clients about basic business planning, to helping them with strategy in pre-litigation negotiations, to drafting complex transactional documents. Although the reasons vary, when senior lawyers request such a memo, they need the writer to fully analyze the assigned question. To provide this information in formal internal office memoranda, new legal writers should understand the audience and purpose of such memos, tailor the style of the presentation accordingly, and determine the appropriate format of the document for their office.

An example of a formal internal office memorandum is included in Appendix 3A.

1. Audience and Purpose

When preparing formal office memoranda, writers should assume that a variety of attorneys in the office could use the memo for different purposes. Therefore, rather than tailoring a memo specifically for the colleague who assigned the project, writers should prepare a memo so that any attorney could read it and fully understand the client's situation and the relevant legal issues. Furthermore, writers should assume the reader is very busy and expects a succinct answer. Therefore, writers must provide complete objective analyses to support their conclusions, but provide the conclusions and supporting analyses as quickly and concisely as possible.

The purpose of the formal memo is to fully evaluate the legal issues relevant to the client's situation and to provide an outcome-neutral prediction of a likely result. Thus, writers should provide an objective analysis of the law and a neutral prediction of how a court would likely apply that law to the client's situation. In most memos, writers should predict how a trial court in the jurisdiction would likely resolve the matter. Therefore, writers must analyze the law and apply the analysis to the client's facts without being influenced by how the outcome will affect the client, even if they predict a negative result. The attorneys reading the memo need the benefit of an analysis that provides a fully objective prediction of the likely result.

New legal writers also should be aware of another, somewhat unrelated purpose of formal memos: They often play an important role in the performance evaluations of junior lawyers. In some offices, senior colleagues who do not work directly with the junior lawyers may read their memos and evaluate the projects as part of the job review process. Thus, formal memos produced early in a lawyer's career may have an important effect on advancement decisions.

2. Style of Presentation

The audience and purpose of a formal memo should guide the writer's presentation. Writers should write such a memo in a formal style because any lawyer in the office could use it to help advise a client about the matter, including colleagues who did not assign the project. Memos should be formal enough not to offend potential readers with casual writing or by seeming too familiar, without being pedantic or stuffy. Writers should use clear and concise wording, but avoid casual language, including colloquialisms and overuse of contractions. Similarly, writers should consider carefully how to refer to the client or other parties relevant to the analysis so that the references are not too informal.

Furthermore, writers should avoid gender-exclusive language and expressions or language that may exclude or offend groups of people. Thus, writers should try to avoid using gender-specific pronouns, and should carefully consider the impact of all words and expressions to be sure they are not gender-exclusive or exclusive in some other way, such as race, religion, sexual orientation, or cultural identity.

Finally, as in all objective writing, the purpose of a formal memo—to provide an outcome-neutral evaluation of the situation—should affect how writers convey their ideas. Writers should carefully avoid stating their opinion or providing commentary about the analysis. To help accomplish this goal, writers should express the analysis in the third person so the reader understands that they are presenting an objective analysis of the situation and not their opinion.

3. Formal Memo Format

The specific format of formal memos varies from workplace to workplace, so when new lawyers are assigned this type of project, they should follow the form used by their office. Generally, most formal memos include a heading, a question presented and brief answer, the discussion, and a conclusion.

a. Heading

The Heading provides information about the recipients, author, date, and subject of the memo, typically including "To," "From," "Date," "Re:," and "CC." Conventions regarding use of titles and honorifics (such as "Mr.," "Ms.," and "Esq.") in the Heading differ from office to office. The amount of information included in the subject line also varies, but generally includes the client name and topic of the memo for record-keeping purposes.

For an example of a Heading, see annotation 2 to Appendix 3A.

b. Question Presented

The goal of the Question Presented is to provide a very quick summary of the central legal issue discussed in the memo. Readers use the section only to determine if they should spend the time to read the memo in depth. Thus, for memos that include only one major issue, writers should express the main question in one concise sentence without referring to the specific client so the reader understands the legal question more generally. For memos that include several complex issues, writers should draft the section so readers can quickly skim it and understand the legal issues discussed in the memo. Waiting to draft the Question Presented until writers have finalized the memo is usually most effective because at that point in the writing process, they will be best able to quickly and concisely summarize the relevant issues in the memo.

For an example of a Question Presented, see annotation 4 to Appendix 3A.

c. Brief Answer

The Brief Answer is directly related to the Question Presented because the goal of the section is to provide a quick answer to the issues outlined in the Question Presented. Thus, writers should provide a very short–one word, if possible–response to the Question Presented, followed by a quick summary of the answer to the specific client's situation. Most writers will write the most effective Brief Answers after they have finalized the discussion of the memo, rather than attempting to summarize an answer before they have fully analyzed the situation in the memo.

Not all law offices include a Brief Answer in their memos, but instead place the Conclusion Section before the Discussion Section of the document. The Conclusion Section is discussed below.

For an example of a Brief Answer, see annotation 4 to Appendix 3A.

d. Facts Section

Formal internal office memoranda include a section where writers lay out the facts that they will use in the Discussion Section to analyze the client's situation. The main challenge when drafting a Facts Section is providing the essential facts concisely so the reader is not overburdened with unnecessary information. To strike the appropriate balance, writers should consider the amount of detail that is necessary, the overall organizational options, and the presentation of the information.

For an example of a Facts Section, see annotation 5 to Appendix 3A.

1. Amount of Detail

To provide a complete yet concise summary of the facts, writers should only include factual information. No legal analysis or legal conclusions should be added. However, the procedural context of the situation is often necessary factual information. For example, writers may be asked to draft the memo as part of pre-filing strategic planning for a summary judgment motion. In this situation, they should probably include procedural context.

Furthermore, writers should include all relevant factual information, even though much of the information will be repeated in the discussion of the memo. Therefore, writers should include all legally significant facts and any other factual information that is necessary for the reader to understand the context of those legally significant facts.

Determining which facts are legally significant is fairly simple if writers wait to draft the facts until after completing the Discussion Section of the memo. Any fact that they use in the discussion is legally significant. Thus, all they have to do is read the Discussion Section and add all facts included in the discussion to the Facts Section. If the Discussion Section included different outcomes depending on contested facts, the section should include explanations of the relevant disputed facts.

Determining the other contextually relevant information that should be included can be more challenging. Writers should include any information the reader would need to understand why a legal memo was necessary to analyze the situation. In other words, they should include the information that explains why the reader is reading the memo. For example, if lawyers are drafting a memo evaluating the chances of success for a motion for summary judgment, they should include all information necessary for the reader to understand why the case is at the summary judgment stage, even if some of that information is not directly related to the legal issues raised by the motion.

2. Organizational Options

Writers should organize the facts to help the reader access the information quickly and efficiently. To accomplish this goal, they should most often provide the factual information in full narrative form, rather than attempting to truncate the information by using bullets or lists of facts. Providing a concise narrative will help the reader absorb the information quickly and in context.

When drafting the facts in most memos, writers have a choice of organizing the facts chronologically or topically. A chronological approach is helpful when the story of the situation itself provides a natural narrative to present the legally significant facts within the context of how the situation developed. Using the chronology of the story in this situation can be effective and concise.

Another organizational option is to group the facts around the different topics that writers will discuss in the legal analysis. Although the reader will not know the analysis when reading the Facts Section, if the factual information is organized so the facts are clustered around the different issues the writer will explain in the Discussion Section, readers will be able to more easily recall the information and how the facts relate to each other when reading the Discussion Section.

In many memos, writers should consider organizing the facts using a combination approach. The chronology of the situation may help provide some basic information, including a variety of contextual facts, while organizing the legally significant facts may be more effective if explained topically.

3. Presentational Considerations

Writers should explain the facts using short paragraphs with concise sentences to help the reader move through the section quickly. Similarly, writers should not burden the reader with detailed information that will not be helpful in the analysis. To reduce unnecessary information, writers should consider using short-references to parties by the role of the parties in the analysis rather than expecting the reader to retain the name of the parties throughout the memo. Using role references instead of names is particularly helpful in complex situations involving multiple parties. For example, in a memo regarding enforceability of an employment agreement related to a sale of a business, the writer could refer to the "seller," "buyer," and "employee" after introducing their names at the beginning of the section. Using their roles throughout the memo would be easier for the reader, rather than expecting the reader to remember that Smith is the seller; Jones is the buyer; and Gonzales, Ameri, and O'Brien are the employees. The one exception to this idea is that writers should usually be able to refer to the client by name, rather than by role. However, in complex problems, writers might consider referring to the client by role if doing so will assist the reader.

e. Discussion Section

In formal memos, writers must provide in the Discussion Section a full narrative discussion of their evaluation of the situation. Once writers have fully formulated the substance of the predictions, as explained in Part A above, they can draft this section, using the choices made during the formulation process to guide the presentation. When presenting these ideas in a formal memo, writers need to carefully consider their introductions and the amount of detail necessary to fully explain and support their analysis and application of each issue.

For an example of a Discussion Section, see annotation 6 to Appendix 3A.

1. Introduction

To begin a Discussion Section, writers must introduce the issues they will discuss in the memo and provide sufficient background for the reader to understand the context of those issues. Thus, they need to lay out the overall structure of the analysis and supporting policy. Writers also should provide a clear roadmap to the discussion so the reader understands how they will organize the presentation. For example, if a statute governs the question and courts have interpreted that provision, writers should include the relevant portion of the statute in the introduction as well as the policy behind the law so the reader has a basic understanding of what the court is trying to accomplish in its interpretation. Then, they should use the basic structure of the court's analysis as the roadmap to the rest of the discussion.

For an example of an introduction, see annotation 7 to Appendix 3A.

2. Explanations of Law

For each issue, writers must fully explain the component parts of the questions, including the explanation of the legal principles and the policy behind those principles, as explained in Part A above. Once they have provided that explanation, they should add some specific examples—usually from decisions—that illustrate how the explanation and its reasoning work on the decisions. The number of illustrations that they should use varies depending on the complexity of the analysis, but generally writers should not burden their readers with excessive illustrations. As explained in Part A above, in predictive writing, writers should not include illustrations to prove the analysis. Rather, they should only add examples to illustrate their ideas.

Generally, legal writers include examples of decisions with positive outcomes first and then move to decisions with negative results. For example, if writers are explaining when the subject matter requirement of a non-competition clause is reasonable, generally they would provide examples of cases where the court found that the restriction was reasonable and then give examples of cases where the restriction was not reasonable.

Writers should always consider illustrating some decisions with parenthetical citations in addition to textual examples to make the example portion of the discussion more concise. They can use a parenthetical illustration of a decision instead of a full textual example if they can explain the information in a fairly short phrase. The parenthetical is included as a part of the citation to the decision.

The main challenge when determining whether to use a parenthetical illustration is ensuring that writers have not packed too much information in the parenthetical, making it dense and hard for the reader to follow. Any parenthetical illustration should be no longer than one concise sentence, without the use of a semicolon or other punctuation that combines two sentences. Generally, such illustrations should be no more than a couple of lines of text. However, they must include all of the same information that would be included in a textual example of a decision—namely, the relevant facts and an explanation of why those facts are relevant using the general principles of the law. In complex analyses, therefore, writers often find that providing examples with a citation parenthesis is not practical because they are unable to reduce all the necessary information to one fairly short sentence. Thus, writers may need to provide full textual illustrations of the decisions. Nonetheless, for some issues with fairly simple analysis, parenthetical illustrations are a good tool to make the Discussion Section more concise because writers can string together additional support from a variety of decisions. For an example of an illustration of a decision with a citation parenthetical, see annotation 13 to Appendix 3A.

For an example of an explanation of a topic, see annotation 8 to Appendix 3A.

3. Applications

After fully explaining the legal analysis for an issue, writers should apply the law to the facts of the situation, as explained in Part A above. To provide a complete application, writers should concisely state the prediction for the issue and then apply the analysis that they explained in the discussion of law for the issue to the facts relevant to the question. As further support of the prediction, writers should compare the client's facts to the facts of some of the decisions that they used to illustrate the law for the issue in the discussion of law. As explained in Part A above, writers generally should organize comparisons to decisions by comparing the client's facts to decisions that have the same result as the writer's prediction and then contrasting the client's facts to decisions with a different result than the prediction. Finally, in much the same way that decisions may be explained using a citation parenthetical, sometimes writers will be able to use a parenthetical citation in place of a textual comparison to a decision.

For an example of an application for a topic, see annotation 11 to Appendix 3A.

4. Counter Predictions and Possible Arguments

If writers determine that they should include a counter prediction for an issue—as discussed in Part A—they should fully explain it after the prediction, including the same level of support as for predictions. In addition to counter predictions, sometimes writers will feel that, despite their prediction and counter predictions, they should include possible arguments that might help the client. While most readers do not expect writers to include arguments in a formal predictive memo, if writers feel the supervising attorney wants such information, they should include the arguments—possibly in a separate section—only after the prediction and counter predictions.

If writers include possible arguments, for each one they should clearly support the argument first and explain how a court could accept the reasoning of the argument. Once they have fully supported the argument, they should separately explain why a court, however, could reject the argument based on the legal analysis. The form of the argument and counter arguments is similar to the prediction and counter predictions explained in Part A, but writers need to be very clear that they are only including possible arguments to assist the reader in evaluating the client's situation. Writers should not suggest that the arguments would lead to a likely outcome for the client.

For an example of a counter prediction, see annotation 15 to Appendix 3A.

5. Citation

Writers should use citations to support the ideas in the memo, but do not need to use citations to prove the analysis, as they would do in a persuasive document. To provide adequate citation, writers must provide support for all ideas in the memo; use concise citations that include appropriate signals and pinpoint references; and decide whether to cite when applying the law to the facts.

Support all ideas. While writers do not need to prove the analysis in the memo, they do need to provide complete support for all ideas. Any lawyer reading an objective analysis needs to know that the law fully supports the ideas and, therefore, expects to see complete and accurate citation throughout the memo. Thus, writers must provide support for every idea in the analysis by generally citing after every sentence when explaining the law. Since writers should only include ideas that the authority supports, adding a citation after every sentence should not be a difficult task, and the full citation will give the reader confidence that the relevant legal authorities fully supported the analysis.

Avoid long string citations. At the same time, writers should not overburden the reader with long, repetitive citations. Therefore, even though they should support every idea—and generally that means citing after every sentence—writers should provide concise citations. Rather than providing a long string citation with every possible piece of authority that supports the idea, they should carefully choose the best support for the idea and only include additional support selectively.

Use signals and pinpoint references. Writers must choose authority carefully and pinpoint the specific sections or pages of the authority that support the idea they are citing. The various citation manuals provide signals that explain to the reader the level of support that the cited authority provides for the idea. Writers should become familiar with the different signals in the appropriate citation manuals. The most common citations used in predictive memos will include citations without a signal, "see," "see also," and "e.g."

A citation without a signal indicates to readers that the cited authority directly supports the proposition being cited. A piece of authority may directly support an idea even if it does not state the idea in the same way that the writers express the concept. In other words, a citation without a signal does not mean that the writers are quoting the language from the source, though if they were quoting information, the citation would not include a signal either.

The "see" signal indicates that the cited authority indirectly supports the idea. Indirect support means that an inferential step is necessary to understand how the authority supports the idea, even though the authority does not expressly state the concept. Often, writers are confident about this inferential step because they are relying on several different pieces of authority together that suggest the same inferential or implicit idea. Thus, the "see" signal before a citation with several decisions is the best way to explain to readers that they would have to consider all of the decisions together to fully understand how the authority fits together to support the expressed idea. The signal "see also" explains to the reader that the cited authority is even less direct support than the authority introduced with a "see."

The "e.g." signal is another signal that will help writers prepare concise memos. "E.g." indicates that the authority cited is a sampling of the support available, but more support exists. "E.g." can be combined with other signals, so writers may provide a sampling of direct support, indirect support, or other levels of support using "e.g." with other signals.

When choosing the authority to include with an "e.g." signal, writers should consider the quality of authority. For example, if writers are primarily relying on lower appellate court opinions, but one higher court opinion supports the idea, they should probably include the higher court decision along with the best lower court cases. Similarly, if they primarily are using older cases, they should consider using a more recent case to indicate that newer cases are following the same line of reasoning, even though the older cases may better express or illustrate the ideas.

Writers also should use pinpoint references in citation to identify the precise place in the authority where they found the support. The pinpoint reference is an important guide if the reader refers to the cited authority. Therefore, writers should rarely cite to a long statute or refer the reader to an entire decision or a long range of pages from an opinion. Rather, writers should direct readers to a specific part of a long statute or a specific page or two from a decision that the writer has determined are most supportive for the idea expressed. Referring readers to long portions of text from several different authorities would not be very helpful because the readers would have to spend time figuring out exactly how the authority supports the idea. Sending readers to specific portions of text with the appropriate signal allows them to quickly understand how the authority supports the analysis.

Finally, writers should use parenthetical explanations of decisions when helpful to the reader or when the relevant citation manual recommends a parenthetical. Most citation manuals suggest parenthetical explanations when using particular signals, including "see also." In addition, writers can use parenthetical citations to illustrate the facts of decisions, rather than describing the facts in the text. When drafting parenthetical information in a string of citations, writers should construct the information using parallel sentence structure, usually beginning with the gerund form of a verb, such as "finding." Parenthetical explanations, however, are only appropriate when providing relatively short amounts of information. Parenthetical explanations can only be one sentence and should be no longer than two or three lines of text. Writers should include longer descriptions in the text. For a discussion of using parenthetical citations to illustrate cases, see Part B.3.e.2 of this chapter. For an example of a parenthetical citation, see annotation 13 to Appendix 3A.

Citation in application. Whether writers should use citation in the portions of the discussion where they apply the law to the client's facts varies from office to office. Some practitioners do not include citation to support predictions. They take the position that citation in the application is unnecessary because writers are applying ideas that they have already explained and supported with citation in the discussion of law. Others, however, include citation throughout the memo, including the application sections, because they want to remind the reader that the legal authority supports the ideas they are applying to the facts. Due to this split, new practitioners should probably err on the side of providing full citation in the application sections of predictive memos until they become familiar with the practices of their office or senior lawyers.

When using citation in an application, writers must remember that the citation alone is not the analysis. They must apply the ideas as explained when analyzing the law for the issue to the client's facts. The citation should include references to the same authority the writers used when laying out the analysis. Thus, much of the citation in the application section will be very similar in terms of signals and amount of authority that the writer used when explaining the analysis for the particular issue. For an example of using citation in an application, see annotation 11 to Appendix 3A.

f. Conclusion Section

The Conclusion Section of a formal memorandum should provide readers with a summary of the answer to the question introduced in the Question Presented. The purpose of a conclusion is not to re-explain the analysis that the writers have fully explored in the discussion of the memo. Rather, they should quickly add a conclusion regarding the overall question in a sentence or two and summarize the answers to all of the different issues discussed in the memo. Generally, they should try to condense the summary of each issue to about a sentence or so.

Because the goal of the conclusion is limited to summarizing the answers that they explained in the memo, writers should not include citation or discussion of specific legal authority. Similarly, writers should not lay out the law in the abstract for a specific issue and then re-apply that explanation to the facts. Instead, they should simply support the overall conclusion by providing a prediction for each component of the analysis.

One drafting technique that helps reduce the time spent on the Conclusion Section is to state in the first sentence the response to the Question Presented. Then, simply review the memo, lift the topic sentences for each prediction for the different issues, and add them to the conclusion. Once writers have pasted all of the predictions together, they should be able to quickly edit the section to provide a clear and quick summary of the different predictions to support the overall conclusion.

As discussed earlier, some offices use only a Conclusion Section rather than including both a Brief Answer and Conclusion Section because the Brief Answer usually states the same information that is included in the first sentence or so of the Conclusion Section. If a memo does not include a Brief Answer, writers should consider putting the Conclusion Section between the Question Presented and the Discussion Section so the reader has the benefit of a quick answer to the problem at the beginning of the memo.

For an example of a Conclusion Section, see annotation 16 to Appendix 3A.

C. OTHER COMMUNICATIONS WITH COLLEAGUES

In the busy environment of law practice, senior colleagues often ask junior lawyers to research and analyze legal questions without preparing formal memos. Instead, they request a quick written summary via email or short informal memo. Sometimes, they may ask junior lawyers to simply provide copies of the authority with a short answer to the question attached. Other times, the junior lawyers may be asked to give an oral presentation about the analysis in a meeting or casual discussion.

These informal tasks may give new lawyers the false sense that such projects are easier and will not be given the same scrutiny as more formal assignments. In fact, completing short-cut projects sometimes can be more challenging for new lawyers than preparing a complete formal memo. Even when preparing a shorthand answer, they must fully understand the underlying analysis. Unfortunately, senior lawyers sometimes forget the amount of time that new attorneys require to fully analyze complex legal issues. They often believe that asking new lawyers to provide the answer to a legal question without preparing a complete memo will save time. This assumption is often wrong because the bulk of the effort when preparing a memo is analyzing the law rather than completing the formalities of the document. Many legal writers use the steps of finalizing a memo to put it into the formal format as a double check on the analysis.

Thus, preparing a formal memo may not take much more time to complete than shorthand assignments. Furthermore, senior lawyers will rely on the analysis no matter what the form of the presentation, and thus they will scrutinize the substantive accuracy of the new lawyer's work in the same manner that they would evaluate formal projects. Therefore, to successfully complete such shorthand assignments, lawyers must provide the most complete analysis possible and carefully consider the format of the final presentation.

An example of an informal internal office communication is included in Appendix 3B.

1. Analyze the Question

When new practitioners present an analysis in some short form, they should recognize that they still need a complete analysis of the question. Therefore, they should go through all of the analytical steps to fully understand and verify the relevant legal analysis and how it will be applied to the client's situation, as explained in Part A of this chapter. Once they have a full understanding of the analysis, they should consider the best format for presenting that analysis in the manner that the senior colleague requested.

2. Format of Informal Written Communications

As new lawyers become familiar with their colleagues, they will quickly learn to adapt their writing in the situations where senior attorneys assign shorthand projects, and they will determine the appropriate format of the documents accordingly. Even though the format and the amount of detail that should be included in these types of assignments will vary from project to project, writers always should consider including some basic information.

Informal memos or emails usually should provide a clear answer to the question at the very beginning and then include a concise version of all the analytical steps included in a formal memo. Therefore, writers may begin with something similar to the Question Presented and Conclusion sections of a formal memo as a general format of the presentation. Once the question is clearly stated, the body of the writing should provide a quick answer and a summary of the analysis, providing only slightly more detail than the Conclusion Section in a formal memo. At that point, writers should introduce the relevant analysis and a quick explanation of each component, even though they may not support the informal writing with complete explanations, citation, or illustrations of the authority. In addition, if writers have been provided with the facts of the situation, most often they should include a clear prediction by applying the relevant analysis to those facts. Writers should consider using headings, bullets, and other formatting to help readers understand the relevant ideas quickly and efficiently.

Sometimes senior colleagues will ask junior lawyers to research a specific question and simply provide copies or citation to the relevant authority, without including any analysis. Even in this situation, however, junior lawyers must begin analyzing the question to find the relevant authority. Therefore, when transmitting the results of this type of assignment, they should consider including a cover memo or email explaining that they were directed to find the relevant authority without fully analyzing the question, but that they could complete a full analysis if necessary. This cover memo will help remind senior colleagues that they had not requested an analysis of the question.

When preparing these types of informal communications, including quick email communications, new lawyers should avoid using a casual tone and submitting assignments that appear to have been completed hastily. Although informal communications are expected to be more succinct than complete formal memos, overly casual writing can appear unprofessional.

Furthermore, new lawyers should carefully proofread and check all correspondence for typos and grammatical mistakes to avoid criticism of sloppy work product.

3. Oral Presentations

Explaining the answer to a question orally often seems like the quickest and most efficient way to communicate information to a senior attorney. However, these informal presentations often take a lot of time for new practitioners to prepare because orally summarizing intricate analyses and providing related predictions can be a complex task.

To prepare, new lawyers must take all the necessary steps to carefully analyze a question that were discussed in Part A of this chapter, even though they may not include all of those steps in the presentation. Then, they must determine how much detail the senior lawyer would like in the presentation. Finding the balance of the amount of information the senior lawyer needs is a skill that often takes time to perfect. Often, this question will not become clear until the presentation itself.

To help make the determination, new practitioners should consider beginning the presentation by quickly summarizing the question that was assigned and then provide a clear answer to that question. The summary of the issue ensures that senior colleagues understand the precise question that the junior lawyers analyzed, which helps avoid ambiguity about the focus of the presentation.

Then, new practitioners should provide a quick answer to that question before laying out detail to support the prediction. Using about the same amount of detail that they would have included in a Question Presented and Brief Answer of a formal memo often is a good starting point. Once they have explained that information, they can try to use the senior attorney's reaction to determine how much analytical support is necessary.

New lawyers also must be prepared for the challenging task of answering the senior colleague's specific questions about the analysis. Often, to fully answer the questions, they may need to provide more detail to the analysis than they included in the initial presentation because the senior attorney does not have the benefit of having read a full memo explaining the analysis.

D. CLIENT LETTERS

Lawyers often advise their clients through letters. Frequently, senior attorneys request that new practitioners prepare drafts of such correspondence, usually based on an analysis they explained in a previous memo or research assignment. To prepare effective client letters, legal writers must understand the audience and purpose of the documents and tailor the form and style accordingly.

An example of a client letter is included in Appendix 3C.

1. Possible Audiences

The exact audience of client letters is difficult to identify because the range of lawyers' clients varies dramatically in practice—from individuals with family law questions to small public interest organizations to large governmental agencies or multinational corporations and everything in between. Sometimes, clients are lawyers themselves.

In the situation where the client is an attorney, the audience of the letter would not be much different than a memo or other communication to a colleague discussed in the previous part of this chapter. Therefore, many of the ideas regarding those documents should guide writers in drafting a letter to that client.

In most situations, however, clients are not lawyers. Therefore, the writers' main challenge is to communicate advice based on the result of a carefully reasoned legal analysis to a non-lawyer. The clients must understand that the lawyers based the advice on the law, but most clients would not benefit from a full explanation of the legal analysis, as another lawyer would. Furthermore, clients hire lawyers for guidance and most do not expect a thorough analytical justification of that advice, but rather a straightforward answer to their problem.

Thus, lawyers must lay out the recommendations they feel are appropriate based on the law, without overcomplicating the recommendations by providing a complete examination of the underlying legal analysis. While this task may be simple to state, it is not easy to accomplish because writers cannot assume that clients understand even fairly basic principles of the process of the legal system that a writer would assume when writing to other lawyers. Therefore, writers must carefully consider the amount of background regarding the particular legal question, but also the amount of other information about legal analysis that a non-lawyer would need to fully understand the lawyer's advice.

2. General Purpose

The purpose of client letters is directly related to the audience. In most situations, lawyers are writing to the client to provide guidance on a particular legal question. The letter is not to fully explain the legal analysis, but to provide bottom-line advice so the client may decide on a course of action. Thus, the usual purpose of a client letter is to explain the course of action that the lawyer recommends based on the relevant legal analysis instead of laying out the legal analysis itself. While lawyers need to be clear that they used the law to determine their advice, most clients need an explanation of the lawyer's recommendations and the legal consequences of alternative courses of action, rather than an explanation of the underlying analysis.

Thus, in most client letters lawyers should lay out the legal consequences of the client's different options. Writers may advise clients about which option they feel is best given their understanding of the client's needs, but most often lawyers need to be clear that the client must make the final decision about what course of action to choose.

3. Basic Format

The goal of quickly summarizing recommendations concerning legal issues to non-lawyers directly affects the form of client letters. The writer should fully summarize the legal question and explain the legal consequences of different courses of action concisely and in simple terms. Thus, most letters should include a quick introduction, an explanation of the recommendations, and a summary.

a. Introduction

The introduction of a client letter should state the specific legal question or questions the writer is addressing in the letter. A summary of the legal issues is important to ensure that the client understands the precise question that the lawyer is answering.

Once lawyers have introduced the issues, they should quickly summarize the answer to the questions by providing a quick synopsis of the recommendations that they will explain in detail in the body of the letter. Usually, clients are most interested in the lawyer's bottom-line advice, so including a summary of that guidance at the beginning of the letter helps accommodate expectations of the clients.

For an example of an introduction in a client letter, see annotation 2 to Appendix 3C.

b. Evaluation of the Legal Question

The body of the letter should concisely explain the lawyers' evaluation of the legal issues. When explaining the evaluation, they should focus on consequences of different actions based on their understanding of the law. They should clearly summarize the legal reasoning that supports the recommendations, but should not provide a complete legal analysis. Instead, they should explain the consequences of taking certain actions based on their legal analysis.

Thus, writers should rarely cite authority or explain details of different pieces of the authority. Citing to authority is usually not helpful because the client is a layperson who does not understand the legal process. Non-lawyers would have difficulty understanding the relevance of citation or what different pieces of legal authority signify because they probably would not understand the relationship between different types of authority or the process of reconciling interpretations of the authority. Rather than attempting to provide an explanation of all of this information, lawyers should focus on the end result by quickly summarizing the law and how it affects the client's situation.

However, sometimes writers may decide that they should lay out statutory or regulatory provisions or language from decisions because the language will help a non-lawyer client understand the lawyer's recommendations more quickly. Lawyers should not use such language to justify the advice to the client, but only to help explain the information the client would need to make a reasoned decision.

Providing guidance without fully supporting it with the underlying analysis is particularly challenging when the lawyers' advice based on the law may be in conflict with the desires of the client. In this situation, they may need to provide a more thorough legal analysis, but they should remember that the client has hired them because the client feels confident about relying on their legal expertise. Therefore, they should not use the letter to justify the advice, but rather focus on explaining what the law suggests the consequences of different courses of action would be.

Providing guidance to clients without full justification can be further complicated when the law is ambiguous and therefore lawyers cannot state with certainty how the law affects the client's question. In this situation, writers must again be careful not to be tempted to provide a full legal analysis of the situation to justify why they cannot provide more certain guidance. Instead, they should express the advice in terms of what they think is most likely given the status of the law. If the law is unclear, writers should deal with that ambiguity by explaining that the legal analysis has uncovered a lack of clarity in the law and explain how that ambiguity could affect the consequences of different courses of action.

For example, if advising a client about whether a contractual term would be enforced in a purchase agreement when the law is unclear because several recent decisions have analyzed the question differently, lawyers should be careful not to provide too much information about the legal authority. Rather than explaining the details of how the cases are in conflict, they should simply state that a recent conflict in the law creates an ambiguity and what that ambiguity means for the client. While the reasoning from the different cases would be helpful to another lawyer dealing with the issue, the client would benefit most from understanding the consequences of the lack of clarity rather than an explanation of the legal reasoning that creates the ambiguity in the law.

For an example of an evaluation of a legal question in a client letter, see annotation 3 to Appendix 3C.

c. Recommendations and Conclusion

At the end of the letter, writers should summarize the advice that they explained in the letter in short, simple terms, quickly providing the different options open to the client.

For an example of recommendations in the conclusion to a client letter, see annotation 4 to Appendix 3C.

4. Style of Presentation

Writers should avoid legalese or any legal terms that would be unfamiliar to non-lawyers when writing client letters. In addition, as in any good writing, the use of clear topic sentences, succinct sentences, and short paragraphs is very important. These good writing tools will help writers condense complex legal ideas into more accessible language for non-lawyer clients.

SUMMARY

New lawyers may be required to present objective predictions to senior colleagues or clients in a variety of forms. To ensure that new practitioners accurately present such predictions in all such projects, they should consider a few key steps when preparing such assignments:

- Remember the purpose of neutral predictions: Do not advocate.
- Develop and explain the law before applying it.
- Determine the overall structure of the analysis.
- Discuss the law for a specific issue:
  - Explain the law.
  - Illustrate the law.
- Apply the law:
  - Fully support predictions.
  - Include counter predictions only after fully explained predictions.
- Refine presentation of predictive writing:
  - Edit illustrations of decisions.

    - Replace possible arguments with predictions and counter predictions.
    - Verify consistency of language.
- Learn format of formal memoranda.
- Understand how to prepare informal communications with colleagues.
- Use neutral analysis to prepare client letters.

CHAPTER 5

Persuasive Writing

Most lawyers—even non-litigators—frequently advocate positions for their clients. For example, business lawyers negotiate deals for clients, family law attorneys advocate for clients in negotiating prenuptial agreements or divorce settlements, and public interest lawyers lobby legislators on behalf of their clients. In all of these settings, lawyers use legal arguments. In addition, much of the give and take of everyday law practice involves persuading colleagues of a point of view to help determine the best strategy. Therefore, new legal writers often work on projects that involve some persuasive writing even if they do not prepare formal court filings.

As in any legal document, the legal analysis is the core of persuasive writing, although the way in which the lawyers use that analysis is very different than in other types of legal writing. In predictive documents, writers must analyze the law neutrally and predict how a court likely would determine the outcome. In transactional writing, lawyers use the law as a guide to structure documents that protect the client's interests. In persuasive writing, the goal is to convince the reader of what the law should mean and how it should be applied to a specific situation. Thus, while persuasive writers must understand the parameters of the law—as they would when writing any other type of legal document—the outcome that the law might suggest should not restrain them. Instead, they must use their analysis to convince the reader of what the outcome should be.

To develop convincing arguments, most legal writers use the drafting process to work through the underlying analysis before concentrating on polishing the arguments. Preliminary drafts tend to focus on developing the analytical foundation of the various arguments, while later versions experiment with using the analysis strategically to convince the reader of the writer's point of view. The final drafts help writers refine and polish the presentation to make the document as persuasive as possible.

As in most writing, preparing convincing arguments requires writers to use a recursive process, moving back and forth between developing analytical support for arguments and refining their presentation. While the stages may not be completely sequential for all legal writers, most lawyers generally use writing to confirm their understanding of the law and ensure that they are presenting the ideas in the most convincing way as they move from early drafts to final documents.

To enable new practitioners to fully benefit from their own writing process to prepare persuasive documents, this chapter begins with a discussion of the analytical basis of most types of legal arguments. The chapter then explores strategies to use that foundation to prepare formal court documents and other types of persuasive assignments that lawyers may encounter early in their careers.

A. USING THE WRITING PROCESS TO DEVELOP AND CONSTRUCT ARGUMENTS

Similar to most projects new practitioners receive early in practice, their persuasive writing assignments usually involve questions based on cross-decision interpretive analysis because the underlying source of law—constitutional, statutory, regulatory, or common law—includes decisions interpreting it. Therefore, new lawyers should be prepared to use cross-decision interpretive analysis to create and present arguments. To assist in that process, new lawyers must first develop arguments grounded in an objective understanding of the law. Then, they should use basic argument construction to draft those arguments before refining them so the arguments are as effective as possible.

1. Build Arguments from Objective Analysis

The first step in preparing an effective argument is to be able to fully assess its strengths and weaknesses. To make such an assessment, writers must analyze the law objectively to evaluate how the analysis affects the client's position. They should then use that objective understanding to brainstorm potential arguments, develop a theme, and evaluate the strengths of possible arguments to determine which ones should be included in the final presentation.

a. Develop a Neutral Understanding of the Law

To accurately assess the strength of an argument, lawyers must have a thorough understanding of the objective analysis of the question, as explained in Chapter 3. When new practitioners are asked to draft arguments, they may have already analyzed the law objectively by preparing a memo or some other type of predictive writing. For example, a senior colleague may ask a junior lawyer to prepare a predictive memo regarding an issue so the senior lawyer can evaluate the client's case. Then, the senior attorney may ask the junior lawyer draft an argument based on the same legal analysis. In this situation, the writer would benefit by having analyzed the different issues objectively in the memo before attempting to draft the argument.

However, even in situations where new practitioners are asked to draft arguments without having first written a neutral evaluation of the analysis, they must evaluate the law objectively to determine the best strategy for the client. If writers only consider the question with a bias for the client's position, they may not undertake an adequate analysis of the situation and may miss some important ideas. These ideas might be weaknesses that the other side could exploit, or creative support for the argument that they could understand only by analyzing the question objectively.

Thus, legal writers should complete all of the analytical steps necessary to neutrally analyze the different issues before drafting arguments. If they are unable to complete a memo, they should still take time to work through the law objectively—possibly drafting a rough outline of the objective analysis—to fully evaluate the strengths and weaknesses of the situation.

b. Brainstorm Potential Arguments

After working through the analysis objectively, legal writers should brainstorm to find potential arguments. During this process, they should not feel overly constrained by their objective understanding. Rather, they should use that understanding to find arguments that might convince the reader of their position. At this stage, writers should trust that their objective understanding of the law will guide them in the creative process of uncovering possible arguments and ensure that they do not go too far afield when thinking of possibilities.

To encourage this exploration stage, many new legal writers benefit from using free writing to explore new ideas. During this process writing, writers should begin by laying out all positive arguments that come to mind. Then, they should spend time listing points that could be made to counter those arguments. Once they have written down those counter points, the writers should add ways of attacking those negative arguments. This back and forth process may uncover ideas that they had not yet considered.

c. Determine a Theme

Once legal writers have objectively analyzed the issues and brainstormed potential arguments, they should use that information to find a theme that quickly expresses the core theory of the case. To develop a theme, writers should ask themselves what they want the reader to think the central idea of the case is. If they had to explain the essence of the case in one sentence, what would it be?

Often, the legal analysis allows writers to present the arguments around a theme that helps creates sympathy for their client or characterizes the opponent in a negative light. Emphasizing this contrast may help tie the arguments together thematically. For example, in arguments supporting a plaintiff's claim of sexual harassment at work, the harassing behavior would be legally relevant and create sympathy for the client personally. Developing a theme around that behavior would allow the writer to use that sympathy to connect the arguments.

Other times, however, finding a theme may be more challenging. The facts themselves may not create a sympathetic story, or a more nuanced thematic connection might be more effective than the most obvious. For example, in a tax case where a plaintiff opposes the government, trying to paint the Internal Revenue Service as a governmental bully—while possibly a tempting theme—may not be the most relevant legal concept. Instead, utilizing the policy behind the specific provisions might allow the writer to develop a more useful theme around how other typical taxpayers would be affected by the outcome of the case.

d. Evaluate and Select Best Arguments

Once writers have brainstormed possible arguments and determined a theme, they must evaluate the strengths and weaknesses of those arguments to winnow strong from weak, using the theme as a guide. At this point, writers need to carefully consider the objective analysis to prioritize the best arguments that they will fully develop in writing. Writers should keep track of which arguments they reject at this stage, however, because they may find that some arguments that initially appear weak may become stronger as they develop and complete their final arguments. Thus, writers should keep track of the ideas that they discount and review them as they finalize the presentation of their arguments.

2. Basic Argument Construction: The Rough Draft

Once writers have a sense of the best potential arguments, they should prepare a draft of the document. When first drafting arguments, new practitioners sometimes struggle to move away from an objective presentation of the ideas once they have analyzed the issues neutrally. When this happens, the neutral analysis controls too much of the arguments, and the presentation is very similar to predictive writing.

A technique that often helps new legal writers move away from an objective format is to use the different goals between presenting analysis neutrally and persuasively as a basic guide to prepare a first draft of an argument. The rough draft may be a fully written argument or some type of outline of the ideas. Whatever the form of the rough draft, the different goals should help the writers use the parts of the analysis to their advantage, even if they will have to revise the final argument.

In predictive documents—as discussed in Chapter 4—the purpose of analyzing the situation objectively generally means that writers should begin with an explanation of the law regarding the issue by laying out the legal principles and policy along with examples of how those principles and policy have been used by decision makers. Then, they should neutrally apply the legal concepts that they have explained to the relevant facts of the situation to predict a likely result if the question were answered by a court.

When writing an argument, the goal is very different: Writers should prove to the reader how the law dictates a certain result given the client's facts. To convince readers of their desired results, legal writers must include all of the components of an objective analysis—including relevant legal standards, the policy behind those standards, examples from the cases or other decisions, the facts of the client's situation, and conclusions based on those facts. However, the persuasive goal of advocacy writing affects how writers present these different components.

In the rough draft, the conclusions based on the client's facts should control all organizational choices. To begin, writers should personalize the arguments by weaving the law and the client's situation together as much as possible from the beginning to the end of the argument without providing a long, abstract discussion of any one analytical component. To help ensure that writers effectively combine the law with the facts, they should first state the result they want the reader to accept based on the client's situation. Then, writers should prove that assertion with the relevant legal standards and policy. They also should use factual comparisons to decisions as further proof of the conclusion. Finally, they should review each draft to verify that they are using the analytical components persuasively.

a. State the Conclusion First

To help write a persuasive first draft of an argument, writers should begin with a strong statement of the conclusion they want the reader to reach based on the situation. Beginning with the conclusion helps writers focus on the result the reader must accept for the argument to be successful. Furthermore, starting in this fashion helps writers determine the best way to present all of the other analytical components to prove that conclusion. Therefore, in the first draft of an argument, writers should attempt to state in the topic sentence the exact conclusion that they want to prove to the reader. Generally, writers should try to articulate this conclusion by applying the basic legal standard to the key facts in one sentence.

b. Support the Conclusion with the Legal Standards

After stating the conclusion, writers should explain the legal standards that prove the accuracy of that conclusion. Writers must explain these standards in much the same detail that they would use in predictive writing. If the decisions explicitly articulate the legal principles, this step can be fairly easy. When the decisions only include implicit principles that writers have to reconcile and refine to prove the desired result, this step may take much longer. In either situation, however, writers should lay out the standards in the context of the argument by applying these principles to the client's facts as they are explaining them. Long, abstract discussions of the law, unrelated to the factual conclusions, tend to lose the reader's attention and thus lack the necessary impact to be helpful.

c. Explain the Policy

In all arguments, writers must prove that relevant policy supports their position. As they explain and apply the legal standards to the client's situation, they should use the spirit behind the law to prove that the legal principles and the reasons behind those principles support their conclusions. They should use that policy to support the legal standards that they have explained and how those standards should apply to the client's situation.

d. Compare Facts to Decisions

When drafting preliminary arguments, writers should carefully consider placement and detail of factual comparisons. To begin, writers should avoid discussing details of decisions at the beginning of an argument. Specific information from decisions—especially factual information—is usually not helpful until writers have fully explained the legal standards and the policy that supports those standards. Thus, writers should prove the conclusion on the client's situation that they have stated at the beginning of the argument with the relevant legal standards and policy before providing further proof with examples and comparisons from judicial or administrative decisions.

When including comparisons to facts of decisions, writers generally should avoid providing abstract discussions of the facts of decisions. Typically, descriptions of decisions are more effective when writers provide the factual information, along with an explanation of its relevance, as they compare the information to the facts of the client's situation. In objective writing, these two steps are often divided.

e. Use of Authority

Unlike objective writing, citation to authority alone is usually not sufficient support for an argument. Writers must prove their analysis instead of simply supporting it. To begin, writers must demonstrate that the reasoning of the authority supports their arguments. Simply citing to authority would not sufficiently explain this support. In addition, if the other party could use certain decisions to undermine the writer's analysis, the writer must distinguish those decisions to explain why they should not be used to reject the writer's position. Depending on the strength of those counter arguments, writers may decide to attack them directly in the text or to distinguish them in footnotes so that they do not overemphasize counter arguments. To help use authority to their advantage, new practitioners should familiarize themselves with all citation signals from the appropriate citation manual. A discussion of the most common citation signals is included in Part B of Chapter 4.

f. Check Each Draft for Objective Discussion

When writing preliminary drafts of arguments, new practitioners often need to explain some of their ideas objectively to fully articulate the concept. Rather than stopping to revise the format of the presentation, most writers should allow themselves to write out the ideas with that objective focus so they fully develop the relevant ideas. Once they fully articulate those ideas, they should revise the argument to make it more persuasive, using the basic construction ideas outlined in this part of the chapter. Comparing the basic objective and persuasive presentation formats often assists writers to quickly make such initial revisions. The chart below outlines the basic differences between presenting an analysis objectively and persuasively:

Objective Presentation: Basic Outline of Analytical Components	**Persuasive Explanation: Basic Outline of Analytical Components**

• Description of law
  • Introduction of topic
  • Explanation of legal principle
  • Policy behind legal principle
  • Examples from decisions to illustrate legal principle and policy
• Prediction: Application to facts
  • Prediction on client's facts
  • Application of legal principle to facts to support prediction
  • Application of policy to support prediction
  • Comparisons of examples from decisions to client's facts to support prediction
	• Conclusion for client
	• Application and explanation of legal principle to client's facts to support conclusions
	• Discussion of how policy supports explanation of legal principle and application to client's facts
	• Examples and comparisons to decisions to support explanation of legal principle and policy and to compare to client's facts

For an example of an argument using basic argument construction, see annotation 6 to Appendix 4.

3. Argument Refinement: The Next Draft

Once writers have completed preliminary drafts of arguments, they should evaluate the best strategy to refine the final presentation. While all the analytical components from the rough draft should be included in the final argument, legal writers often change the structure of the argument to creatively use the analysis most persuasively. Every argument has a specific combination of how the writer should apply the law and the reasons behind the law to the facts. The placement, emphasis, and blend of the different analytical pieces vary from argument to argument.

The basic argument structure outlined in the previous part of this chapter may be an effective organization when the analysis applied to the situation clearly supports one conclusion and that conclusion is best for the lawyer's argument. However, in other arguments, some parts of the analysis support the argument more than the others. Therefore, writers often must revise their rough drafts to create the strongest argument possible by experimenting with different combinations of the analytical components. To help this process, writers should rework the rough draft and experiment with the best analytical focus for each specific argument.

a. Personalize the Argument: Creatively Weave Law and Fact

Refining arguments to find the optimal final presentation often takes many drafts. Writers must experiment with different ways to use, develop, and prove the different analytical components of the argument. Therefore, writers should revise the rough draft to try out different variations of organizing those components. When experimenting, writers need to be careful not to default back to writing their ideas objectively, but also need to be careful not to be so creative that readers would be reluctant to accept their ideas.

In arguments, the client's situation should control how the ideas are put together. This goal usually means that writers should avoid extensive abstract discussions of any part of the argument. Long discussions of legal principles or the policy behind those principles will not be very convincing unless the writer explains how those ideas relate to the argument by applying them to the client's situation. Similarly, lengthy recitations of the facts of the situation are not helpful because the reader needs to understand why those facts are relevant based on the relevant law. Thus, writers need to personalize all arguments by weaving the law and the client's situation together as much as possible from the beginning to the end of the argument.

When weaving the facts with the law and policy to develop the argument, writers need to state strong positions, but should keep in mind that decision makers, including courts and regulatory agencies, are very cautious about breaking new ground when deciding cases. Thus, lawyers need to support arguments as strongly as they can without appearing to be asking for a dramatically new interpretation of the law.

b. Experiment with Analytical Focus Options for Each Argument

To be as convincing as possible, the analytical focus of an argument depends on the specific relationship between the underlying analysis and the client's facts. The ideal mix of the legal standards, policy, and facts varies depending on the writer's strategy. When determining that strategy, new practitioners should experiment with organizations that emphasize different analytical building blocks: arguments that focus on legal standards, arguments that emphasize the policy supporting the legal standards, and arguments that stress the facts of the situation.

1. Legal Standard-Focused Arguments

When a black-letter standard clearly supports an argument, writers should consider emphasizing that standard in the argument. The standard could explicitly come from a statute, regulation, or interpretive decision. However, writers cannot simply state the standard, cite the authority, and apply the standard to the relevant facts and hope the reader accepts the conclusion. They also must explain how the policy behind the legal principle supports the articulated standard and how that reasoning supports an application of the standard to the client's facts in a way that dictates the result the writer is putting forth. Nonetheless, when creating an argument in which a specific legal principle has been expressed in a way that is helpful for the client's situation, writers may want to take advantage of the language and craft an argument around that stated principle.

Even when the legal standard is not explicitly stated in exactly the way writers would like, they may emphasize strongly implied legal principles in much the same manner as explicit standards. Writers may need to provide more citation and discussion of the policy that supports the implicit standard than if decisions had articulated the legal principle explicitly, but they could still create the argument by emphasizing the standard itself.

To craft arguments focused on legal standards, writers usually should include the standard very early in the argument, sometimes laying out the standard without reference to any facts in the topic sentence. Using the standard early helps highlight the specific language that supports the argument. However, writers should not include a long discussion of the standard without applying it to the relevant facts to personalize the argument to the case being argued. Thus, they should still apply the standard to the key relevant facts early in the argument.

Once writers have stated the standard and used it to support the argument by applying the standard to the key facts of the argument, they need to prove that the standard is accurate. They have two major tools to use to provide this corroboration: policy and examples from the decisions.

Writers should apply the policy to support the conclusion on the client's facts that they are putting forth. They must use the spirit of the law to demonstrate how the court should apply the legal standard to the key facts to find for the client.

Writers should use examples from the decisions as additional proof for the legal standard. Some opinions will help prove the standard with explicit language. Others will help support the standard with implicit ideas that writers must explain. Writers also should use decisions to illustrate and explain relevant policy. Finally, writers must demonstrate how the client's facts are similar to or different than the facts of decisions based on the standard and policy.

The difference between the rough draft of an argument explained in Part A.2 of this chapter and a revision of that argument that focuses on the legal standard is mainly that the legal standard is articulated and explained early in the argument. Thus, writers emphasize the standard before the client's facts. Often, writers use only key facts early in this type of argument. They add more details of the client's facts through the comparisons to decisions. This chart illustrates basic differences between the rough draft and revision of such an argument:

Basic Argument: Outline of Analytical Components	**Legal Standard-Focused Argument: Basic Outline of Analytical Components**
• Conclusion based on client's key facts • Application and explanation of legal principle to client's facts to support conclusions • Discussion of how policy supports explanation of legal principle and application to client's facts • Examples and comparisons to decisions to support explanation of legal principle and policy and to compare to client's facts	• Standard of law to support conclusions • Application of standard to key facts to state conclusion for client • Policy to support standard • Apply policy to key facts to support conclusion • Examples and comparisons to decisions to support explanation of legal principle and policy and to compare to client's facts

When revising a rough draft into a standard-focused argument, writers should avoid being too objective. Because the standard strongly supports the main premise in the argument, writers may default into objective writing by laying out an abstract discussion of the standard and related policy, providing examples from decisions to support those ideas and only toward the end apply the ideas to the client's situation.

To help reduce the risk of writing a standard-focused argument that is too objective, writers should avoid long, abstract, and objective explanations of legal standards and supporting policy without personalizing the argument to the situation by applying the standard to the client's situation. Thus, standard-focused arguments should emphasize the legal principles early in the argument, but writers should still combine the standards with the client's facts, policy, and decision examples throughout the argument. An easy technique to verify that the writer is taking these necessary steps is to ask, "So what?" after each paragraph. If a reader would not understand why the statement is relevant to the client's situation, the writer probably needs to connect the ideas more fully to the client's facts.

A comparison between an objective discussion of an issue and a standard-focused argument is included in this chart to help illustrate the differences between an objective discussion of a question and a standard-focused argument:

Objective Presentation: Basic Outline of Analytical Components	**Legal Standard-Focused Argument: Basic Outline of Analytical Components**

• Description of law
  • Introduction of topic
  • Explanation of legal principle
  • Policy behind legal principle
  • Examples from decisions to illustrate legal principle and policy
• Prediction: Application to facts
  • Prediction on client's facts
  • Application of legal principle to facts to support prediction
  • Application of policy to support prediction
  • Comparisons of examples from decisions to client's facts to support prediction
	• Standard of law to support conclusions
	• Application of standard to key facts to state conclusion for client
	• Policy to support standard
	• Apply policy to key facts to support conclusion
	• Examples and comparisons to decisions to support explanation of legal principle and policy and to compare to client's facts

To help illustrate the construction of a standard-focused argument, imagine in a non-competition argument that a writer taking the position that the employer has a legitimate interest in restricting an employee from competing against it, an idea that is the threshold requirement in most jurisdictions when analyzing enforceability of non-compete clauses in employment agreements. The court has explicitly stated that the employer is presumed to have a legitimate interest if the employee is the only contact with the employer's customers. The court has explained that such exclusive contacts suggest that customers likely would follow the employee to the competitor. The client's employee had exclusive contacts with the customers.

In this situation, the writer probably would want to focus the argument on the explicit legal standard about exclusive contacts because it clearly supports the best conclusion for the client. Early in the argument, the writer would lay out the articulated standard and apply it to the client's situation. Even if the court had not stated that exclusivity of contacts was the most important consideration, if all of the courts found that the relationship was sufficient in all of the cases where the contacts were exclusive, the writer could lay out the implicit standard regarding exclusivity and use it persuasively.

However, the writer would not simply quote the relevant cases and cite to the authority as complete support for this argument. Rather, the writer would need to prove that the articulated legal principle is the correct standard based on the relevant policy. The writer would want to convince the reader not only that the contacts that the client's employee had with customers were exclusive, but why those very contacts and their exclusive nature would likely mean that the client's customers would follow its employee to a competitor. Thus, the writer would be using all of the analytical building blocks to support the argument—the standard, the policy, and the client's facts—while emphasizing the reasoning step that would be most convincing to the reader.

For an example of a legal standard-focused argument, see annotation 9 to Appendix 4.

2. Fact-Focused Arguments

Legal writers must use relevant facts of the client's situation to convince the reader of the right conclusion in any argument, but in some arguments, the facts themselves so strongly favor the argument that the writer should emphasize them early. They should not simply state factual conclusions, however. Writers should emphasize the facts, but also prove their position with necessary legal standards and supporting policy.

When revising a rough draft into this type of fact-focused argument, writers should provide the key facts at the beginning of the argument, often in the first sentence or two. While usually not all of the facts can be included at this point, the key facts will help set the stage to develop the rest of the argument. Writers should avoid long, abstract discussions of nothing but facts, however. As soon as they state the argument with the key facts, they should provide legal support for those conclusions.

The best way to support a fact-centered argument with the necessary legal standards, policy, and comparisons to decisions varies. However, rarely should writers begin with examples from decisions. Examples will only be helpful once writers explain the law with the legal standards and policy. Thus, generally, writers should first support the factual conclusions with discussions of the legal standards and supporting policy. As they explain the standards and policy, they should apply the ideas to more details of the client's facts as further support.

Finally, writers should include comparisons of decisions to prove and support such an argument. At this point, writers should use the examples from decisions to show similarities and differences between the client's facts and the decisions. In addition, writers should demonstrate how those similarities or differences support the argument by fully explaining the comparisons using the standards and policy.

The main risk when using a fact-centric argument is that writers do not provide enough objective support from the law because they overly rely on the factual emphasis. In this situation, writers do not thoroughly explain the standards and policy to support the argument. Long discussions of only the client's facts and then comparisons to facts of decisions are not sufficient. The reader must understand how the facts are similar based on relevant legal standards and the policy behind those standards.

A comparison of the analytical components of an objective analysis to an outline of a fact-centered argument is included in this chart to help illustrate all of the analytical components that must be included in the fact-centered argument, even though the writer will emphasize the key facts early in the argument:

Objective Presentation: Basic Outline of Analytical Components	**Strong Facts Argument: Basic Outline of Analytical Components**

• Description of law
  • Introduction of topic
  • Explanation of legal principle
  • Policy behind legal principle
  • Examples from decisions to illustrate legal principle and policy
• Prediction: Application to facts
  • Prediction on client's facts
  • Application of legal principle to facts to support prediction
  • Application of policy to support prediction
  • Comparisons of examples from decisions to client's facts to support prediction
	• Conclusion highlighting best facts to support conclusion
	• Explanation of legal principle and policy to support conclusions
	• Apply explanation of legal principle and policy to more facts
	• Examples and comparisons to decisions to support explanation of legal principle and policy and to compare to client's facts

Using the legitimate interest argument discussed in the previous section as an example, imagine that rather than suggesting that exclusivity of contacts is the most important question, the court has only found that exclusivity is one idea among several others. The court has suggested that exclusivity, along with regularity and duration of the employee's customer contacts, determines if the customers would likely follow the employee to a competitor. Imagine that the client's employee was the exclusive contact, but only met with each customer fairly infrequently and only worked for the client for a year.

By focusing early in the argument on the exclusive nature of the relationship, before explaining the law, the writer would help plant the idea in the reader's mind that such exclusive contacts would mean that the employee developed the kind of relationship with the customers that would create a threat to an employer. The specifics of the standard might dilute the impact of the exclusivity idea if the writer emphasized the equal nature of the different factors too early. Thus, the writer would have created sympathy for the client's situation by emphasizing facts before moving on and explaining the relevance of the exclusive contact idea as one among several factors that the court considers. While the writer would use all of the factors, focusing the reader on the exclusive nature of the client's situation early on could help influence the reader's use of the court's standard and related policy, leading the reader the writer's point of view.

For an example of a fact-focused argument, see annotation 7 to Appendix 4.

3. Policy-Focused Arguments

Beginning an argument by explaining the spirit of the law before laying out specific legal standards or discussing the client's factual situation can be effective if the policy will influence readers to accept the argument more easily than the legal standard or an application of the standard to facts. In some situations, if readers do not understand the policy behind the stated legal principle, they might come to the wrong conclusion about how it should be applied to the facts. However, once readers appreciate the policy, they will grasp how that the policy supports the argument about how the law should be applied to the situation. In such an argument, writers could lay out the reasons behind the law before launching into a discussion of the specific standards. They would demonstrate that the policy behind the law should lead to the desired result given the facts of the situation. Thus, writers might be arguing for a slightly revised standard so that the result is consistent with the spirit of the law.

This type of argument is often necessary when the relevant law has not been fully developed or when the client's situation presents very different facts than the court has faced when analyzing the issue. The court's explicit legal principles may not have had time to develop to accurately reflect the spirit behind the law when applied to these new situations. By fully explaining the policy behind the law, writers should be able to guide the reader to understand why a court might need to adjust the legal principle to ensure that the result is consistent with the spirit of the law.

To begin this type of argument, writers should provide a statement of the policy that will support their contention. However, to avoid a very abstract discussion of policy, they should apply the policy ideas to the client's facts to demonstrate that the spirit behind the law supports the result they are seeking. Next, writers must either explain why the court should revise the stated standard to accomplish this result or propose a specific standard since the court has not articulated one. To support a new or revised legal principle, writers may need to provide more policy at this point to convince the reader of the accuracy of the standard. How straightforward writers should be that they are suggesting a new standard depends on the specific argument. At times, writers may simply be suggesting a slight variation to a previously accepted idea. They may decide that the best strategy is to simply offer the new language as a reflection of the true meaning of the previously stated analysis. Other times, writers may have to request a bolder change in the law, and the best strategy may be to candidly argue for the change by explaining why the requested refinement is a necessary modification.

Once writers have explained a new legal principle, they must continue to prove its accuracy by demonstrating how the standard would support comparisons to the examples from decisions that would make sense based on the policy. For example, writers might need to demonstrate that using the old, non-revised standard would lead to an incorrect finding that the client's situation is similar to the facts of a decision when the policy strongly suggests that the situation should be seen as very different. Then, they could prove the accuracy of the proposed standard by showing that the new standard would result in an accurate comparison of the client's situation and the facts of the decision based on the policy.

The challenge of drafting policy-focused arguments is to ensure that they are not too defensive or weakly supported with the decisions. Thus, writers need to carefully include all the analytical components, even though they are seeking a new or revised interpretation of what has been articulated in the past.

This chart compares the objective discussion of analysis with a breakdown of a policy-focused argument to demonstrate that all necessary analytical components are included in the argument:

Objective Presentation: Basic Outline of Analytical Components	**Policy-Focused Argument: Basic Outline of Analytical Components**

• Description of law
  • Introduction of topic
  • Explanation of legal principle
  • Policy behind legal principle
  • Examples from decisions to illustrate legal principle and policy
• Prediction: Application to facts
  • Prediction on client's facts
  • Application of legal principle to facts to support prediction
  • Application of policy to support prediction
  • Comparisons of examples from decisions to client's facts to support prediction
	• Explanation of policy
	• Conclusion on client's key facts based on policy
	• Explanation of new or revised standard
	• Application of new or revised standard to facts
	• Explanation how new or revised standard accomplishes policy concerns
	• Examples and comparisons to decisions to support explanation of legal principle and policy and comparison to client's facts

Using the same legitimate interest example in the non-compete clause argument from the previous two sections, imagine that the court has stated that the purpose of its analysis is to determine whether customers would likely follow an employee to a new employer because in that situation the former employer's business would be threatened. In all the cases, the employees were the only contact with the employer's customers. The opinions state that those exclusive customer contacts were the most important consideration in determining the question, though the length and regularity of the relationships were also important.

If the lawyer had to argue for an employer with employees who were not the exclusive contact with the customers, but the employees had a multi-year relationship with those customers and met with them several times monthly, the lawyer might be able to use a policy-centered argument. The lawyer could begin by emphasizing that the court's goal in the analysis is to determine whether clients would likely follow an employee to a competitor because the employer's business would be threatened in that situation. The writer could apply this general policy idea to the client's situation before dealing with the non-exclusive nature of the relationship. The court's stated goal of determining if clients would likely follow the employees to a competitor would help the lawyer use the facts of how long and regularly the employees had met with the customers to lead the reader to the conclusion that the customers would likely follow the employees, before dealing with the non-exclusive nature of the relationship. Thus, in effect, the writer would be arguing that the policy should shift the standard from using the exclusive nature of the contact as the most important factor to its being just one factor among several because the court's policy supports that change.

For an example of a policy-focused argument, see annotation 8 to Appendix 4.

B. PRESENTING ARGUMENTS IN COURT DOCUMENTS

When new practitioners prepare drafts of court memoranda, they must include all necessary information to create strong arguments based on the law, as discussed in the previous part of this chapter. After writers have completed those initial analytical steps, they will be ready to use them to prepare the appropriate court document. When preparing such documents, writers must consider the specific audience, the purpose of the brief, and the prescribed format of the document for the specific court.

An example of a court brief is included in Appendix 4.

1. Audience of Court Briefs

When preparing a brief, new lawyers must adjust their writing because they are addressing a court. However, rather than thinking of the reader as an abstract court, understanding that the readers are actual judges and people who assist the judges should help new practitioners tailor their writing to be more effective.

a. Judges as Primary Audience

When preparing a brief, writers must keep in mind that they are writing to the judge or judges who will decide the question. Therefore, briefs should be formal documents that give full deference to the judge and the decision-making responsibilities of the court.

To begin, writers should write with appropriate formality, avoiding casual or colloquial language. At the same time, writers should avoid using an overly stuffy tone and legalese. In addition, writers should be deferential to the court. They need to remember that they cannot force a judge to do anything. Therefore, writers should not express arguments in a threatening way or in a manner that attempts to bully the judge into a decision. Rather, they should use the strength of the analysis to convince the judge to come to the conclusions they are seeking. To be convincing, arguments must include all the detail a judge would need to make the decision. Writers should fully support their arguments with the law, policy, and facts of the situation so the judge has all the necessary information to decide the question.

Similarly, the court's decision-making role requires writers to carefully articulate and support all arguments without overstating their positions.

Judges have a responsibility to decide the questions based on the law and the facts. Although judges understand—and expect—lawyers to use creative arguments to help guide the decision-making process, writers need to be careful of overly zealous arguments that could affect their credibility. Thus, writers should use all factual information—good and bad—and deal with any authority that may weaken their argument so that the reader fully trusts their analysis.

b. Law Clerks as Secondary Audience

While the judge is the primary audience of any brief, new practitioners should realize than other people, such as law clerks, also work with the documents when assisting judges. Typically, law clerks read all arguments made by the different parties and then evaluate them on their own by doing independent research and analysis. The law clerk may prepare a memorandum to the judge objectively analyzing the issues and suggesting a decision.

Thus, new practitioners should keep in mind that a law clerk could be part of their audience as they are drafting their arguments. Law clerks are often new law school graduates who have not analyzed a large number of legal issues. If the brief provides the type of detail that will help that clerk accept the analysis in a way that supports the writer's argument, the law clerk is more likely to include the writer's ideas in the recommendation to the judge. Realizing that another new lawyer may be an important reader can help guide writers in determining the appropriate amount and type of support and detail when finalizing court briefs.

2. Purpose of Court Briefs

The purpose of court briefs is to provide the court with the information it needs to find in favor of the lawyer's arguments. To provide this information, writers must persuade the court of the arguments and inform the court of the information it needs to decide the question.

a. Persuading the Court

The purpose of presenting written arguments to the court is to convince the judge of the positions that will get the client the best result. Unlike objective writing, where the purpose is to explain the ideas to the reader who trusts the substance of the analysis, a brief must prove its ideas. Therefore, writers must provide all the information necessary to prove that the law should be applied to the client's facts in certain way, as discussed in Part A of this chapter.

b. Informing the Court

When lawyers file court documents, they are acting as officers of the court and therefore have a responsibility to provide the information the court needs to resolve the question. Local court rules and the rules of ethical conduct require court briefs to inform the court of certain information, even though that information may negatively affect the lawyer's argument. Therefore, when preparing a court brief, writers should be familiar with all of the relevant rules to ensure that they provide the required information. Generally, lawyers are required to disclose to the court legal authority that is directly adverse to their positions, but are not required to include all negative facts regarding their argument. However, leaving out negative facts that the other side may be able to use against the lawyer's argument generally is a risky strategy.

3. Format of Court Briefs

Writers should refer to the court rules to determine the appropriate format of the brief. While the format may change from court to court, most court filings are required to include several distinct sections: a caption and other introductory information, a statement of the relevant facts, an argument section, and a conclusion.

a. Caption and Preliminary Tables and Indexes

Court filings must include a caption that identifies the parties and the case filing information, such as the docket number. The court rules outline the required content and formatting of captions. In most situations, new practitioners will be drafting a court filing in ongoing litigation, so they should be able to find an example of the caption for the case in the client's file. However, they should confirm the accuracy of the caption with the local court rules before submitting a draft to a senior lawyer.

In addition to the caption, court rules often require other introductory information to assist the court, depending on the type of filing. For briefs supporting dispositive motions, such as motions to dismiss or motions for summary judgment, the court rules may require a table of contents, an index of authorities cited in the brief, and directories of other information. While such introductory information may seem like a formality, writers must be sure that the information is accurate and formatted according to the local rules.

For an example of a caption, see annotation 2 to Appendix 4.

b. Statement of Facts

Memoranda supporting court motions should include a section that provides a statement of the relevant facts. Most local court rules require citation to sources of the factual information, such as hearing transcripts, depositions, affidavits, interrogatories, and other discovery information. When drafting a brief, lawyers should refer to the court rules to determine what factual information they must cite and the form of the required citation.

To provide this information effectively, writers must carefully consider what information the court will need to decide the issue and determine the best way to present the information persuasively. To help make these evaluations, writers should consider the timing of drafting the Facts Section.

For an example of a Statement of Facts Section, see annotation 3 to Appendix 4.

1. Include All Information Necessary for Court to Accept Argument

To ensure that the court has all the necessary information to accept their arguments, writers must include all facts necessary for their argument and any other factual information that is necessary to put those facts in context for the reader.

Argument-reliant facts. Writers must include in the statement of the case any factual information that they use in the Argument Section of the brief. Thus, once writers have completed a fairly good draft of the relevant arguments, they should carefully review the Argument Section for all factual references and incorporate that information into the statement of the Facts Section.

Contextual facts. In addition to the facts used in the arguments, writers should include any other information necessary to understand the context of those facts. Contextual information should include all facts the reader needs to understand why the legal question is before the court, including relevant procedural information, as well as any information about the parties that would be necessary to fully understand the controversy. Similarly, writers might need to include information about the situation that the other party might use even though they have not included those facts in their argument. Otherwise, the reader might have the impression that they are trying to hide or avoid negative factual information.

2. Presenting Factual Information Persuasively

Presenting the statement of the case persuasively is challenging because writers must organize the factual information in a way that prepares the reader for the arguments without making the arguments. Therefore, writers must use their understanding of the arguments to guide choices about presenting the facts, including theme and perspective, persuasive organization, and effective language.

Theme. One important tool in preparing an effective statement of facts is using the theme of the argument to convey the core theory of the case through the story itself. As explained above in Part A, writers usually develop a theme to connect the different arguments together. They should use that theme as a guide to present the facts.

Perspective. The theme of the case also helps writers determine the best perspective to use when presenting the factual information. Often, writers use the client's perspective to tell the story, because they want the reader to understand the situation through the eyes of the client. However, different perspective choices are sometimes more helpful. If writers believe, for example, that the other party is unfairly benefitting from a situation, they, might decide that telling the story from the other party's perspective would help convey that theme. Similarly, if writers decide that the client or the client's position is not very sympathetic, they could use the perspective of a neutral third party when presenting the story.

Overall organization. The theme should also help writers determine the overall organization of the facts. Writers use the organization to emphasize good facts and downplay information that is less helpful. This strategy can be as simple as putting helpful information early in the section, while holding damaging information until later in the presentation or combining the good facts with damaging information to help reduce the impact of the bad information.

When considering overall organization to achieve these strategic choices, writers have a few options. In many circumstances, using the chronology of the situation is a good method for presenting the facts persuasively for the client. The story itself may help writers use the theme and perspective to set the stage for the arguments that will be included in the Argument Section.

Other times, however, writers may decide that a chronological organization is not the best choice. The facts of the situation may not lend themselves to a chronological recitation or using a timeline of events may not be the most persuasive narrative. In those situations, writers should consider a topical approach to group the facts around the issues that they will argue in the Argument Section. A topical approach allows them to connect different facts around the ideas that the reader will encounter in the Argument Section.

Writers will sometimes decide that a combination approach of mixing a chronological narrative with a topical presentation of the facts is most effective. For example, writers may decide that they should present the argument-reliant facts topically, but a timeline of the events will help the reader understand the context of those facts most effectively. Thus, they could begin the Statement of the Facts Section with a timeline of events and then group the other facts topically.

Micro-organizational strategies. Careful consideration of paragraph and sentence construction will also help writers draft effective statements of facts. Writers need to use these techniques to promote the theme by emphasizing some facts and downplaying others, without hiding relevant information. Placing certain facts at the beginning or the end of paragraphs and inserting other facts in the middle of those paragraphs will often highlight some facts for the reader and help the other facts fade in the reader's mind, or at least leave an impression that they are less important.

Similarly, construction of sentences can accomplish many of these same goals. Long sentences can help downplay facts, while shorter sentences highlight information. Subject and object placement can increase the impact of certain information as well. Grammatical construction, such as use of the passive voice, may also help de-emphasize information. However, writers should be careful with some grammatical techniques, such as use of the passive voice. Often, the intent of using the technique to hide or downplay information is too obvious and has the opposite effect.

Strategic word choice. Writers should carefully consider the language they choose to describe people, entities, and events in the Statement of the Facts. Specific word choice can highlight the theme of the arguments, emphasize helpful information, and alleviate the impact of damaging facts.

3. Timing for Drafting Facts Section

New practitioners should consider waiting to write the Statement of the Facts Section until they have a fairly final draft of the arguments. Until the arguments are fairly well developed, writers may have difficulty determining which facts should be included and how to present those facts persuasively. If writers have already worked through the relevant arguments by brainstorming and refining the ideas in the arguments, they will be able to quickly determine which facts to include and the best way to persuasively present them.

c. Argument Section

The Argument Section is the part of the brief that explains and supports the writer's positions. Once writers have developed the relevant arguments as explained in the previous part of this chapter, they are ready to prepare this section. To draft it, they must decide how to organize the different arguments and include headings and introductions for those arguments.

For an example of an Argument Section, see annotation 5 to Appendix 4.

1. Organizing and Dividing the Arguments

The major strategic decision when drafting the Argument Section is determining the best organization to highlight the strengths of the case. While briefs usually include at least one major argument, many of those major arguments have components. Writers may divide and organize those different parts to highlight their strongest points. For separate arguments or sub-arguments, writers may use headings and introductions to highlight key ideas.

First, writers should organize most Argument Sections around the different claims or grounds for relief. Each section should begin with a major heading and introduction to support the major claim, followed by the arguments for that claim. If, however, writers combine several independent grounds of relief in the brief, they should organize the Argument Section around those different claims and include separate headings and introductions for each independent argument. For example, in a brief in support of a motion seeking declaratory judgment that a non-compete clause is enforceable, the result the party is seeking is enforcement of the clause. Thus, the major point heading and overall introduction should focus on that claim. If, however, the brief were in support of a motion for declaratory judgment or, alternatively, a motion for summary judgment seeking damages for breach of the clause, the Argument Section should include a major point heading for each of those grounds for relief.

Writers can divide major arguments into sub-arguments if the supporting legal analysis has different components. Leading the reader through the argument with short, concise sub-arguments that are well reasoned and easy to explain is often the most effective persuasive tool. Some arguments may have stronger impact if they are included in a stand-alone section. Other arguments are more effective when combined in sections with other related sub-arguments.

Therefore, dividing large, complex arguments into component pieces can be very convincing because shorter sections tend to make the information easier for the reader to follow and absorb. The less taxing the task of following the argument, the more likely the reader will stay focused and follow the writer's point of view from argument to argument. Thus, writers should try to divide arguments into manageable parts so that they do not ask readers to read complex arguments for several pages without a break.

On the other hand, dividing arguments into too many small pieces may lessen the impact of the main idea or the relationship between the different sub-arguments. Therefore, writers should avoid dividing arguments into too many very short sections that cause the writing to feel choppy and disconnected. Instead of using too many separate sections, writers can use good topic sentences and other clear transitions to connect short related arguments in the same section.

In addition to strategically dividing the Argument Section, writers must carefully consider where to place each argument to be as persuasive as possible. One technique is to begin the section with the strongest argument, placing weaker positions in the middle of the section, and ending with a convincing idea. While beginning with the strongest point and burying weaker arguments are good basic guidelines, often the legal analysis dictates an organization that may not allow writers to highlight strong ideas first and wait to discuss weaker arguments. Therefore, writers must determine the most effective placement of each argument within the confines of the analysis itself.

2. Headings

One important reason for dividing the brief into sub-arguments is to have headings to highlight the major ideas in the brief. Writers should use each heading to convey the theme and emphasize the key ideas in the arguments. To make headings as effective as possible, writers should consider several ideas.

First, headings should be a clear, vivid, and concise summary of the argument in the section. Writers should avoid using headings that only introduce abstract legal ideas. Instead, most headings should personalize the argument to the client's situation by applying the main legal idea to the key facts to state the contention they are asserting in the section.

In addition, headings should be as concise as possible. Most headings should only be one short sentence and no more than about three or four lines of text. Since headings are only a summary of the argument that the writers will fully support in the section, they should not include any citation.

Furthermore, writers must remember that headings are independent from the text of the argument itself. Headings do not replace the topic sentences of sections, though they often may be similar. However, writers should not simply restate the topic sentence as the heading. Rather, writers should draft headings that emphasize the key ideas differently than the related topic sentences, though both should be persuasive summaries of the main argument in the section.

To help ensure that the headings are independent from the text, writers can use a fairly simple technique. After they have written the headings, writers can copy and paste the headings and subheadings into a separate document to verify that the headings alone provide a complete outline of the arguments. This outline alone should highlight the best facts for the client and provide a cohesive theme to the arguments. In addition, writers should read the entire brief without referring to any headings to ensure that they are not using the headings to replace necessary transitional topic sentences in the text itself.

Finally, writers must conform the headings to the local rules. Most court rules dictate the numbering and formatting for headings. In addition, writers should follow basic outlining guidelines. If writers divide a section into subsections, they must include at least two subsections. The only exception to this rule relates to the overall major heading. Briefs should always begin with a major heading, even if the argument only includes one major argument. For all other sections, however, if writers use any subheadings under an argument, they must be able to use at least two subheadings in that argument.

For an example of a heading, see annotation 4 to Appendix 4.

3. Introductions

For each argument with a heading, writers should begin with an introduction of how they will prove to the reader the position they are asserting in that specific argument. Writers should not simply provide an objective summary of the different topics that they will explain in the section. Rather, they must use the introduction to persuasively introduce and tie together the ideas that they will handle in the section.

To be effective, introductory sections should be as short and concise as possible to quickly introduce the ideas that writers will argue in the section. In fact, some experienced brief writers take the position that introductions should only be one paragraph. However, introductory sections may vary in length depending on the complexity of the arguments.

In addition, most introductions should begin with a clear statement of the main point the writers are asserting in the section. For introductions to the major arguments, writers should state the relief the party is seeking from the court. For introductions to sub-arguments, they should introduce the major idea that they will prove in that argument. Thus, writers must state in a fairly short sentence exactly what the result should be in the client's situation for the argument or sub-argument.

Once writers state the overall conclusion, they must provide the legal mechanism that supports that result. They must use the client's key facts and the relevant policy ideas to explain the overall structure of the law that they will use when making the arguments in the discussion. They may have to include abstract information about the law and policy behind the legal concepts, but the focus should be on how those ideas will lead the reader to the writer's desired result given the client's key facts.

Finally, writers must provide a roadmap of the ideas that they will explain in the argument. However, writers should not attempt to fully support those ideas in introductions. Thus, they should not include detailed information about the law or decisions that support specific arguments. Rather, the focus should be on the overall conclusion and a basic framework of arguments that they will fully support in the rest of the argument.

Writing a persuasive introduction is not a simple task. Many new practitioners are unsure of how to craft introductions to make them persuasive, while still including the right amount of detail. Many of the uncertainties when drafting introductory sections are often a result of trying to write introductions too early. Most writers will more effectively write introductory sections by waiting until after they have completed a good draft of all of the sub-arguments. Once all of the arguments have been written, they will often have a better understanding of how to introduce all of those ideas persuasively by highlighting the key facts and broad policy that establish the theme for the arguments and providing the reader with a roadmap to the arguments included in the section.

4. Use of Authority: Citation and Quotations

The goal of a brief is to prove the arguments to the judge, rather than just analyzing and summarizing the law objectively. Therefore, when using authority in a brief, writers should imagine that they are taking the reader through the authority and showing how it precisely supports their arguments piece by piece. Writers cannot simply state propositions and provide citation.

Therefore, conclusory statements with long citations generally are not helpful. Sometimes, string citations with several authorities may show that the weight of the law supports the arguments, but even in those situations, the reader needs more than just a long citation as proof of the argument. To prove their arguments, writers must explain in detail how the authority supports their positions. Sometimes, this proof requires extensive discussion of individual pieces of authority as well as an explanation of how different sources of authority relate to each other in a way that supports the assertions.

Some lawyers quote too much from the authority when drafting arguments because they mistake the use of quotations with proof of how the authority supports their assertions. While quotations sometimes do help prove arguments, simply stringing long quotations from a variety of sources is not persuasive. To be effective, quotations should be used sparingly and only in combination with a thorough explanation of the arguments. When using quotations, writers must show how the quoted language specifically supports the arguments. Therefore, they must explain how the quotation should be used along with ideas from other pieces of authority and the relevant policy goals to prove their contention.

5. Citing the Facts

When referring to facts in the Argument Section, some local court rules require citation for the factual information even though the writer has provided citation to the facts in the Statement of the Facts Section. Thus, when drafting a brief, lawyers should refer to the court rules to determine how to provide the necessary citation for factual information used in the arguments.

d. Conclusion Section

Briefs can include two different types of Conclusion Sections. Local court rules usually provide which form writers should use. The shortest Conclusion Section simply requests that the court decide the issue in favor of the lawyer's client for the reasons stated in the brief. Thus, this conclusion is a simple, one-sentence statement followed by the signature of the lawyer filing the brief with the court.

The more complete conclusion is one that substantively summarizes the major arguments in the brief to support the claim for relief. In this type of conclusion, writers must begin with a clear statement of the overall relief and support that claim with a quick summary of the major arguments. This section gives writers another opportunity to use the theme to highlight the key facts that support the major arguments. Therefore, this type of conclusion should not be an abstract summary of the law. Rather, the conclusion should be a persuasive summary of why the policy and main legal concepts argued in the brief, when applied to the key facts, should result in a finding in favor of the their position.

For an example of a Conclusion Section, see annotation 10 to Appendix 4.

C. OTHER TYPES OF PERSUASIVE WRITING

In law practice, even non-litigators write a variety of persuasive documents based on legal arguments. For example, business lawyers may write demand letters to other parties on behalf of clients or write to opposing counsel to persuade the other side of their client's position. Transactional lawyers often send cover memos or emails with the marked-up documents supporting the proposed changes. Other lawyers write to regulatory agencies putting forth positions for their clients in formal filings or more informal letters. Even some internal-office writing may be persuasive because lawyers write emails and memos trying to persuade their colleagues or clients of their point of view when determining strategy in litigation or transactions. To effectively prepare these different types of persuasive documents, new practitioners must carefully consider the audience and purpose of the writing and adapt their persuasive technique to fit the different documents.

1. Audience and Purpose of Non-Court Persuasive Writing

The main challenge when writing a persuasive document that is not a court filing is determining the appropriate amount of detail. As with any writing, fully understanding the audience and the purpose of the document will guide writers when deciding how much information to include. When writing to a court, the document must fully articulate and prove the arguments based on the law, policy, and facts because the court is the decision maker who will decide the question. In other types of persuasive writing, the level of detail that should be included to support the assertions varies depending on to whom the document is written and why.

Some non-court persuasive writing should include the same amount of support that writers would include in a court filing. Often, they are trying to prove to the reader that the law fully supports the claims to convince the reader to take a certain course of action. For example, in some pre-litigation negotiations, lawyers may try to convince the other side that the strength of their case should dictate a favorable settlement. By fully presenting the arguments, they are attempting to demonstrate the strength of those claims. Thus, a complete explanation of the legal arguments could help move the other side to settle the case more favorably for their client.

At the other end of the spectrum is persuasive writing that does not include much support for the claims made. Often, lawyers write letters or other documents to simply outline the legal rights of their clients to provide notice of those claims to begin negotiations or litigation. For example, lawyers write demand letters to another party to state all potential claims rather than to prove the strength of those claims. The purpose of the letter is to demonstrate the power of their position by stating all possible legal theories that the opposing party must evaluate if that party does not concede to the demands. In these situations, because the goal is only to provide notice of the different claims, often the best strategy is not to include any support because the other side might recognize weaknesses of the position and respond accordingly.

At this stage, lawyers usually do not want to reveal too much about the strengths or weaknesses of the case. Because they simply stated the demands, the other side must fully evaluate the claims.

In between a fully supported argument and a simple outline of demands falls most other non-court persuasive writing. In these documents, writers usually include an outline of the different claims and some basic legal support for the arguments. Determining exactly how much legal support such a document should include is a decision that they should make with the advice of the supervising lawyer. Therefore, new practitioners should seek guidance about how much information to include when drafting these types of documents.

However, writers should have an idea of the strategy they feel is best when requesting that advice. If possible, they should prepare a draft of the document with the level of support they think appropriate so they can use the draft to ask for specific guidance as to how much detail they should add to or delete from the draft as they finalize the document. Supervising lawyers will usually have an easier time making the final strategic evaluation if they have a draft document to use when making the judgment.

2. Techniques to Develop Arguments for Non-Court Persuasive Writing

Preparing persuasive documents that do not include full support of the various arguments can be as challenging as drafting fully supported court documents. To prepare non-court filing persuasive documents, writers must fully understand all the various arguments, determine the most effective theme to connect the arguments, and prioritize those arguments to choose only certain points they will include in the writing. Thus, preparing these documents is somewhat similar to preparing the opening statement for an oral argument. To prepare an opening statement, lawyers must fully understand the intricacies of all the different arguments because they can only choose a few points to highlight in the statement. When writing letters or other documents that include only an outline of the arguments or some selective support, writers are making a similar judgment as to what to include.

Generally, the most effective way for new practitioners to prepare non-court persuasive writing is to prepare the arguments as fully as they would if they were supporting them in a court brief. This step ensures that writers have all the necessary information to determine how much detail they should include based on the specific audience and purpose of the writing. This determination will be most accurate if the lawyer has gone through the process required for drafting a court brief—even though the form of the final presentation will be different—because the steps of developing, refining, and perfecting the argument that writers use to prepare court documents is usually the best method to fully evaluate final arguments. Trying to short-cut this analytical process is not ideal. If possible, writers should write out all arguments as they would for a court document, without the formalities of headings and introductory sections.

Most often, however, practitioners do not have the time to prepare a full draft of the arguments before writing their persuasive documents. In these situations, writers should use the steps for developing arguments and brief writing that are outlined in this chapter. They should try to find the time to sketch out or outline the various arguments even if they cannot fully write them out. By composing an outline or some type of shorthand sketch and the support behind the arguments, writers will have worked through enough of the analytical process to help determine the amount of detail that should be included in their specific document.

SUMMARY

New lawyers may be required to argue on behalf of clients in a variety of settings and in different types of writing. Therefore, learning to compose effective legal arguments is an important skill for new practitioners. To draft most types of persuasive writing that they may be assigned early in practice, new practitioners should consider a few key steps:

- Use the analysis strategically:
    - Begin with a neutral understanding of the law.
    - Use the neutral understanding to brainstorm potential arguments.
    - Determine a theme.
    - Evaluate and choose best arguments.
- Learn basic argument construction:
    - Understand differences between presenting an analysis neutrally and persuasively.
    - State conclusion based on client's key facts.
    - Apply legal principle to client's facts to support conclusions.
    - Use policy to support argument.
    - Use factual comparisons to support argument.
- Refine basic arguments:
    - Legal standard-focused arguments.
    - Fact-focused arguments.
    - Policy-focused arguments.

- Know how to present arguments in court documents:
  - Consider the audience and purpose of the specific document.
  - Learn the appropriate format for the specific court:
    - Caption.
    - Statement of the facts.
    - Argument.
    - Citation.
- Develop techniques to present arguments in other persuasive writings.

CHAPTER 6

Fundamentals of Agreement Drafting

Agreement drafting is an integral part of law practice. Transactional lawyers advise clients about legal issues raised by their deals and memorialize the transactions with documents that protect their clients' interests. Non-transactional lawyers often draft short agreements for their clients as well. For example, a litigator may draft a settlement agreement or a release of claims for a client who settles an action. Therefore, new lawyers in any area of practice may be asked to assist with drafting an agreement. Although these documents take many forms—from very long bond indentures to simple contracts regarding the sale of personal property—most are some type of agreement that explains the rights and responsibilities of the different parties.

Preparing agreements is a different kind of writing than drafting other types of legal documents. In most legal writing, writers articulate the relevant legal analysis and tailor the presentation of that analysis to the purpose of the document. In most agreements, however, writers do not explain the underlying legal ideas. Rather, the point of the document is to specify the parties' rights and obligations. Legal requirements may require the lawyers to construct the agreement in a particular way, but they typically do not explain those ideas in the document itself.

Therefore, the process that most novice legal writers should use to draft agreements is often different from the methods they use to prepare other types of legal writing. To help develop that process, the first part of this chapter explores methods to develop the substantive foundation of agreements. Then, the chapter explains basic drafting techniques to help writers use the foundational underpinnings to complete effective agreements.

A. UNDERSTANDING THE SUBSTANTIVE FOUNDATION OF AGREEMENTS

Although the relevant analysis controls all legal documents, because agreements typically do not include an explanation of the underlying law, new practitioners need to carefully consider how the substantive foundation of the agreement affects the writing process. When preparing a predictive or persuasive assignment, writers develop the underlying legal analysis as they complete the project. The final document is an expression of that analysis and how those analytical ideas apply to the relevant factual information. The writing process helps the writers understand, verify, and refine the ideas that they express in the final document. When drafting an agreement, however, the writing is not an expression of the underlying analysis. Rather, the function of the language in the agreement is to describe the parties' rights and responsibilities. While legal requirements may affect agreement formation, the purpose of the document is not to explain that legal analysis. Writers must draft the language to fulfill certain legal parameters, but rarely would they include an explanation of the analysis underlying those parameters.

For example, when writing a memo or a brief dealing with the requirements for enforcing an indemnity agreement, lawyers would explain the legal analysis for the requirements and use that analysis to predict or advocate the result on the given facts. The writing would explain the different requirements and the policy behind those requirements so that the reader fully understood the legal analysis. If composing the necessary language for the indemnity agreement itself, however, lawyers would carefully draft the language to satisfy the jurisdiction's legal requirements, but the underlying analysis of the requirements would not be included. They would describe the actions to which the parties have agreed without an explanation of how the legal analysis affects those obligations.

Therefore, when drafting agreements, lawyers must determine the relevant analysis and then use that understanding to draft an agreement that satisfies the client's needs within the legal parameters. A clear sense of the audience and purpose of agreements will help novice legal writers take the necessary steps to fully develop the ideas to support agreement drafting—even when those ideas are not part of the document itself. Writers also need to consider techniques to determine the clients' needs and how those requirements interact with the law that relates to the transaction.

1. Audience and Purpose of Agreements

Agreements are forward-looking documents, prepared to outline the actions the parties must undertake and the consequences if they do not fulfill those obligations. As in any writing, the first step in preparing agreements is to fully understand who will read the document and how the reader will use it. This information helps writers determine the amount of detail that they need to include and the appropriate style of the presentation. For most other types of law-practice documents—memos and briefs, for example—novice legal writers understand the audience fairly easily because either they know the ultimate readers personally or they can imagine who those readers are. Furthermore, new lawyers quickly appreciate how the purpose of writing a memo to a colleague to provide a neutral assessment of the situation dictates different writing choices than they would make if they were writing to persuade the reader of a given position. Understanding the audience and purpose of transactional documents will also help new practitioners prepare agreements, even though who the audience is and exactly how documents will be used by that audience may be less obvious to new lawyers than in other forms of legal writing.

The audience that drafters should use as a guide when preparing agreements is a neutral observer, such as a judge or arbitrator, without any prior knowledge of the parties or any details of the transaction. Unfortunately, some novice legal writers construct agreements using the parties as their target audience. While the parties themselves are important, the problem with using them as the primary audience is that the nature of their relationship or the parties themselves, through death or assignment of the agreement, may change over time. In fact, case law is replete with examples of friendly transactions turned hostile. Thus, writers should include all information that a disinterested observer—with no knowledge of the transaction—would need to fully understand the rights and responsibilities of all parties.

Once writers have a neutral observer in mind as the audience, they must consider how that observer will use the agreement. Writers must assume that the neutral observer would be reading the document to arbitrate a controversy regarding the transaction without any previous knowledge of the matter. Thus, the reader would use the document to determine the rights and responsibilities of the different parties to make a decision as to what a particular party must do to comply with the agreement or what a party's duties are once the agreement has been violated.

Understanding that a neutral observer—as opposed to a friendly or hostile party to the transaction—will use the document to determine the rights and obligations of all parties will help guide writers to explain the terms and conditions in agreements more clearly and completely.

2. Determining the Client's Interests

Writers must fully understand the client's needs to prepare an agreement that would fully protect the client if an impartial arbiter used it to resolve a conflict. The most obvious way to obtain this information would be to handle a client's situation from beginning to end, allowing lawyers to work directly with the client to obtain the relevant information about what the client is hoping to accomplish in the transaction. In this situation, lawyers would interview the client to determine the client's needs and wishes, research and analyze the relevant legal issues, negotiate with the other parties, and finally draft the agreement.

While handling the entire transaction allows writers to understand more fully the client and the context of the client's interests in the transaction, very few new practitioners are given full responsibility of any type of agreement early in their career. Most clients require representation from more senior lawyers who have experience dealing with transactional issues. Even with fairly simple agreements, clients benefit from experienced transactional lawyers who are able to quickly assess the needs of a clients holistically to best accomplish the clients' goals while fully protecting them through the transactional documents

Therefore, most new practitioners who are asked to draft agreements receive all the relevant information from their senior colleagues. In fact, often senior attorneys will ask junior colleagues to draft a portion of a larger agreement or draft a self-contained agreement that is part of a larger transaction.

Nonetheless, junior lawyers must invest the time to fully understand the client, the needs of the client, and how the transactional documents are protecting those interests, even when the particular agreement or clause is just a small part of a larger transaction. Therefore, junior attorneys must study the client and the transaction through the information that senior lawyers provide them, but must also be willing to request more information from senior colleagues when necessary. When drafting a clause or a small portion of an agreement, if writers do not fully understand the larger transaction, they will not be confident that the language they prepare completely fulfills the needs of the client or satisfactorily protects the client's interests.

3. Drafting Within the Parameters of the Law

When preparing agreements, the main duty is to ensure that the document protects clients' interests. To accomplish this task, lawyers must not only understand the clients' wishes, but also how the law will affect the ability of the client to attain their goals. Thus, at the core of all agreements must be a clear understanding of the underlying law that controls the different aspects of the transaction.

In the best situation, the law would allow clients to transact their affairs in exactly the way they believe would maximize their benefit from the transaction.

In reality, however, the law often restricts the ability to optimally protect a client's interests. Thus, the lawyer's job is to negotiate and draft documents that provide maximum benefit and protection to the client within the confines of the law. When drafting agreements, lawyers must identify all relevant legal questions, research and analyze those issues, and use their understanding of the legal analysis to draft an agreement that satisfies the client's needs and protects the client's interests.

In some smaller transactions, lawyers handling the matter analyze all legal questions and draft the agreement according to their understanding of the law. In most situations, however, practitioners do not start from scratch by independently analyzing the law for all the legal issues raised by a transaction. Rather than undertaking a full independent analysis of all the issues for each new transaction, they generally rely on work that others have done on previous transactions to create new agreements.

For example, many practitioners rely on form documents by legal publishers as a starting place for agreements. Similarly, law offices create their own model agreements using the expertise of their lawyers who have handled similar transactions over many years. Those lawyers have often perfected the provisions in the sample documents to represent the best language for the type of transaction.

While form or model documents often provide a useful place to begin, junior practitioners must be careful when using samples to draft new agreements. Although they may not be required to fully analyze the underlying law that various writers have used to construct the agreements, they must understand the legal analysis that is reflected in the documents to tailor the agreements to their specific transactions.

For some transactions, junior lawyers may be asked to assist with the entire transaction—from meeting with the client to drafting the final agreement. Thus, they will help senior colleagues identify and analyze the relevant legal questions necessary to draft an agreement. When, however, new practitioners are asked to handle only a part of a larger transaction—either a clause in an agreement or a stand-alone agreement that is one piece of a multifaceted transaction—they probably will not be able to fully understand all legal issues related to the overall transaction. In fact, rarely would a senior lawyer expect a junior colleague to take the time to learn all facets and related legal issues of a large transaction.

Working on a portion of a larger agreement is challenging because the junior lawyers likely will have to prepare language about one aspect of the transaction without having a full understanding of all relevant issues. In this situation, they should analyze the law relevant to the provision they are drafting to prepare the appropriate language. They should be careful to communicate to the senior colleagues that they have analyzed only the law that relates to that specific provision and they did not analyze any other legal issues that may be involved in the transaction.

When working on an entire transaction or just a portion of an agreement, junior lawyers may be asked to draft new language for agreements based on their own analysis of the relevant law. This situation occurs most often when the law has evolved and sample language needs to be updated or when the particular transaction raises a novel legal issue. The best scenario would be for the senior attorney to ask the junior colleague to prepare a memorandum regarding the law relevant to that portion of the agreement. If so, the writer would analyze the law and identify the different issues that create limitations on the transaction structure. The senior attorney, using that memorandum, would discuss the different options with the client, and the client would decide which is the best one. Then, the senior attorney would direct the junior colleague about what approach to use in the agreement.

Often, however, in the busy world of law practice, agreement drafting occurs as negotiations are ongoing. Therefore, senior colleagues often ask junior lawyers to analyze a legal issue related to a transaction and draft language based on that analysis without writing a formal memo. The junior lawyers may only have time to research and quickly analyze the relevant legal analysis and use that understanding to draft the language, skipping the step of analyzing the question systematically in a memo.

When faced with this type of situation, new practitioners need to develop techniques to ensure that they take all the steps necessary to understand the nuances of the analysis before finalizing the language of the agreement. They need to work from their research notes—charts, outlines, or other short summaries of the analysis—to develop and verify the legal analysis that affects the language of the agreement, going through all the analytical steps that they would have taken when writing a memo.

Handling these condensed assignments typically does not create a problem for writers when the analysis provides clear guidance on the necessary language for the provisions. If the law is clear, lawyers should draft the provision based on that understanding and explain it to the senior attorney, even if the language is contrary to the client's preferred structure. The junior lawyers should be prepared to explain to their supervising colleagues why the language is different from the client's requested structure.

The situation is more complex, however, if the law does not provide clear direction on the necessary language. This problem is compounded when the law—although not entirely clear about the exact nature of the language that should be included—indicates that the client's preferred terms would not be acceptable. When the law only provides a variety of less-than-optimal options, writers must evaluate the different options and determine the best way to explain the different possibilities so the senior lawyer can help the client make a decision.

If junior lawyers do not have time to prepare a formal memorandum, they could present the issues verbally to the senior attorney before attempting to draft the language. Another option would be to quickly draft different versions of the agreement that the law seems to support and present those versions to the senior attorney. Seeing the different options in writing could help the senior lawyer more quickly understand the choices and thus be able to more quickly and efficiently discuss the different options with the client. Annotating the different versions with quick explanations of how the legal analysis affects each variation is often a helpful technique when presenting different options.

B. EFFECTIVE AGREEMENT PREPARATION

Agreement drafting is a skill that can take years to master. For this reason, there are complete law school courses and a variety of treatises that explore the questions of drafting philosophy and technique. However, new lawyers will be able to learn to successfully complete most drafting assignments if they use a few basic concepts. As discussed in the previous part of this chapter, they need to understand the audience and purpose of the document, the client's needs, and the relevant law related to the agreement. Once they have those ideas in mind, they should consider a few drafting techniques and carefully think about drafting new agreements when using form documents or examples of agreements.

An example of an agreement is included in Appendix 5.

1. Basic Drafting Techniques

When drafting any type of agreement, the writer's goal should be to prepare a document that guides the reader through the terms of the agreement in a simple and straightforward fashion. This task can be challenging because often agreements embody multifaceted transactions that balance the interests of the different parties within complex legal parameters. To help draft easy-to-read agreements, junior lawyers should

- Carefully consider the overall organization;
- Make the provisions of the document internally consistent;
- Define certain terms;
- Format the document for ease of reading;
- Use simple language; and
- Verify that the terms of the agreement accomplish the goals of the transaction.

a. Organizational Plan

An agreement is a memorialization of a deal agreed to between the parties. All transactions involve a story that includes the different parties;

what their roles are in the transaction; the obligations and rights of those parties; and the consequences if certain actions are taken or not. Using the narrative as an organizing principle is often the simplest way to structure an agreement. The narrative approach keeps the writer's focus on the reader, who, as an impartial observer without any prior knowledge of the transaction, would use the language to settle conflicts between the parties.

Thus, to use the narrative to guide the organization, in most agreements, drafters should include an introductory section in which they present the different parties. The introduction also should include a short statement about why the parties are entering into the agreement. This summary should help the reader understand how the terms of the agreement fit together. After the introduction, the agreement should include a section that explains the details of the story by specifying the rights and responsibilities of the different parties. Finally, the agreement should conclude with an explanation of the consequences for different parties if they do not complete the actions required in the other provisions.

For an example of an introductory section to an agreement, see annotation 2 to Appendix 5. For an example of the section explaining the rights and responsibilities of the parties and related consequences, see annotation 4 to Appendix 5.

b. Consistent Expression of Ideas

Writers should carefully consider how to lay out provisions to make them easy to follow for a neutral observer to arbitrate the transaction if necessary. To help with ease of reading, writers should express the same ideas consistently throughout the document. The use of consistent expression simply means that writers should state the same idea in the same way in the entire agreement. Once writers determine the best way to express the idea, they should not change the manner of expressing it in a different place in the agreement. Changing even a word or two could create ambiguity.

Similarly, when laying out the different provisions, writers should use parallel construction to ensure that they explain different provisions in similar ways. While drafters do not need to organize all sentences or paragraphs exactly the same, they should use parallel construction whenever possible. Drafters should organize paragraphs by placing major ideas in about the same location in each paragraph. Similarly, they should construct sentences so that they introduce the subject, the action, and the object of each provision in roughly the same place.

Many novice writers feel that expressing ideas in the same way with parallel construction is repetitive and uncreative. But for readers, the repetitive nature allows them to follow the terms of the agreement more quickly, helps them locate and relocate different provisions easily, and reduces ambiguity. Thus, expressing the same ideas in the same way and using parallel construction help make even a complex agreement easy to understand and follow.

Expressing ideas consistently with parallel construction is challenging for many novice legal writers when preparing an agreement from whole cloth, but becomes even more difficult when they must draft provisions in a larger document. When drafting only part of an agreement, writers must spend the necessary time familiarizing themselves with the entire document so they are able to articulate the same ideas in a consistent manner and craft the provisions using the same type of construction that is used in the larger agreement.

c. Defined Terms

Even in fairly short agreements, defining important terms will help provide clarity and precision. However, writers need to carefully select the terms they define and use simple, clear definitions. In addition, writers should determine the best placement of the definitions of terms so they help make the agreement easy to follow and understand. For an example of definitions in an agreement, see annotations 3 and 5 to Appendix 5.

1. Which Terms to Define

Writers should only define terms if the terms have a particular meaning to the specific transaction. Writers should not further define legal terms that they use for their generally understood meaning. However, they should include definitions for terms of art or technical ideas that a neutral observer deciding a dispute regarding the agreement would not understand without the definition.

For example, often drafters define the parties by the role they play in the transaction. Thus, a writer would define the term "buyer" in a business-asset purchase agreement as the specific entity purchasing the assets. Similarly, an agreement might require the seller to purchase a variety of insurance policies during the purchase period, so the writer could define "insurance" as all of those different policies.

Writers should only define a term if they will use the same term repetitively in the agreement. If they will only use the term once or twice, writers should consider explaining the full meaning of the term when they use it—even if they repeat that explanation twice—rather than asking the reader to refer back to the definitional section. For an example of repeating an in-text definition instead of adding the term to the definitional section because the term is used only twice, see annotation 5 to Appendix 5.

2. Clear and Concise Definitions

Definitions should be as simple and concise as possible. Using short sentences with clear transitions between ideas helps the reader grasp and retain the relevant definitions. Writers should not use the term they are defining, or a similar form of the word, in the definition. For example, a writer should not define "Motor Vehicle" as "a vehicle that is motorized."

Finally, writers should avoid definitions that refer to other definitions. While sometimes writers must refer to another defined term in a definition, they should be aware that asking the reader to jump from definition to definition, especially when referring back to the definitional section when reading the agreement, is confusing and time-consuming. Therefore, writers should attempt to provide all definitions in a manner that avoids referencing other definitions as much as possible.

3. Location of Definitions

In a short agreement with only a few simple definitions, drafters may decide that using parenthetical definitions in the body of the agreement is easier for the reader than adding a separate definitional section. For example, at the beginning of an asset purchase agreement, the writer could describe the entity purchasing the assets and then add the word "Buyer" in a parenthetical after the name of the company. The writer could define other terms in similar manner throughout the agreement.

However, parenthetical definitions woven into the text of an agreement can quickly become cumbersome and hard to relocate, so writers should only use the technique if they define a few terms. If the agreement requires more than two or three definitions, writers should probably include a definitional section. Similarly, if some of the definitions are long or complex, they should probably use a separate definitional section rather than defining the term in the body of the agreement, even if the agreement only has a few defined terms. For an example of a definitional section in an agreement, see annotation 3 to Appendix 5.

Sometimes references to exhibits or attachments can help make definitional sections more concise. For example, if a purchase and sale agreement involved a two-page inventory of assets, including that list as an attachment to the agreement and referring to it in the asset definition would be less cumbersome than including a two-page definition in the body of the agreement.

When including a definitional section, writers should place it at the very beginning of the agreement so that they define all the terms before using those terms in the provisions of the agreement. Writers also should consider using simple formatting when laying out the defined terms for ease of reading and quick reference when the reader is working through the body of the agreement.

d. Simple Language

While the use of clear and simple language is a good idea in all legal writing, it is especially helpful when drafting agreements. Writers should strive to use concise paragraphs and sentences to express their ideas. When explaining complex terms in an agreement, writers should split the ideas into separate short paragraphs with clear topic sentences to move the reader from one idea to the next. Similarly, rather than trying to explain several concepts in one long sentence, writers should explain each idea in a short, simple sentence, with a clear transition between the sentences. Using short paragraphs and sentences will often force writers to more clearly explain the relationship between the ideas and thus explain the relevant terms of the agreement more precisely and effectively.

e. Format of Agreement

Writers should choose a format that will assist the reader in following and understanding the terms of the agreement. For short, one-page agreements, writers may find that specifying the terms in separate paragraphs without using section or paragraph numbering is best because the reader can absorb short agreements fairly quickly.

However, writers should divide long or complex agreements into sections. When dividing an agreement into sections, using section and paragraph numbering with descriptive headings often helps writers draft a more effective agreement because it helps them organize the document around related ideas. Such formatting also helps the reader move back and forth between sections more quickly and effectively.

When considering the appropriate format, new practitioners need to be aware that certain types of agreements follow generally accepted organizational formats, providing certain information in specific places. Drafters should follow those accepted guidelines because lawyers are accustomed to such presentations. Thus, when first drafting a particular kind of agreement, new practitioners need to determine if that type of document has a specific format. If so, writers should use that format as a guide for preparing the agreement rather than altering the traditional presentation.

f. Mechanism to Check Agreement Accuracy

To verify that the agreement sets out the terms as intended, writers need to develop a mechanism to check their work. In most agreements, the terms relate to each other in a way that explains the rights and responsibilities of the parties under certain conditions. For shorter agreements, this relationship may simply mean that one party is obligated to do something as a result of an action by the other party. In complex agreements, the triggering actions and related consequences often overlap and relate to each other.

One way to verify that the terms of a complex agreement work is to create a flowchart or outline from the draft of the agreement. Using the agreement provisions themselves, drafters should be able to chart the rights and responsibilities of the parties in a way that accomplishes the intended goals of the transaction. If they are unable to create such a flowchart from the language of the document, the terms of the agreement are probably not clear enough for a neutral observer to fully understand how the agreement works. In that situation, they should refine the language so the terms and their relationship to each other are clear and precise.

2. Use of Forms and Samples

Using a sample agreement is often a helpful way to begin the drafting process. Such a sample could be an agreement from another transaction, a form document produced by a legal publisher, or a form agreement produced by lawyers in the writer's office. No matter what the source of the sample, writers should only use samples as a guide and should independently assess such examples to ensure that their final agreements protect the needs of the clients and accurately reflect current law.

a. Using Samples as a Guide

Writers can use sample agreements and form documents as a guide to determine the best organization and structure of their agreements. Furthermore, model documents often help writers determine the different provisions that should be included in a particular agreement and guide writers in choosing effective and appropriate language. For example, form documents from legal publishers can be an efficient way for writers to determine the necessary provisions that must be included to create a legally binding agreement. Often, those form documents also include annotations with the legal analysis explaining the different provisions. Using such model documents can save time and resources.

However, writers should not rely on such examples to the point that their agreement is not a cohesive representation of the transaction. Writers should use samples or forms only as a guide to determine the format and structure of their own agreements. When using a model document, writers need to be sure to make any additions or changes using the same structure and language to construct new provisions to be consistent with the original document.

Often, however, writers will realize that using sample or model documents as templates for their agreements may not be the most efficient way to prepare a draft document. They may become frustrated and spend too much time trying to adapt their understanding of the transaction into a template that someone else drafted. In those situations, writers will do a better job drafting a cohesive agreement if they write their own agreements using the model only as a rough guide. Preparing their own document often allows writers to more efficiently incorporate language or formatting ideas from a variety of different sources and to draft the transaction-specific language more quickly because they use their own organization and language throughout the document.

b. Independent Assessment of Final Agreement

If writers use language from a model document, they must ensure that the language accurately reflects the transaction and the current status of the law. However, senior colleagues often ask junior lawyers to prepare the first draft of an agreement using a form document as a template, but may not request that they independently analyze the law behind the different provisions included in the form agreement. In this situation, writers may feel fairly confident that they should include the suggested language because a senior attorney has suggested the agreement as a starting point. Similarly, when using published forms from reliable legal publishers, writers may feel secure that current law supports the language in the form. They would probably feel even more confident that the language is appropriately constructed based on current legal standards when using a form that lawyers in the office constantly update and revise.

Nonetheless, when new practitioners include language in the draft of an agreement that they have not been able to verify is based on the current law—no matter what the source of the model agreement—they need to communicate to the senior lawyer the source of the different provisions by identifying the language that came from the model document. When communicating this information, writers should indicate which language is supported by their own analysis, if any, and which provisions they included without undertaking any independent analysis, as well as the source of those unverified provisions. Using the track changes and commenting features of word processing applications often is an efficient method to communicate this information.

When using a sample from a different transaction, writers may attach the sample to their draft of the agreement and highlight the different provisions that they have not analyzed independently and include any questions that they believe the senior attorney should consider when finalizing the agreement. With form documents from published sources, writers can identify the source and highlight the provisions that they changed from the form to tailor the language to the current transaction or the status of the law based on their independent analysis.

SUMMARY

New practitioners quickly learn that attorneys in almost all practice areas may be required to draft agreements. New transactional practitioners will spend much of their time working on projects related to producing the agreements related to their transactions, which may include drafting stand-alone agreements on their own, or revising agreements that other lawyers have drafted. In addition, senior colleagues may ask new lawyers working in non-transactional areas to draft short agreements for their clients, such as a settlement agreement in litigation or a property agreement in a divorce case. Although agreement drafting is different from other types of legal writing, new practitioners can learn to prepare effective agreements by following a few fundamental steps:

- Understand the substantive foundation of the agreement:
  - Consider the specific audience and purpose of the agreement.
  - Know the client's interests.
  - Draft within the parameters of the law.
- Use basic drafting techniques:
  - Consider the overall organization.
  - Make the provisions of the document internally consistent.
  - Define necessary terms.
  - Design the format of the document for ease of reading.
  - Use simple language.
  - Verify that the terms of the agreement work.
- Think about effective use of forms and samples:
  - Use samples only as a guide.
  - Make an independent assessment of the final agreement no matter what form is used.

Part III

THE FINALIZING PHASE
Perfecting the Presentation

CHAPTER 7

Refining and Editing Legal Writing

Final polishing is an important step in legal writing because it ensures that the writer has communicated the ideas to the reader clearly and efficiently. While clear expression is important in all writing, it is critical with legal writing because the writer explains the analysis of the governing law. However, most legal writers should focus on polishing toward the end of their drafting process. If they spend too much time making stylistic and format changes too early, the focus of perfecting the presentation of their writing may get in the way of developing a complete and sophisticated understanding of the relevant ideas. Therefore, during the preliminary drafting stage, most writers should generally use their writing to develop their understanding of the relevant legal analysis, so the focus of the writing is to help them to improve the underlying concepts. As they gain confidence about those ideas, they should shift the focus from developing the concepts to expressing them clearly to the reader. At that point, they should concentrate on polishing the presentation of their analysis.

Some writers prefer to take the polishing steps on discrete portions of a document. They only begin a new section after ensuring that earlier parts are final. Others carefully choose to wait to make any final refinements only after they have a complete draft of the entire document. Most writers, however, tend to move to this finalizing stage naturally, gradually shifting their focus as their ideas become clearer at different places in the document.

Whichever method legal writers use, learning to intentionally shift their attention from developing ideas to perfecting their expression allows writers to refine their writing effectively and efficiently. When they are ready to begin polishing, most writers should first review the document or section to refine the clarity of the ideas. Once they have taken that step, they can quickly focus on tone and detailed copyediting and proofreading issues.

Finally, they should confirm that all the authorities that they rely on in the document are valid law.

A. REFINE CLARITY OF IDEAS

Once legal writers are ready to move to the presentation stage, they should read the document from the point of view of the reader who will only be able to rely on words on the page to understand the ideas. Reading from this perspective helps check the clarity of expression and ease of reading. At this stage, writers should verify that they have articulated the relevant concepts to allow the reader to grasp the ideas quickly and efficiently by checking that they organize around ideas, use clear introductions and transitions, and express their ideas with plain and precise language.

1. Examine Organization

Legal writers should first check that they have organized the presentation around the ideas in the analysis. In most legal problems, writers must develop the relevant analysis by reconciling a variety of different legal authorities. This process requires writers to first focus on individual pieces of authority to develop the broader concepts through that reconciliation process. To explain the analysis clearly and precisely to the reader, writers must explain the ideas that come from reconciling the different authorities before the specific details of the decisions or other authorities are helpful. Therefore, typically, writers should organize the presentation around the ideas garnered from the reconciliation process rather than the specific decisions or other legal authority.

However, in early drafts, many legal writers tend to organize their discussion around the pieces of authority because they use their writing to work through the reconciliation process. Thus, for many writers, structuring the discussion around the major analytical ideas rather than organizing the writing around specific pieces of authority is the major change that they need to implement when moving from the preliminary to final drafts of a document. Therefore, a first step for the final presentation should be verification that the writer has organized the document around the ideas from the reconciled analysis rather than the original sources of those ideas.

2. Review Introductory Sections and Precise Transitions

Once writers have verified that they have organized their presentation around the relevant ideas, they should check for clear introductory sections and precise transitions. Introductions should include enough information to put all the ideas in context for the reader and provide clear roadmaps to the concepts that the writer will develop later in the section, beginning with the overall introduction and introductions to components of the analysis.

After reviewing the introductions, writers must ensure that presentation of the ideas is consistent with the organization they outline in the introductory sections, including use of clear transitions from one idea to the next. To help, writers should ensure that they use clear topic sentences in all paragraphs that lead the reader through the macro ideas in the document, as outlined in the introductory sections.

Drafting clear and accurate topic sentences can be a challenge until a writer is fully convinced of how the different ideas fit together. Thus, writers often must perfect topic sentences so they introduce the idea in the paragraph, and explain how that idea fits in the structure of the analysis.

When taking this step, writers need to carefully look for vague topic sentences. Often, writers use imprecise topic sentences in earlier drafts because they have not fully determined exactly how the ideas fit in the analytical scheme. In this situation, many writers may default to listing of chronological transitions in earlier drafts, such as "first" and "second," etc. When using these types of listing transitions, writers must be sure that the transitions accurately explain the connection between ideas. Sometimes a sequential connection is the most accurate, and thus listing the ideas in chronological order would be appropriate. However, many times writers use some type of listing transition when another, more accurate connection is required. For example, one idea may be a complementary idea, rather than the second idea in the analysis.

Similarly, writers must be sure to use transitions between sentences that tie the smaller ideas together in a coherent way for the reader. Writers need to be wary of simply using transitional words they find on lists in writing guides instead of determining the true connection between ideas. The difference between "however" and "in addition" can be critical in a legal document, so the transitional words that a writer uses must be accurate.

One technique writers can use to verify that they are accurately connecting ideas is to use repetitive transitions in earlier drafts. A repetitive transition repeats the key concept to move the reader to the next idea. For example, the phrase "a repetitive transition" was repeated as a transition from the first sentence of this paragraph to the explanation of the concept in the second sentence.

If the ideas fit together, writers should be able to connect the concepts with such repetitive transitions. However, overuse of such transitions can make the final draft too repetitious and often too long. Therefore, writers should be sure to edit their work to make these transitions shorter and less burdensome on the reader—as explained in the next section.

3. Check for Plain Language

A key component of good legal writing is using plain language. Legal writers should consider a variety of techniques to explain complex legal concepts plainly and efficiently.

a. Avoid Legalese

In many legal problems, writers must use technical language or legal terms of art. However, they should avoid legalese, which tends to express ideas in archaic words and phrases. The use of such legal jargon makes writing dense and hard for the reader to comprehend quickly, which in turn may leave an impression that the writing is ambiguous or the ideas are not well developed. Law school courses stress the importance of using plain language in legal writing, so law school graduates have learned to express their ideas without relying on archaic legal terminology. Nonetheless, novice legal writers sometimes slip into the use of legalese early in practice when drafting complicated legal documents. Most often, these new lawyers seem to employ cumbersome language as references or connections between ideas.

For example, new lawyers sometimes use archaic references for opinions or their client's situation, like "said case," "instant case," or "case at bar." A clear transitional reference is a better option. When referring to a court opinion, they should use something like "that case" or "this case" or refer to the name of the case. When identifying the client's situation, they should choose something like "in our client's situation" or "on our client's facts."

New lawyers also sometimes use cumbersome language when describing transitions from one idea to the next. New legal writers should carefully review their work to be sure that they use precise and simple language when connecting ideas. For example, using "now" instead of "forthwith," "but" for "whereas," or "then" for "furthermore" helps clearly articulate the connections between relevant ideas in simple, crisp terms.

b. Use Quotations Sparingly

Legal writers use quotations to emphasize language when the specific words and construction of the passage are exceptionally important. Readers understand that they must carefully evaluate any quoted excerpts. This emphasis is burdensome because readers must slow down to comprehend the import of the quotation. Therefore, writers should only use quotations when they are necessary to explain or emphasize the ideas. Generally, the most efficient way for writers to express the relevant concepts is to articulate those ideas in their own words rather than relying on verbatim language from legal authority.

In many legal problems, however, writers are required to include quotations because the specific language of the authority is a necessary part of the analysis. For example, the writer may be analyzing a statute or regulation and the exact wording of the provision is essential. In those situations, writers should quote the relevant excerpts when they are focusing on specific language that is essential to the legal issue. However, even when verbatim language is necessary, writers should quote the shortest amount possible to reduce the burden on the reader. Writers should consider quoting only the most specific portion necessary while paraphrasing the remainder of the language to put the quoted language in context. Other times, writers may decide to summarize the entire passage because the language is long and complex. If the writer believes that the reader might need to refer to the verbatim language, the writer can include the entire text in a footnote or in an appendix at the end of the document.

At other times, the analysis does not require quoted excerpts, but writers determine that verbatim language will emphasize a point or help the reader understand the analysis. Nonetheless, due to the burden of quoted passages, writers should be selective in using these types of quotations.

Although quotations are sometimes appropriate, novice legal writers often overly rely on verbatim language in preliminary drafts. When making the transition from their research notes and charts to the first drafts of documents, new writers may insert long portions of quoted language as they reconcile those ideas to express the relevant analysis. As they refine their understanding of the ideas, they should remove much of the verbatim language as they realize that paraphrasing the ideas is the more efficient and accurate way to explain the concepts. Often, writers recognize that they have used quoted language from a variety of sources in places where readers need a synthesized explanation of the ideas from the authority. The writers must use their own words to explain the complete analysis rather than asking readers to reconcile the quoted language and to figure out the relevant concepts on their own. Therefore, as new lawyers are finalizing assignments, they should carefully consider each and every quotation to ensure that the quotation is helpful and necessary to the reader's understanding of the analysis. They should verify that they are not using quotations in place of their own essential explanations.

c. Use Consistent Language

Another technique to make legal writing precise and accurate is to use consistent language. This simple step can be a challenge for some new lawyers because their previous writing training stressed the importance of avoiding repetition. However, in most legal writing, writers should determine the most accurate expression of an idea and use that same language consistently when explaining the analysis. Consistent expression assists the reader in grasping the meaning of the ideas quickly and concisely. When new legal writers are unable to express ideas consistently, that inconsistency is often a manifestation of a lack of understanding about the underlying concepts. Thus, they may need to rework part of the analysis to be able to express their ideas consistently.

d. Precisely Identify Actors and Actions

Writers can make their writing more precise by carefully considering and identifying the relevant actors and actions in each sentence. In legal writing, the reader often needs to easily grasp "who does what to whom" in order to fully understand the ideas. Writers can use a few techniques to refine their writing to clearly identify these ideas.

1. Favor Active Verbs

To help the reader understand "who does what to whom," writers should always consider making the subject of the sentence the main actor and using an active verb to clearly identify what the actor must or must not do. An active verb clarifies what the subject of the sentence is doing—it is an "action" word. In contrast, a passive verb does not.

For example, in an analysis about a bystander's cause of action for negligent infliction of emotional distress, part of the analysis is that the courts require that the bystander witness the negligent act. To clearly communicate this requirement, a writer could write:

> The bystander **must witness** the negligent act.

This sentence communicates clearly that the analysis is all about the main actor, which is "the bystander." It also makes completely clear what that bystander must do, which is to "witness the negligent act." Compare the above with a sentence that uses the passive:

> The negligent act **must be witnessed** by the bystander.

In this version of the sentence, the reader will have a more difficult time focusing on the main actor—the bystander—and what that bystander must or must not do. The use of the passive verb quickly makes understanding "who does what to whom" more difficult.

However, writers should use passive verbs when they want the reader to focus on what is being acted upon rather than the actor. Some analyses are not centered on a specific actor but only on the object of the action. For example:

> The structure **must be secured**.

Here, the use of a passive verb is appropriate because the analysis focuses on what must be secured—the "structure"—and not about "who had to secure it."

If the structure had to be secured by the owner, the following sentence with an active verb would be better:

The owner must secure the structure.

2. Question Use of "There Is"

Writers should consider reworking sentences that include variations of "there is." By expressing an idea in this manner, they may not make clear enough "who did what to whom." In addition, they are generally using more words than necessary to express the idea. The following examples illustrate these ideas:

There must be a bystander who witnesses the negligent act.

Using the phrasing "there must be" makes the idea of "who does what to whom" harder to figure out and the sentence unnecessarily wordy. A more precise and concise articulation of the idea is:

A bystander must witness the negligent act.

3. Avoid Turning Active Verbs into Nouns

In general, writers should avoid changing active verbs to nouns. Often, this kind of sentence joins two of these nouns with a "to be" verb. Analogously to passive voice, this type of sentence makes less clear "who does what to whom" because the "action" is hidden and often so are the actors. The "bystander" example from above will help illustrate this idea:

Witnessing the negligent act is **what the courts require**.

In this sentence, the writer has taken two active verbs and turned them into nouns. First, the writer took an active verb—to witness—and turned it into the noun "witnessing." Second, the writer took an active verb—to require—and turned it into the noun phrase "what the courts require." By constructing the sentence in this manner, the writer has completely obscured "***who*** must witness" and made it difficult to figure out "***who*** requires" the action. The result is a sentence that does not spell out clearly "who is doing what to whom."

Revising the sentence to use active verbs makes it easily apparent who is doing the act of "requiring" and who must do the act of "witnessing":

The **courts require** that the **bystander witness** the negligent act.

4. Watch for Dangling Modifiers

Writers also impede the readers' ability to understand "who is doing what to whom" when they fail to place modifying phrases in a manner that makes clear what they modify. These problems are often described as dangling modifiers, because the modifying words "dangle" in such a way that the reader is uncertain which idea is being described by the modifiers. The following sentence illustrates such a problem:

> **Witnessing the negligent act**, the court requires the bystander to encounter the injuries of the direct victim first-hand.

The preceding sentence is problematic since the phrase "witnessing the negligent act" is placed in the sentence so that it modifies the subject of the sentence, which is "the court." In fact, however, this idea should modify "the bystander." To correct this problem, the writer would need to reconstruct the sentence so that the phrase "witnessing the negligent act" clearly relates to the "bystander" and not to the "court." For example:

> The court requires that the bystander encounter the injuries of the direct victim first-hand **by witnessing the negligent act**.

5. Use Precise Pronouns

New legal writers should also check that they are not creating ambiguity with use of vague pronouns. For example, the use of a plural pronoun to refer to a singular noun in the following sentence creates ambiguity:

> **A bystander** must encounter through **their** own senses the serious injuries of the direct victim.

While the practice of using a plural pronoun to refer to a singular noun is becoming commonplace in our language, lawyers should avoid it when writing for busy law practice readers. Encountering this inconsistency, readers will have to stop and think about whether the plural pronoun refers back to the antecedent noun that is singular. The following revised sentence is clearer because the pronoun and the noun that is referenced are both plural:

> **Bystanders** must encounter through **their** own senses the serious injuries of the direct victim.

Similarly, writers often create ambiguity with the vague use of variations of the pronoun "this," including "that," "these," and "those." These pronouns can confuse readers if writers use them in a manner that can describe more than one previous idea. These two sentences illustrate this problem:

> The court requires that bystanders encounter through their own senses the injuries of the direct victim and that the injuries be serious. **This** is important because it helps the court determine how reasonable the reaction is.

The pronoun "this" in the second sentence is vague because the reader would be unsure if it refers to the court's requirement, the idea that bystanders must "encounter" the injuries, or that the injuries must be "serious." To avoid such ambiguity, writers can identify the relevant idea by repeating or specifying it after the variation of "this." These revised sentences illustrate this idea:

> The court requires that bystanders encounter through their own senses the injuries of the direct victim and that the injuries be serious. **This encounter** is important because it helps the court determine how reasonable the reaction is.

By repeating "encounter" after "this," the writer clearly identifies which of the two previous ideas "this" refers to in the second sentence. Often, writers can simply use the previous ideas in this fashion. However, to avoid excessive repetition, they may describe the previous idea with a synonym or other phrasing.

6. Avoid Unnecessary Subject and Verb Separation

When writers include sentences with too much information between the subject and verb, readers struggle to figure out "who does what to whom" and how all the ideas in the sentence fit together. Typically, to solve this problem, writers can either restructure the sentence or divide the sentence in two. The following sentence illustrates this problem:

> **Bystanders** who encounter through their own senses the serious injuries of the direct victim **will react** with serious and genuine emotional distress.

This sentence is potentially confusing because the subject is separated from the verb by a long string of ideas. To clarify the sentence, the writer should place the subject and verb closer together:

> When bystanders encounter through their own senses the serious injuries of the direct victim, **they will react** with serious and genuine emotional distress.

e. Double Check for Concision

Concision is essential in legal writing because of the nature of law practice. All readers of legal documents are busy and expect the writer to convey the necessary information as quickly and efficiently as possible. However, being concise is not the primary responsibility of legal writers. Their first obligation is to develop the law that governs the situation fully and accurately. Therefore, new legal writers should consider waiting to revise their work for concision until they are confident that they have fully developed and explained the relevant concepts.

Once they have edited the draft to refine the accurate presentation of the analysis through the organization, connections, and clarity of their ideas, they should then spend time going back through the draft to edit for concision. When editing for concision, they should begin by reevaluating the structure of the document to ensure that it presents the ideas as efficiently as possible, specifically focusing on overall organization and introductory summaries. Then, they should check the structure of paragraphs and sentences, concentrating on length and non-substantive guidepost statements. Finally, writers should assess word choice in phrasing the different concepts.

1. Be Willing to Change Final Organization

Even at the final editing stage, writers should evaluate whether the organization of their writing conveys the ideas as concisely as possible. Often, when polishing the final presentation of a document, a simpler, more efficient, organization becomes apparent. By simply moving pieces around to different places, the writer may combine ideas, reducing introductory language and transitional sections.

2. Reevaluate All Summary Passages

At this stage, writers should also reevaluate any place where they have summarized ideas, whether to provide the reader with a roadmap for a section that follows or to sum up the prior discussion. Writers should keep summaries that sufficiently help readers even though they repeat ideas, but delete the rest. In many instances, this decision will be a judgment call where reasonable writers might reach different conclusions.

3. Recheck for Short Paragraphs and Sentences

Writing is easier for readers to understand when writers use short paragraphs and sentences. To help ensure such concise writing, writers should skim their drafts to visually evaluate the length of paragraphs and sentences. When they see a paragraph that is very long—three-quarters of a page to over a page—they should stop and figure out whether to shorten it. Similarly, they should revise sentences that are very long—about two or more lines. Often, when writers try to divide long sentences or paragraphs, they find a missing link or an idea that was buried in the writing. Breaking ideas into shorter pieces often helps writers use more precise language and better transitions between ideas.

If the paragraph is still too long, writers should first evaluate whether they could logically divide the focus of the paragraph into two or more paragraphs to provide the reader with smaller pieces of the analysis each time. Second, they should assess whether the paragraph contains unnecessary ideas or is repetitious. They might be able to shorten the paragraph simply by rephrasing ideas more concisely or by deleting those that are unnecessary to developing the analysis.

When writers encounter a long sentence, they should stop and read it aloud. If they have trouble understanding what they have written when taking this step, they probably are attempting to convey too many ideas in the sentence. They should try to divide the sentence around those different concepts. Once they have made the separation, they should evaluate whether all the ideas are necessary and whether they could rephrase some of the ideas more concisely. Finally, they should check whether they could revise the sentence construction to present ideas more economically.

4. Delete Non-substantive Guideposts

In addition, writers should remove statements that have no substance, but simply identify what the writer is going to do next in the writing. This type of statement will distract readers from the substantive ideas. For example, the following statement would not provide the reader with any substantive information and should not be used:

> I will now discuss the next topic.

Similarly, writers should remove or rephrase statements with insufficient substance to focus on the substantive point. For example, the following statement would need more substantive information to be helpful:

> I will now discuss the next topic of relationship.

This statement could be revised to focus on the relative substantive point:

> The courts also require that a bystander have a sufficient relationship with the direct victim.

5. Edit Unnecessary Introductory Phrases

Writers should evaluate whether introductory phrases are necessary. Typically, these phrases begin with variations of "it is." In many instances, writers can either delete the phrase completely or replace the phrase with a more powerful verb later in the sentence. Here are a few examples of sentences with introductory phrases and the same sentences revised:

> **Wordy: It is clear that** a plaintiff must satisfy the requirement that . . .
>
> **Revised:** A plaintiff must satisfy the requirement that . . .

> **Wordy: It is important to note that** a plaintiff must satisfy the requirement that . . .
>
> **Revised:** A plaintiff must satisfy the requirement that . . .

> **Wordy: It is necessary that** a plaintiff satisfy the requirement that . . .
>
> **Revised:** A plaintiff must satisfy the requirement that . . .

B. EVALUATE TONE OF PRESENTATION

After legal writers have edited their writing to refine the clarity of ideas, they should evaluate the tone of the presentation. In general, legal writers use a professional, formal tone, though they avoid writing that is stuffy or pretentious.

However, in some offices, colleagues may be comfortable communicating with each other with writing that is more informal. Nonetheless, until new lawyers are familiar with their office and colleagues, they probably should adopt a formal tone in all their writings to avoid offending readers or using language that is off-putting. To help find the appropriate tone, new lawyers should express their ideas in the third person, avoid colloquialisms, respectfully refer to the various parties, and use gender-neutral language.

1. Use Third-Party Neutral Tone

Legal writers should use a third-party neutral tone and generally avoid the first person by not referring to themselves. These steps give the writing an appropriately formal tone and help keep the reader's focus on the relevant ideas as opposed to the writer. Therefore, legal writers typically should not express analysis in terms of their opinion or belief. Rather, they should describe what the law provides or what the appropriate decision maker would decide. For example, writers should avoid sentences like this:

> **My opinion is that** a future court would probably conclude that Energy satisfies the first requirement.

Instead, this sentence should be expressed in the third–person:

> A court would probably conclude that Energy satisfies the first requirement.

However, if writers include instructions or certain assumptions from supervising attorneys, they would want to make those ideas clear using the first person. For example, if a supervising attorney asked a junior colleague to focus on only one of several issues in a problem, the writer could explain that idea using the first person. In many situations, writers find that using the passive voice to explain the instructions they received is better than personalizing the instructions to a specific colleague. Thus, a writer might explain such an instruction by using the following:

> **I was asked** to focus only on the issue of....

2. Avoid Colloquialisms and Casual Language

To help present ideas with a professional tone, new legal writers should avoid colloquial words or phrases that are conversational and therefore more like talking with or writing to a friend. Similarly, in most legal writing, writers should avoid using contractions, like "you're," "it's," and "wasn't." Contractions are informal because they give the impression that the writer is speaking to the reader.

New legal writers will quickly recognize the casual language they tend to use, if any, and should carefully review their own writing for that specific language. However, when using writing to develop ideas, writers generally should not take the time to replace such casual language with formal alternatives. Rather, they should use whatever language helps them figure out and express the relevant concepts. For example, some writers use contractions without thinking when laying out ideas quickly. Instead of investing time in the preliminary draft to expand the contractions to formal phrasing, those writers should use the contractions in the early drafts. At the presentational stage, however, they should edit their work to replace this language.

3. Describe Parties Formally

Legal writers should consider how to describe and refer to their clients and other parties. On the one hand, they may not need to be very formal, using "Mr.," "Mrs.," or "Ms." On the other hand, they should describe the parties with sufficient formality to be respectful. In general, therefore, writers should not refer to parties by their first names. Ways to avoid this are to use a party's full name, the party's last name only, or the party's relationship to the analysis, such as "our client" or "the employee." When referring to a party throughout a document, a writer could use a party's first name after a more formal reference.

When drafting advocacy documents, writers should make strategic decisions about how to refer to parties and may determine in some situations that informal references to parties or other people are appropriate persuasive tools. Even in those situations, however, writers need to be sure that the informal references are respectful.

4. Use Gender-Neutral Language

Lawyers should always consider using gender-neutral language because they may be writing to an audience—possibly judges, supervising attorneys, or clients—who would be offended by sexist language. Of course, when a writer is describing a situation where the gender of the people is known, referring to those individuals by gender is appropriate. However, when writers are describing abstract ideas, they should express the concepts with language that does not exclude either gender. Therefore, writers should carefully choose the terms and pronouns they use to avoid gender-exclusive references.

Writers should use titles and terms that are not gender-specific. For example, writers should replace gender-exclusive terms, such as policeman and waitress, with gender-neutral labels, such as police officer and server.

Writers also should consider substituting gender-specific pronouns when referring to an abstract person. Writers can employ a variety of techniques to replace gendered pronouns with less awkward neutral references.

a. Avoid Cumbersome or Incorrect Alternatives

Writers should avoid using cumbersome alternatives, such as "his/hers" or "she or he." Similarly, writers should not use plural pronouns, such as "they" or "their," to refer to singular nouns. Although this practice has become accepted in spoken language, and some grammarians now take the position that these plural pronouns should be accepted as suitable references to singular abstract nouns, many readers disagree and consider such usage to be sloppy grammatical mistakes.

b. Consider Plurals

To avoid gendered pronouns, writers might choose to use plurals. Using plurals avoids the very awkward "he/she" or "he or she" and avoids the confusion of a plural pronoun referring back to a singular noun. To use plurals to accomplish this goal, writers typically only need to make some minor editing adjustments. For example:

> **A bystander** must witness the negligent act so that **he or she** encounters the injuries of the direct victim.

can be edited to:

> **Bystanders** must witness the negligent act so that **they** encounter the injuries of the direct victim.

c. Repeat Nouns

Another method to avoid gendered pronouns without using cumbersome double pronouns or incorrect plural pronouns to refer to singular nouns is to repeat the noun instead of using a pronoun. For example:

> **A bystander** must witness the negligent act so that **he/she** encounters the injuries of the direct victim.

can be edited to:

> **A bystander** must witness the negligent act so that **the bystander** encounters the injuries of the direct victim.

C. FINAL COPYEDITING

Once legal writers have revised their documents for clarity of ideas and expression, the next step is to edit the writing to be sure all grammar, spelling, and punctuation are perfect. At this point, writers also should finalize citations, footnotes, and other necessary references to authority. Writers also should use a spelling and grammar checker and carefully proofread the document to correct any other errors in formatting.

Before taking the final copyediting step, new practitioners often should spend time reviewing the appropriate citation or style manual for proper citation and formatting guidelines for the particular document. Any writer who is unclear about the rules for citation and formatting should review a writing book or style manual for a complete discussion. When they have a choice about a grammar rule or style format guideline, writers should make their choice and use it consistently throughout the document.

Most writers have some idiosyncratic issues with their writing, such as repeating certain spelling mistakes or grammatical errors. New lawyers should learn to identify their personal writing problems and take extra care to correct them in final documents. Some new practitioners may benefit from a quick review of certain grammar rules that seem to trip them up. Below is a list of common writing questions that often create ambiguity in legal writing. Understanding these issues and making a determination about the best way to handle them in their own writing can help make new lawyers' writing more accurate and easier to understand.

1. Punctuation Questions

a. Serial Comma

A serial comma (also referred to as the Oxford or Harvard comma) is a comma placed before the conjunction in a list of three or more items. Although style and grammar manuals differ on whether use of the serial comma is required, many style manuals recommend it to avoid ambiguity. Furthermore, grammarians agree that the serial comma is never incorrect. Therefore, legal writers should consider using the serial comma because it can help clarify ideas. This sentence is an example of how the lack of a serial comma creates ambiguity:

> The trust documents required that equal shares of the proceeds go to: John, Jason, Jim and Jim's children.

In this sentence, the reader is not sure if one share of the proceeds goes each to John *and* Jason *and* one share is shared by Jim and his children, or if one share of the proceeds should go to John *and* Jason *and* Jim *and* one share goes to Jim's children. Using a serial comma would resolve this ambiguity:

> The trust documents required that equal shares of the proceeds go to: John, Jason, Jim, and Jim's children.

A serial comma can also clarify if the writer is using a comma to add a phrase to describe a previous item, or using a comma to include new items in the list. For example:

> The subject of the talk was George, an actor and a lawyer.

Here, the reader is not sure if the topic was only George, who is an actor and a lawyer, or if the subject was three people: George *and* an actor *and* a lawyer. A serial comma would clarify that the focus of the talk was three people:

The subject of the talk was George, an actor, and a lawyer.

b. Semicolons

Semicolons are helpful to link to independent clauses that are closely connected. For example:

The employees are very experienced; they have worked there for years.

Writers need to be careful not to use a semicolon, however, when a comma is the appropriate punctuation because the two clauses are not independent. For example:

Incorrect: The employees seem young; but not inexperienced.

Correct: The employees seem young, but not inexperienced.

Writers also use semicolons to divide a series of items in a list if any of the items contain commas. For example:

The restaurant served vegan appetizers; meat, seafood, and vegan entrees; and fruit sorbet, fruit pies, and pastries for dessert.

c. En Dashes and Em Dashes

An "en" dash (a short dash, just a little longer than the length of a hyphen) is used to replace "to." For example, in dates, instead of writing, "The events took place from March to July," a writer could use the en dash:

The events took place from March–July.

Writers use the "em" dash (a longer dash, about the length of two hyphens) for emphasis in place of other punctuation marks, including parentheses, commas, semicolons, and colons. In formal writing, writers should use the em dash sparingly because it is an informal tool that can make documents feel too casual. However, if the writer wants to emphasize a point by setting off ideas differently than the formal punctuation, the em dash can be effective. For example:

The clause included two important restrictions—a time limitation of two years and a geographical restriction limiting the employee from working in any part of the state.

The formal form of this sentence with a colon might not give the same emphasis to the two requirements:

The clause included two important restrictions: a time limitation of two years and a geographical restriction limiting the employee from working in any part of the state.

2. Repetitive Phrasing

a. "And" or "Or" vs. "And/or"

Writers should avoid using "and/or." Most often, either "and" or "or" is a more accurate connection between the two ideas.

b. "Whether" vs. "Whether or Not"

Although grammar rules can be complicated about when to use "whether" or "whether or not," writers should consider omitting the "or not" in many situations. Writers can generally decide if "whether" alone is sufficient by rereading the sentence without "or not." If the sentence expresses the correct idea with just the word "whether," they should use that phrasing.

c. "May" vs. "May or May Not"

The word "may" usually implies "may or may not." However, using the longer phrase sometimes helps provide emphasis. Therefore, writers should avoid the use of "may or may not" unless such emphasis is necessary.

3. Homophones

Homophones are words that sound alike, but are spelled differently and have different meanings. Different homophones may create difficulty for different writers. Here are some homophones that cause problems for many writers:

- "Its" and "it's";
- "Your" and "you're";
- "To" and "too";
- "There," "their," and "they're";
- "Affect" and "effect";
- "Discreet" and "discrete";
- "Compliment" and "complement";
- "Principal" and "principle";
- "Foregoing" and "forgoing"; and
- "Capitol" and "capital."

D. GOOD-LAW VERIFICATION

Before submitting a final work product that relies on cited authority, the writer must be sure to undertake a final citator verification to confirm that the authorities are still good law. Due to the hectic pace of law practice, many new lawyers work on several projects at the same time, and their work on any assignment is often interrupted, sometimes for long periods. Even though their initial research process would include verification that the authorities are valid, they need to ensure that the sources they are using in the final version of the document are still good law.

SUMMARY

Although polishing writing is important in legal writing, most legal writers should only take this step toward the end of their drafting process. Otherwise, they may spend too much time making stylistic and format changes instead of developing a complete understanding and expression of the relevant concepts. When writers are ready to polish their writing, they should review their work for a few key ideas:

- Refine clarity of ideas:
    - Organize around concepts.
    - Use introductions and precise transitions.
    - Express ideas with plain language.
    - Check for concision.
- Evaluate tone of presentation.
- Review for final copyediting:
    - Check for idiosyncratic grammar mistakes.
    - Check for typographical and formatting errors.
- Perform a final citator good-law verification.

CHAPTER 8

Working with Feedback

New practitioners often find receiving feedback on their written work to be a a challenging experience. Typically, they have only received extensive comments on legal writing in law school, during the first-year legal writing course and possibly in advanced writing or seminar courses. This type of feedback is generally very different from the kind of comments senior practitioners make on new lawyers' written work. To successfully work with feedback in practice, new practitioners need to think about the nature of the feedback they receive and develop techniques to use the comments to their advantage when reworking their documents.

A. UNDERSTANDING THE NATURE OF FEEDBACK IN LAW PRACTICE

Although most new lawyers have received critique on writing in law school, comments from a professor on course assignments are different than the type of feedback most senior lawyers provide in practice. A professor's assessment is a teaching tool designed to help students refine the analytical and presentational skills necessary to complete the assignment. Professors choose topics carefully to teach these skills and often have a good—if not complete—understanding of the underlying analysis. Furthermore, the professors generally have experience providing comments that help students perfect their analysis and writing. When professors read and comment on assignments, they use their own understanding of the analysis of the problem and their commenting experience to help provide feedback that will help students refine their writing.

In practice, however, when senior lawyers comment on a new practitioner's writing, their primary goal is to ensure a good work product for the client. While a tangential purpose may be to train the junior colleague, the teaching objective usually takes second position to completing the work efficiently and effectively. This efficiency goal usually means that the senior colleagues do not have time to study the underlying authority and develop a complete understanding of the relevant legal analysis. Therefore, when they review their junior colleagues' assignments, they often only provide very succinct margin and copyediting remarks and rewrite portions of the document because it is often the fastest way to finalize it.

B. BENEFITING FROM COLLEAGUES' COMMENTS

The short editing-type feedback most senior attorneys provide poses several challenges for new practitioners. At times, new lawyers may be inclined to quickly accept the revisions so they can finalize the assignment, assuming that the suggestions are correct. However, when new practitioners receive feedback on their work, they must remember that the senior probably does not know the analysis as well as they do. If the revisions change the meaning so that the document is not an accurate expression of the law, junior lawyers obviously cannot make those changes, even if the revised writing seems clearer and easier to read. While ease of understanding is a goal in legal writing, accurate analysis must always control the writer's final editing decisions.

Other times, new lawyers may want to minimize the comments because the senior colleague does not understand the analysis or because the suggestions seem to be a difference in style or some other superficial issue. Even when junior lawyers are not able to accept revisions as proposed, they should use the comments to guide their revision process because the comments or suggested changes identify places where the senior colleague—as the reader—had difficulty grasping the meaning or felt that the writer had not expressed the ideas clearly.

To avoid prematurely adopting or rejecting suggestions, new practitioners should develop techniques to translate feedback from senior colleagues into the substantive assistance that they need to effectively revise their documents. Although senior colleagues' succinct comments may not specifically emphasize analytical flaws over other writing issues, new practitioners can often use the shorthand feedback to do this for themselves. Using specific steps when working with the feedback will help writers find clues regarding conceptual problems that they need to correct before tackling copyediting and other technical writing revisions, even though the senior colleague may not have identified those specific analytical issues.

1. Consider the Feedback Holistically

New practitioners should carefully consider all comments together to fully comprehend their significance before revising the document. When evaluating the entirety of the feedback, writers must remind themselves that most problems in legal writing are not due to poor grammar or other basic writing issues. Even when a reviewer has uncovered such basic writing issues, writers probably need to do more than just correct those mistakes to accurately rewrite the document. Elementary writing problems often indicate that a writer has not fully understood some of the underlying ideas. That misunderstanding often is affecting the writer's ability to express the concept. Writers must resolve those analytical flaws rather than simply fixing the superficial writing mistakes.

2. Do Not Dismiss Comments that Seem Incorrect

If a senior colleague misidentifies a portion of the writing as grammatically incorrect, but the author determines that the grammar is accurate, the author should not simply reject the comment. The author should carefully review the part of the writing where the colleague thought the writer had made a mistake. Often, when readers review a document quickly, they will imply a grammatical mistake at a point in the writing where they were unable to follow the ideas. For example, readers may highlight a sentence as a run-on sentence or a sentence fragment when the sentence is correct grammatically. Even though the sentence may be grammatically correct, the idea seems incomplete to the reader, or the ideas seem to collide together without sufficient explanation. Therefore, the author should carefully reconsider the sentence conceptually and grammatically to help refine the idea so the reader can grasp it more easily.

3. Carefully Contemplate Macro-Organizational Suggestions

When senior colleagues suggest major organizational changes by moving large sections to different places or reordering ideas, authors should reevaluate their understanding of the analytical framework of the problem before implementing the suggestions. Such recommendations may seem like superficial changes, which do not affect the meaning of the analysis. However, comments or suggestions regarding large structural ideas often indicate that the author has not clearly determined the relationship between the different parts of the analysis, even though the reader did not pick up on this analytical problem. In this situation, after rethinking their understanding of the overall organization, authors will often find that the writing needs to be reorganized to more accurately reflect the analysis, but not in the way that the senior colleague suggested.

4. Examine Revisions to Topic Sentences and Transitions

When senior colleagues suggest changes to topic sentences or transitions from one idea to another, they are often uncovering a weakness in the writing that may go deeper than the particular sentence or transition. Writers may find that the actual deficiency is not in the location that the reviewer has identified, but may be found a few paragraphs earlier. Thus, correcting the specific transition is not the solution. They may have to revise some other portion of the writing. Other times, they may need to reorder and rewrite entire sections because the editing uncovers a larger flaw in their overall understanding of the analysis. The accurate way to correct it is to rewrite large sections of the document.

5. Isolate Personal Writing Idiosyncrasies

Most writers have individual writing quirks. They should learn to identify these shortcomings so they can isolate them from comments about other writing problems. Comments about the personal writing issues are often superficial errors or stylistic weaknesses that authors can quickly fix. However, comments regarding writing mistakes that do not normally appear in their writing may suggest that they are struggling with the underlying ideas. The writing mistake may be a manifestation of that misunderstanding. Simple writing problems often identify a fairly simple analytical problem that they can easily correct, but sometimes even these seemingly small blunders uncover fundamental misconceptions about major analytical ideas.

To help determine the level of the problem, authors should look for patterns of new writing issues. In situations where reviewers identify a similar new writing problem in different places in the writing, authors may realize that the comment reappears at every point where they were discussing a particular analytical concept. This situation can indicate that they were struggling to understand the idea clearly and that the writing mistake is related to that misunderstanding. For example, if authors usually do not overuse passive voice when writing, but a senior colleague identifies several places where they used passive verbs, they should take time to reflect on why passive voice appeared at those particular points. The use of passive voice in those particular places may be an indication that they were unclear about the underlying concept. If so, they would need to do more than simply edit the sentences from passive voice to active. They would only be able to accurately correct the problem by reworking the analysis so that they clearly understand the idea they are expressing. While the superficial writing mistake may identify the problem, simply correcting the writing error may not fix it.

6. Focus on Comments Regarding Long Sentences or Paragraphs

Comments about long sentences or paragraphs often highlight a flaw in the writer's understanding of the issue. Authors should not simply divide sentences or paragraphs as suggested by the reviewer, but need to reflect on why they used such complex writing to express the idea. To effectively articulate the concepts in smaller pieces, authors often need to unpack the long sentences or paragraphs. In the process, they may uncover several layers of ideas that they had not fully handled in the earlier draft. Therefore, the best way to fix these types of problems may not be to simply divide the current writing into smaller pieces, but to add new ideas that bridge the gaps in the analysis. Once they fill those holes, they will have an easier time expressing the ideas with short sentences and paragraphs.

7. Reevaluate Criticism Regarding Awkwardness and Wordiness

When most writers receive criticism about word choice, excessive and repetitive writing, or awkward language, they immediately choose a different word or copyedit the writing, trying different ways to reformulate the same idea. Sometimes, writers are simply clumsy in their expression, so these quick-fix solutions may solve the problem. Often, however, the problem is not that the writers were too sloppy in the initial draft, but that they had not fully developed the relevant idea. Rather than spending time trying to re-express the same idea, most writers should rework the idea itself when they receive these types of comments. Once they have a clear understanding of the concept, they will have an easier time expressing it with language that is more artful.

8. Develop Your Own Clues

As new practitioners receive more feedback on their writing, they will begin to see patterns in the types of changes or suggestions that the senior colleagues propose. As they use the feedback from different colleagues to revise their projects, they will begin to learn that certain types of comments suggest analytical problems, while others indicate more superficial issues. Learning to quickly recognize which comments identify analytical issues will help new lawyers use any feedback they receive more efficiently and effectively because they will be able to prioritize their revision process to focus on the most important problems. Understanding the revision priorities is critical when reworking documents under the time constraints of practice.

SUMMARY

The type of feedback that new practitioners receive from colleagues can be very different from the kind of comments they have received in other situations. To use colleagues' feedback effectively, new lawyers should consider several key concepts:

- Think about the nature of feedback in law practice.
- To fully benefit from senior colleagues' comments:
  - Use feedback holistically:
  - Do not dismiss incorrect comments,
  - Carefully consider macro-organizational suggestions.
  - Examine changes to topic sentences and transitions.
  - Separate personal writing issues from other problems.
  - Be on the lookout for comments regarding long sentences or paragraphs.
  - Pay special attention to comments about word choice.
  - Learn to develop clues about your writing from others' comments.

APPENDICES

APPENDIX 1

Illustration of Cross-Decision Interpretive Analysis

This appendix illustrates the process of reconciling a group of decisions by applying the methodology discussed in Chapter Two to analyze part of the question regarding enforceability of a non-compete clause in an employment agreement in Minnesota. Although an analysis of the entire enforceability question is not included here, this example will demonstrate how a lawyer would use the analytical problem-solving steps discussed in Chapter Two to develop one part of the analysis. Although in this example several cases interpreting Minnesota common law govern the question, the methodology would be similar if the analysis were statutory or regulatory and required interpretation of judicial or administrative decisions relevant to the question.

A. THE LEGAL QUESTION

Assume that a senior lawyer has asked for an analysis regarding enforceability of a non-compete clause in an employment agreement in Minnesota. Specifically, the senior lawyer needs to know what language must be included in the clause to ensure that it is enforceable against a salesperson who had personal contact with the employer's customers, but who did not receive any type of confidential information, trade secrets, or specialized training.

B. UNDERSTANDING THE ANALYTICAL FRAMEWORK: DETERMINE WHAT LAW APPLIES

The first step in understanding the analysis is to find the analytical framework of the problem. Recognizing that the question is a contract issue and therefore state law applies, the lawyer would begin by determining whether the Minnesota constitutional or statutory provisions govern the question. The research would reveal that Minnesota constitutional and statutory law is silent regarding the issue. Therefore, Minnesota common law controls. The lawyer would understand from a quick review of the Minnesota court system that the highest court is the Minnesota Supreme Court, and the state added the Minnesota Appellate Court in 1983. The case research would uncover a dozen or so relevant cases from the Minnesota Supreme Court and the Minnesota Court of Appeals. The lawyer also would find some federal cases dealing with the issue, but because the federal cases would only be persuasive authority, the lawyer would focus on the state cases to answer the question.

C. ANALYSIS OF MINNESOTA COMMON LAW

1. Overall Structure of the Court's Analysis

To reconcile the court opinions accurately and effectively to answer the question, the lawyer should first determine the overall structure that the court is using for its analysis, as well as the policy considerations supporting the court's approach. Beginning with what appears to be the central opinion is a good place to start. Based on reading the cases while researching the question, the lawyer would probably have a sense that one of the cases that courts most rely on is *Bennett v. Storz Broadcasting.*[1] Therefore, the lawyer could decide to begin with that case to determine the overall structure of the question.

Bennett is a 1965 Minnesota Supreme Court decision. In the opinion, the court clearly explains that Minnesota courts disfavor non-compete clauses in employment agreements because they restrict the right of employees to find work and generally depress competition. Nonetheless, the court recognizes that employers have a need to protect themselves from employees using advantages they gained during employment to compete against their former employers. The opinion states that courts must therefore carefully evaluate such agreements to balance the rights of the employees and employers. Although the court seems to outline its analysis in different ways at several places, at one point the court articulates the test as follows:

> Where the [non-compete covenant in an employment agreement] is for a just and honest purpose, for the protection of a legitimate interest of the party in whose favor it is imposed, reasonable as between the parties, and not injurious to the public, the restraint has been held valid.[2]

1. Bennett v. Storz Broad. Co., 134 N.W.2d 892 (Minn. 1965).
2. *Id.* at 898.

Since the court apparently has explicitly outlined a clear structure of the analysis, the lawyer would need to verify the approach on the cases as a group. As explained in Chapter Two, moving from the major case that seems to provide the structure of the analysis to a recent—if not the most recent—case is often the good way to determine if the court has changed its overall approach. One of the most recent opinions regarding the issue in Minnesota is *Dynamic v. Bloch.*[3]

In *Dynamic*, the lawyer would see that the court does seem to change the overall test that was outlined in *Bennett*. In *Dynamic*, although the court cites *Bennett* as authority for its articulation of the overall structure of the analysis, the court seems to alter the overall approach when it lays out the analysis as follows:

> [Non-compete covenants in employment agreements] are upheld ... if the restriction is necessary for the protection of the business or the good will of the employer. If the court finds the covenant to be necessary, it must consider the reasonableness of the scope of the covenant. The covenant must not impose any greater restriction on the employee than is necessary to protect the employer's business.[4]

At this point, the lawyer would want to verify the new approach from *Dynamic* on all the cases to verify that the court's analysis has evolved and to understand why the court made the change. Understanding why the court changed the overall structure of the test should help the lawyer understand the policy concerns driving the court's analysis.

A review of all the relevant cases would verify the lawyer's understanding of the policy from *Bennett* and the shift of the overall approach from *Bennett* to *Dynamic*, with a few clarifications. The cases as a group confirm that courts only enforce a non-compete clause if it narrowly protects the employer because such restrictions limit the right to employment and diminish competition. The cases also confirm that to ensure that non-compete clauses only protect employers in this limited way, the court applies a multi-part test to determine enforceability. First, the employer must have a legitimate interest in restricting the employee. An employer can establish such an interest if the employee has a sufficient relationship with the employer's customers. Next, if the employer has a legitimate need in restricting the employee because of the employee's relationships with the employer's customers, the covenant must reasonably protect those relationships in terms of subject matter, geography, and time. Finally, if the employer has a legitimate interest but the covenant is unreasonable, the court has the discretion to modify the covenant to make it reasonable.

---

3. Dynamic v. Bloch, 502 N.W.2d 796 (Minn. Ct. App. 1993).
4. *Id.* at 799.

Interestingly, a review of the cases does not uncover an explanation of what happened to the ideas from *Bennett* regarding how the covenant affects the public or whether it overburdens the employee, except a brief reference to the questions in one later case. In many jurisdictions, these two questions remain a central part of the court's analysis. While the cases as a group do not explicitly explain why the court's analysis has evolved, they do seem to confirm that the court abandoned these two issues or incorporated them into other parts of the analysis.

The diagram provides a flowchart of the overall analysis of the non-compete analysis.

Overall Framework of Non-Compete Analysis

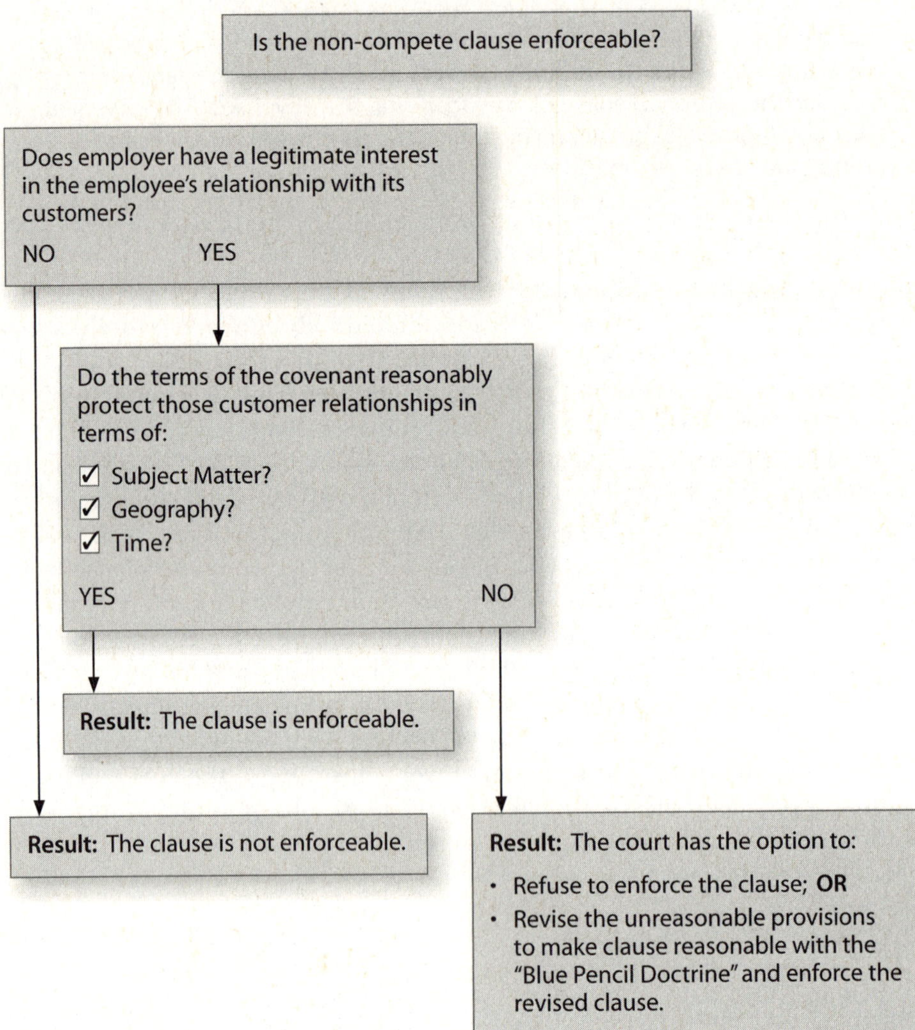

2. Analyzing Components of the Analysis

For purposes of this example, assume that the employer can satisfy the threshold requirement that it has a legitimate interest in the employee's relationships with its customers. Based on the overall structure of the court's analysis, if the employer has a legitimate interest in the employee's client relationships, the covenant must reasonably protect those relationships. To decide if the covenant satisfies this requirement, the first topic that the lawyer would have to determine is how the court decides if the subject matter of a covenant is reasonable. To begin the analysis of this question, the lawyer should prepare a chart or notes of all the relevant cases for the issue as described in Chapter Two, including the following information for each case:

- Case name;
- Citation;
- Date;
- Facts regarding the subject matter issue;
- Result the court came to regarding subject matter; and
- All the explicit language from the opinion regarding subject matter.

A chart of the relevant cases with all of this information is included below.

a. Verifying Explicit Analysis

After completing the chart, as explained in Chapter Two, the lawyer's next step would be to use the chart to determine if the court has explicitly laid out an explanation of when the subject matter restriction of a covenant is reasonable. By examining the chart, the lawyer would see that the court has not explicitly explained its analysis, even though the court does reach a decision regarding the subject matter restrictions in several of the cases.

However, the chart does uncover some language that helps explain the reasoning behind the subject matter restriction. This language confirms the court's overall goal that a covenant must be limited to protecting the employer's legitimate interest. From the chart, the lawyer sees that in *Davies*, the court states:

> If a former employee were prohibited from selling any insurance in the area, the customers not served by him would not necessarily choose the [employer] from all other insurance agencies.

With this language, the court explains that the reasonable subject matter requirement is to protect the employer from losing business because of the former employee's relationships with the employer's customers. If the employer's legitimate interest in restricting the employee is due to the employee's relationships with its customers, the employer only has a reason to restrict the employee in a way that protects those relationships.

Chart for Subject Matter Requirement:
"The subject matter of the covenant must be reasonable."

Facts	Result Reasonable = ■ Unreasonable = ■	Specific Language Regarding the Issue
Minnesota Supreme Court Cases		
***Eutectic v. West,* 160 N.W.2d 566 (Minn. 1968)**		
Covenant: The clause" precluded [employee], for the ... period of 2 years, from ... competing with or taking employment with a competitor ...." p. 568 —Employee "sold directly to consumers when employed by [former employer] but in his present employment sells only to distributors, in which selling work he uses no [former employer] sales secrets." p. 569	Subject matter restriction is too broad.	"We agree with the trial court that the covenant should not be so enforced in the circumstances of this case because plaintiffs had unreasonably extracted from defendant a commitment far broader than his actual functions and status could reasonably require." p. 570 "Restrictive covenants that serve primarily to prevent an employee from working for others or for himself in the same competitive field so as to discourage as to discourage him from terminating his employment constitute a form of industrial peonage without redeeming virtue in the American enterprise system." p. 571
***Walker v. Parkhurst,* 219 N.W.2d 437 (Minn. 1974)**		
Covenant: Employee forbidden to "engage in the business of, or accept employment by an employment agency within the County of Hennepin." p. 438 —Employee worked as counselor for employment agency.	Subject matter apparently reasonable because the covenant enforceable as written	There is no specific language regarding subject matter, but in finding the covenant reasonable the court said "the restrictive covenant further was not unduly restrictive in that the restrictions only applied for one year after leaving employment and to Hennepin County only. There was no unreasonable in the extent of time or area ..." p. 441
***Davies v. Davies,* 298 N.W.2d 127 (Minn. 1980)**		
Covenant: Employee precluded "from engaging in the insurance business ...." p. 129 —Employee became solely responsible for selling court and probate bonds to some customers. p. 131 —Trial court modified the agreement "to prohibit [employee] from engaging in the sale of bonds ...." p. 131	Subject matter restriction preventing employee from engaging in the insurance business was overbroad. Minnesota Supreme Court further modified trial court's modification restricting employee from selling bonds to prohibiting employee from soliciting former employer's customers.	"It appears that the agency's actual need for protection is limited to prohibiting its former employees from actively soliciting business from agency customers. A broader restriction than this could not enhance the agency's business: If a former employee were prohibited from selling any insurance in the area, the customers not served by him would not necessarily choose the [employer's] agency from all other insurance agencies. Instead, a blanket prohibition would only hurt the former employee's livelihood." p. 131 "[Employer] implied that this would be the general effect of enforcing the terms of the noncompetition agreement. He gave as a reason for not enforcing it, 'We had an agency policy that recognized that people in the insurance industry had the right and the necessity to make a living ...' and '... I recognize the fact that they have to have a right to make a living. The insurance industry is what they are involved in, where their experience is, they can go and work for an insurance company or another agency if they just leave us alone.'" p. 132

Continued on next page

Continued from previous page

Facts	**Result** Reasonable = ■ Unreasonable = ■	**Specific Language Regarding the Issue**
		"Thus, based upon this practice of the agency, a prohibition against active solicitation of agency clients by a former employee is all that is reasonably necessary to protect the agency's interest in the insurance area." p. 132
Minnesota Court of Appeals Cases		
***Dean Van Horn v. Wold*, 395 N.W.2d 405 (Minn. Ct. App. 1986)**		
Covenant: Employee prohibited "from soliciting or lending similar services to any customer he advised during his employment with [employer]" p. 406 —Employee prepared tax returns and advised clients on tax and accounting matters.	Subject matter apparently reasonable because covenant enforced with modifications only to the time of restriction.	None regarding subject matter of covenant.
***Webb v. Fosshage*, 426 N.W.2d 445 (Minn. Ct. App. 1988)**		
Covenant: Employee not allowed to "directly or indirectly, engage in or solicit [publication business] for any customer that has done business with the custom publishing division of [employer] within ... one year immediately prior to [employee's] termination of employment." p. 447 —Employee solicited business and assisted employer's clients in developing marketing strategies.	Court suggests that subject matter is too broad, but remands to trial court for determination.	"However, the scope of the restriction suggests overbreadth in light of its purpose. [Employer's] only asserted interest is to protect itself from [employee's] solicitation of his former customers. If [employee] had access to information on other [employer] customers which would aid him in soliciting their business, then restricting him from doing so would not be unreasonable. However, the record does not indicate such access ..." p. 450
***Overholt v. Bredeson*, 437 N.W.2d 698 (Minn. Ct. App. 1989)**		
Covenant: Employee prohibited from soliciting any business from customers he personally serviced while employed with employer and from working in the "insurance business." p. 703 —The term "insurance business" is not defined in the agreement. —Employee sold crop insurance for employer.	Subject matter restriction is reasonable.	"Testimony at the hearing indicated that the parties understood the provision to prevent contact by former employees with existing policyholders. Such an understanding is consistent with the term 'insurance business,' and is limited to protect legitimate interests of [employer]. We find the noncompetition agreement was not overbroad as to subject matter." p. 703
***Dynamic v Bloch*, 502 N.W.2d 796 (Minn. Ct. App. 1993)**		
Covenant: Employee restricted from "soliciting [employer's] customers with whom he had worked." p. 797 —Employee worked as a full-time sales application engineer. —Trial court found the covenant unreasonable because it did not include a territorial restriction.	Remands to trial court because a covenant may be reasonable even without a territorial restriction if the covenant includes certain type of subject matter restriction.	"Common sense suggests that a territorial limitation is often an irrelevant factor for [a covenant that prohibits the employee from soliciting the employee's former customers]. In Rollins Burdick Hunter of Wis., Inc. v. Hamilton, ... the Wisconsin Supreme Court, construing Wisconsin law, noted that a territorial limit is irrelevant in a nonsolicitation covenant because the restriction to former clients is sufficiently narrow. We find this reasoning persuasive." p. 800

This idea is confirmed from the language on the chart from both *Webb* and *Overholt,* where the court explains that an employer may only protect the employer's interest in its client relationships. Using this reasoning will help guide the lawyer through the next step of using the court's implicit ideas to determine an explanation of when a subject matter restriction is reasonable.

b. Determining the Analysis from the Implicit Reasoning

Since the court has not articulated an explicit explanation of when the subject matter of a covenant is reasonable, the lawyer needs to develop an accurate implicit explanation—as explained in Chapter Two. By using the reasoning that the covenant should be limited to protecting the employer's interest in the relationships that the employee established with the employer's customers, several ideas emerge from the pattern of the cases on the chart.

First, to hypothesize an explanation, the lawyer could use the court's stated policy, which is to protect employers from employees using the relationships they established with customers to take those customers away from the employer. If employees began working for a competitor, they could use their relationships with the customers to draw business away from the employer to the competitor. Thus, one way to protect the employer would be to prevent the employees from working for a competitor. Using this idea, the lawyer could hypothesize the following explanation of when a subject matter restriction is reasonable:

> To be reasonable, the subject matter restriction must only limit the employee from competing in the same business or industry.

The lawyer would check this potential explanation on the cases as a group. Testing the explanation first on the Minnesota Supreme Court cases, the lawyer would see a conflict regarding this idea. In the earliest case on the chart, *Eutectic,* the Minnesota Supreme Court seems to find that the subject matter of a covenant that included a restriction prohibiting the employee from working for a competitor was unreasonable. However, in *Walker,* the court found a similar restriction to be reasonable.

In the third case on the chart, *Davies,* the court provides relatively clear support that a restriction that simply restricts the employee from working in the same industry is too broad and, thus, unreasonable. In that case, the trial court found a covenant that prohibited an insurance salesperson from working in the "insurance business" was too broad, but found modifications to the covenant to restrict the employee from selling the types of products he had sold during employment to be reasonable. The Minnesota Supreme Court seemed to make a further change to the subject matter restriction, apparently modifying the restriction to prohibit the insurance salesperson from "active solicitation of agency clients [because that is] all that is reasonably necessary to protect the agency's interest in the insurance area."

Based on the first three cases, the lawyer would reject the hypothesis that a subject matter restriction is reasonable if it *limits the employee from competing in the same business or industry.* Using the non-solicitation idea from *Davies,* the lawyer might revise the hypothesized explanation as follows:

> A subject matter restriction is reasonable if it restricts the employee from actively soliciting the employer's customers.

The lawyer would then move to the other cases on the chart to verify the revised explanation to determine if further modification is necessary. *Dean Van Horn* seems to suggest that the new explanation may be too broad. In that case, the court enforced a covenant that included a subject matter restriction that prohibited the employee from soliciting the customers he had advised during his employment, rather than all of the employer's customers. In fact, this narrower restriction seems more in line with the basic reasoning that the court expresses in *Davies* and that later cases confirm. Those cases suggest that the employer's interest in restricting employees is only to protect the employer from harm they can cause because of the relationship they established with the employer's customers. If employees only had a relationship with a subset of customers, why would it be reasonable to restrict them from contacting all of the employer's customers?

Webb seems to confirm that restricting employees from contacting any of the employer's customers is too broad. In that case, the subject matter of the covenant basically restricted employees from soliciting any of the employer's customers. The court remanded the case to the trial court, but it did not hold that the subject matter restriction was unreasonable. However, the court did say that the employer's only interest appeared to be to restrict the employee from contacting his former customers, as opposed to all of the employer's customers.

The other cases on the chart do not seem to give much more guidance on the question of whether restricting employees from contacting all of the employer's customers is too broad because they come to different conclusions. While *Overholt* seems to find as reasonable a restriction that prohibited an insurance salesperson from contacting the insurance company's policyholders, *Dynamic* suggests that the appropriate restriction regarding customers would be limited to the customers with whom employees had contact.

Based on all the cases, whether the courts require that the subject matter be restricted to all of the employer's customers or just the customers with whom employees had contact is not clear. However, given the number of cases following the more restrictive approach, along with the express reasoning in several of these cases, it is reasonable to imply that the restriction should only restrict employees from contacting the employee's former customers. Therefore, the lawyer could refine the explanation as follows:

> A subject matter restriction is reasonable if it restricts the employee from actively soliciting the employee's former customers.

The lawyer at this point would need to verify this explanation on all the cases to be sure that the idea fully explains the results in the cases regarding subject matter restriction. Thus, the lawyer should apply the explanation to the cases where the court found that the subject matter restriction was reasonable to verify that it explains the results of the cases.

The lawyer would quickly realize that the explanation is too broad by considering the policy that the court has expressed. Simply restricting employees from soliciting their former customers is overly burdensome because they should only be restricted from contacting the customers if the contact would threaten the employer's business. What if an employee had sold insurance policies for the former employer but now sells hospital supply equipment? Obviously, the former employer's business would not be threatened if the employee contacted former customers for a different type of business. Therefore, the lawyer would need to revise the explanation to incorporate this idea, as follows:

> A subject matter restriction is reasonable if it restricts the employee from actively soliciting the employee's former customers on behalf of a competitor in the same business or industry.

This more specific explanation tests back on the cases as a group and seems to work based on the court's reasoning behind the subject matter restriction.

However, *Dynamic*, the last case dealing with the subject matter issue, seems to suggest an idea that the lawyer's final explanation does not incorporate. The question in *Dynamic* was whether a covenant could be reasonable with no territorial restriction. The trial court interpreted the cases to mean that all covenants must include a reasonable territorial restriction and therefore held that the covenant was unacceptable because it included no restriction regarding geographical area. The Minnesota Court of Appeals disagreed. The Court of Appeals found that a territorial restriction might not be necessary in *Dynamic* because of the subject matter restriction that precluded the former employee from soliciting customers on behalf of a competitor. The court suggests that the covenant reasonably restricted the employee by including the customer non-solicitation provision, even though the covenant did not include any restriction regarding territory.

The result in *Dynamic* would make the lawyer question whether the hypothesized explanation that a subject matter restriction is reasonable if it prohibits the employee from contacting former customers on behalf of a competitor is completely accurate. The court in *Dynamic* is suggesting that when a restriction against contacting customers on behalf of a competitor is included, a territorial restriction might not be necessary. However, the court does not state that a geographical restriction is always unnecessary. If a territorial restriction may still be required in some situations, the court seems to be suggesting that some broader subject matter restriction may be acceptable when combined with the territorial restriction. Thus, the lawyer would need to determine if the cases support another explanation for subject matter restriction.

The first case on the chart, *Eutectic,* does seem to put the focus of the question on the type of job employees should be restricted from doing rather than whom the employees should be restricted from contacting. However, the goal of the restrictions seems to be the same. The court in *Eutectic* suggests that employees should only be restricted from working in positions that would allow them to use their relationships with the former employer's customers to the advantage of the new employer. In fact, the lawyer would quickly learn from secondary sources that this job-based restriction seems to be the more traditional approach in many jurisdictions. Therefore, the lawyer could conclude that there are two ways to satisfy the subject matter restriction in Minnesota:

1. A subject matter restriction is reasonable if it restricts the employee from actively soliciting the employee's former customers on behalf of a competitor in the same business or industry; or
2. A subject matter restriction is reasonable if it prohibits the employee from working in a position for a competitor that could put the employee in contact with the employee's former customers.

Probably the easiest way to be sure that a court would find the restriction to be reasonable would be to use the first restriction and restrict employees from contacting their former customers on behalf of a competitor because it is the narrowest and least burdensome restriction on employees. The court's stated goal is to restrict employees only narrowly.

The lawyer's next step would be to determine if this narrow non-solicitation subject matter analysis would affect the court's stated geographical requirement. The lawyer might decide that the subject matter and territorial restrictions are merging because a non-solicitation subject matter restriction could render the need of a geographical restriction unnecessary. An analysis of the geographical restriction is not included as part of this illustration.

APPENDIX 2

Illustration of Handling Legal Ambiguities in Different Documents

Using the Minnesota non-compete question from Appendix 1, this appendix demonstrates approaches for handling legal ambiguities from cross-decision interpretive analysis when preparing different documents in practice.

To begin, imagine that an employer has retained a firm for advice regarding a salesperson who recently resigned and is considering a sales position with a competitor. The client is a small company that sells and installs wind turbines and other green power generation systems for farms and small businesses in Minnesota. The former employee signed the following non-compete clause as part of her original employment agreement when she joined the client's sales force:

> Employee agrees that upon termination of employment with Employer for whatever reason, employee will not, for a period of two years after the termination, take an ownership interest in or enter into employment with a competitor within 25 miles of the city limits of any city where Employer has an office or other business location.

The agreement provides that Minnesota law applies and defines "competitor" as a business selling the same type of products as the client. The company that the former employee may join as a salesperson is located about ten miles from the client's main office, where the former employee was assigned. Assume that the two-year time restriction is enforceable.

A. PREDICTING THE RESULT

Imagine that the client does not want the former employee to work for the competitor and has sought advice about whether it should seek a preliminary injunction to stop her from taking the new position. To help make this determination, the senior lawyer has asked a junior colleague to analyze whether a court would enforce the non-compete clause.

The junior lawyer would analyze the entire question and possibly identify a variety of issues, including a problem with the subject matter of the clause. The clause prohibits the employee from working for a competitor, without limiting the type of job or position. Thus, the language of the clause restricts her from working for a competitor in any capacity. Although the court's analysis of what it will accept as an enforceable subject matter restriction is somewhat unclear—as explained in Appendix I—the junior lawyer would understand that a court is not likely to enforce a provision restricting a former employee from working for a competitor in any capacity.

The junior lawyer would fully analyze the issue and provide an explanation of the court's analysis regarding the subject matter restriction question, which was discussed in Appendix I. In this explanation, the lawyer would explain that the courts might be moving from a job-based restriction to a client-based approach. Then, after fully explaining and illustrating these ideas, the lawyer would apply the analysis to the client's restriction.

In predicting whether a court would enforce the clause, the lawyer probably would include a prediction that it would not be enforced as written and then include several counter predictions of how the court could handle the question. The lawyer would include a prediction that the clause would not be enforced as written because it is too broad under any of the approaches that the cases suggest are acceptable. However, the author would need to include counter predictions regarding how a court could handle the clause because the Minnesota analysis gives a trial court several options when faced with an unenforceable non-compete clause.

Therefore, the author would need to predict that a court would probably not enforce the restriction as drafted, but explain that the result of what a court would do is hard to predict because of the court's different options. First, the courts are clear that a trial court may refuse to enforce a non-compete clause entirely if it is overbroad in any way. Thus, the lawyer would explain that the court would have the option of refusing to enforce the clause because the subject matter restriction is too broad.

Next, the author probably would include a counter prediction that the court might decide to enforce the clause, but not with the subject matter restriction that was included in the original agreement. Minnesota courts have adopted the "blue pencil" doctrine that gives them the discretion to revise unreasonable non-compete clauses to make them reasonable. The author would explain that if the court chose to modify the restriction instead of throwing it out entirely, the court could revise it in two different ways. The author would need to explain that which option the court would exercise is unclear, but first provide the result that the author believes is most likely and then explain the other possibility.

If the author felt that the court would most likely choose the approach that would restrict the employee the least—as explained in Appendix 1—the choice would be clear. The author would first provide a prediction that the court could revise the restriction to only restrict the employee from dealing with the employer's customers with whom she had contact during employment with the client. Therefore, the lawyer would predict that a court would allow the employee to take the new job with the competitor, but it would not allow her to contact any of the former customers with whom she worked while employed by the client.

Next, the author would include another counter prediction that the court could revise the restriction differently because the cases suggest that this analysis is in flux and the courts have not clearly chosen one approach. Thus, the author would explain that a court could revise the subject matter of the restriction to prevent the employee from working as a sales representative for a competitor. However, the author would need to explain that if the court chooses this approach, enforceability of the clause would depend on the geographical restriction.

B. MAKING ARGUMENTS

If the client decided to file the motion for preliminary injunction, despite the risk that the court could decide that the entire non-compete clause is unenforceable due to the overly broad subject matter restriction, the junior lawyer would have to determine the most effective way to use the analytical ambiguities to support the arguments. The first strategic choice would be whether to argue that the court should enforce the subject matter restriction as written. The former employee likely would argue that court should throw out the entire clause because the subject matter restriction is unenforceable given the court's analysis. While the restriction does seem overly broad based on the cases, the lawyer might be able to create an argument that the court should enforce it as written by focusing on the policy behind the analysis.

The court has explained that employers have a right to narrowly protect themselves from competition from former employees and therefore courts enforce non-compete clauses if they include restrictions that prevent former employees from taking advantage of the relationships they developed with the employer's customers. If the facts suggested that the green power generation businesses in Minnesota tend to be so small that customers develop a relationship with all of the employees in the business, the lawyer might be able to convince the court that a restriction from working in any capacity for a competitor is a reasonable restriction. The lawyer could argue that a new employer could take advantage of the employee's relationships with the former employer's customers in any position in the new company since customers develop relationships with all of the company's employees.

Depending on the facts, this argument could be risky because the restriction would prevent a former employee who worked as a sales representative from working in any position at all for a competitor. For example, the former salesperson could be restricted from working as a maintenance person or some other position that would not naturally put the employee in contact with any customers. Convincing a court that restricting a former salesperson from taking such a position with a competitor would actually protect the former employer might be a stretch. Therefore, the junior lawyer might decide that the better strategy would be to concede that the subject matter restriction might be too broad as written, but that the court should use the "blue pencil" doctrine to enforce a modified restriction.

At this point of the argument, both the lawyer for the employer and the lawyer for the employee would be using the same legal ambiguity from the group of relevant cases to develop very different arguments. The employer's lawyer likely would argue that the former employee should be restricted from working for a competitor as a salesperson or in any capacity that would put her in contact with customers. The employee's lawyer likely would argue that the cases support the idea that the she should be restricted as narrowly as possible, and therefore she should only be restricted from contacting her former customers. In both arguments, the lawyers would use specific language from the cases, the policy, and case examples to try to convince the court of their point of view. Both sides would have very strong arguments given the status of the law in Minnesota, but neither side would know for certain what the court would ultimately decide.

C. DRAFTING A NEW AGREEMENT

The legal ambiguities discussed above would pose problems if the client planned to hire new employees and asked advice about what language to include in the new non-compete clause so that it will be more likely to be enforced while restricting new employees as much as possible. The lawyer's task obviously would be easier if the client requested a clause that a court would most likely enforce, even though it would not restrict the employees as much as possible. To draft such a clause, the junior lawyer would probably include a provision that restricted employees from contacting former customers on behalf of a competitor in a reasonable geographical area. While a court would likely enforce this restriction because it includes a narrow subject matter restriction combined with a reasonable geographical restriction, it probably is not the clause that restricts the employees as much as possible based on the cases.

When trying to determine a clause that would most fully restrict the employees and that a court would enforce, the junior lawyer probably would not be sure of the best option given the status of the law. Therefore, the junior lawyer would probably draft alternative clauses for the senior attorney to consider and include explanations of both provisions.

The junior lawyer might decide that the safer option that would still be relatively restrictive would be to restrict former employees from contacting—on behalf of a competitor—any of the employer's customers with whom they had worked, but not include any geographical limitation. While the junior lawyer would have to explain that courts might be unwilling to uphold a clause that does not include any geographical limitation, only preventing employees from contacting customers might be sufficiently narrow because the employees would be allowed to work anywhere and for any competitor, as long as they did not contact former customers. Therefore, the court would probably accept it, even without a related territorial restriction.

The other option that the junior lawyer probably would include for the senior attorney's consideration would be a clause that prohibits employees from working for a competitor as a sales representative or in any position that puts them in contact with customers, along with a reasonable geographical restriction. While this prohibition might restrict the employees more broadly and thus appeal to the client, the junior lawyer would need to explain that the cases suggest that this type of clause might be too restrictive. A court might rewrite it to only prevent the employee from contacting former customers. However, given the status of the law, most courts probably would enforce such a restriction.

The senior lawyer would have to work with the client to determine which of these options should be included in the new agreement. Therefore, the junior lawyer probably would provide drafts of the different language with attached notes explaining the pros and cons of each alternative.

APPENDIX 3

Samples of Predictive Writing

A. SAMPLE OF FORMAL INTERNAL OFFICE MEMORANDUM

1. For a discussion of formal internal office memoranda, see Chapter 4, Part B.

MEMORANDUM

2. For a discussion of the heading, see Chapter 4, Part B.3.a.

To: Senior Attorney
From: Junior Colleague
Date: January 3, 2014
Re: Mike Long: Enforceability of Employment Agreement Non-compete Clause

<u>Question Presented</u>

3. For a discussion of the Question Presented, see Chapter 4, part B.3.b.

In Minnesota, can an employer enforce a non-compete clause in an employment agreement against a departing employee who had contacts with former customers if the clause restricts the employee from working in a similar position for a competitor for three years in any state where the employer does business?

<u>Brief Answer</u>

4. For a discussion of the Brief Answer, see Chapter 4, Part B.3.c.

Probably not. A Minnesota court probably would not enforce the non-compete clause as written. Although a court likely would find that the employer has a legitimate interest to restrict the departing employee because of his relationships with its customers, a court probably would find that the clause itself is too broad to reasonably protect those relationships. While the subject matter restriction is reasonable, the time and territory provisions are not. Therefore, a court probably would revise the clause with the "blue pencil" doctrine to make it reasonable. However, what modifications a court would make are unclear.

A court could revise the clause so it restricts the employee from contacting any of his former customers on behalf of a competitor in the northern part of Minnesota for one year. On the other hand, a court could modify the clause so it only restricts the employee from working in a similar position for a competitor in the northern part of Minnesota for one year.

5. For a discussion of the Facts Section, see Chapter 4, Part B.3.d.

Facts

Our client, Mike Long, has sought advice about whether Energy Resources, Inc. (Energy) can enforce the following non-compete clause that was included in his original employment agreement with Energy:

> [E]mployee will not, for a period of 36 months after Termination, enter into employment as a service representative or salesperson with any Business that sells or markets Generator Equipment.

Energy, a Minnesota corporation, provides large energy generators to commercial enterprises, such as hotels, hospitals, military installations, law enforcement offices, and shopping malls. Energy sells and services its equipment throughout the Midwest.

Energy uses a team approach to market and service its equipment. It assigns a team of four employees for each region. Although Energy trains all team members to be competent to handle all the servicing needs of the customers, each member is mainly responsible for one of four areas: mechanical upkeep of generators; on-going customer training; maintenance of computer equipment; and updating the computer software. Mr. Long was the team member responsible for customer training.

Before a sale, the teams meets with customers as a group several times a week for about six months to evaluate equipment selection, installation, and long-term servicing options. Once a sale is completed, the team works with the customers for regular upkeep and servicing. Each team member meets with the customers for approximately the same amount of time, which typically includes a regular quarterly meeting and additional meetings about once a month.

Energy assigned Mr. Long to the team in the northern region of Minnesota (approximately the northern half of the state). He was a member of that team for the approximately six years he was employed with Energy. Mr. Long did not become friends with any of his customers during that time. The team did not contact all potential customers in its territory.

Energy trained Mr. Long for about a year to fully familiarize him with the equipment and technical information. Energy provides the same training to all team members. For purposes of the memorandum, I have been asked to assume that Energy did not disclose any of its confidential information to Mr. Long.

Several months ago, Mr. Long left Energy and began working as a salesperson for a competitor, Bright Lights Unlimited, Inc. ("Bright Lights"). His territory is all of Minnesota. Since leaving Energy, Mr. Long has not solicited or contacted any of Energy's customers.

Mr. Long has sought our advice about the non-compete clause because his new employer, Bright Lights, has expressed concern about his ability to continue working as one of its sales representatives if Energy attempts to enforce the clause against him.

6. For a discussion of the Discussion Section, see Chapter 4, Part B.3.e.

Discussion

7. Introduction. For a discussion of introductions, see Chapter 4, Part B.3.e.1.

Minnesota has not enacted a statute regarding the enforceability of non-compete provisions in employment agreements. When evaluating such clauses, Minnesota courts disfavor them because they restrict employees' right to work and earn a livelihood.

2

See, e.g., *Bennett v. Storz Broad. Co.*, 134 N.W.2d 892, 899 (Minn. 1965); *Davies & Davies Agency, Inc. v. Davies*, 298 N.W.2d 127, 131 (Minn. 1980); *Webb Publ'g Co. v. Fosshage*, 426 N.W.2d 445, 450 (Minn. Ct. App. 1988). However, the courts recognize that employers need to be able to protect their businesses from employees using advantages they gained during employment to compete against them. *See, e.g.*, *Bennett*, 134 N.W.2d at 898; *Davies*, 298 N.W.2d at 131. To balance these competing concerns, a court will only enforce a non-compete clause if the employer has a legitimate interest to restrict the departing employee and the terms of the clause reasonably protect that interest. *See, e.g.*, *Bennett*, 134 N.W.2d at 898; *Davies*, 298 N.W.2d at 131.

The courts first require that the employer have a legitimate interest in restricting the departing employee from competing against it. *E.g.*, *Bennett*, 134 N.W.2d at 898-99; *Webb*, 426 N.W.2d at 450. An employer has such an interest when the employee acquired the employer's confidential information or developed close relationships with the employer's customers. *See, e.g.*, *Eutectic Welding Alloys Corp. v. West*, 160 N.W.2d 566, 569 (Minn. 1968); *Webb*, 426 N.W.2d at 450. The courts protect these interests because employers need the ability to defend themselves from unfair competition that would result if employees were allowed to use their confidential information or client relationships to compete against them. *See, e.g.*, *Bennett*, 134 N.W.2d at 898; Webb, 426 N.W.2d at 450. For purposes of this memo, I have been asked to assume that Mr. Long did not receive Energy's confidential information. Therefore, the discussion will focus only on Mr. Long's relationships with Energy's customers.

8. Topic sentence introducing first requirement. For a discussion of role of topic sentences, see Chapter 4, Part A.2.b.1.

9. Explanation for the legitimate interest question. For a discussion of explanations of issues, see Chapter 4, Part B.3.e.2.

An employer has a legitimate interest when the departing employee has such close contacts with its customers that the strength of those relationships could draw the customers to the employee's new employer. *See, e.g.*, *Davies*, 298 N.W.2d at 131; *Menter Co. v. Brock*, 180 N.W. 553, 555 (Minn. 1920); *Webb*, 426 N.W.2d at 450. To make this determination, the courts evaluate the totality of the relationships, including exclusivity, length, regularity, and the level of friendship between the employee and customers. *See, e.g.*, *Davies*, 298 N.W.2d at 131; *Webb*, 426 N.W.2d at 450. In addition, if the departing employee has begun working for a competitor and some customers have already followed the employee to that competitor, the court usually finds that the relationships were sufficiently close that more customers could be drawn to the new employer. *See Webb*, 426 N.W.2d at 450.

For example, in *Davies*, the court found that the relationships between the employee and his clients were sufficiently close because the employee worked for the employer for eleven years, eventually taking over the employer's bond business and becoming the exclusive contact for many of those clients. 298 N.W.2d at 129. The court found that customers could follow the employee due to the strength of their relationships with him because he had exclusive contact with the clients for a significant length of time. *See id.* at 131.

10. Illustration of a decision. For a discussion of decision illustrations, see Chapter 4, Part B.3.e.2.

The court also found sufficient relationships in *Webb*, where the departing employee, an account executive, was the exclusive contact with his clients for about seven years and became a friend with several of them during that time. 426 N.W.2d at 449. After the employee began working for a competitor, almost half of his customers canceled their contracts with the employer and followed him to the new employer. *Id.*

3

at 450. The court reasoned that because the employee had worked exclusively with the clients over seven years, and the employee developed friendships with some customers, the relationships between the employee and the clients were such that customers would likely follow him to the competitor. *See id.* Furthermore, because two of the clients actually had followed the employee to his new employment, the court found that more customers would likely do the same. *See id.*

On the other hand, the relationships are not sufficiently close if clients are unlikely to follow the departing employee to a competitor. *See e.g., Davies*, 298 N.W.2d at 131; *Menter*, 180 N.W. at 555. For example, in *Menter*, the court determined that the store manager of a retail-clothing store did not have sufficiently close relationships because he only had irregular and brief contacts with walk-in customers. See 180 N.W. at 554–55. Since these contacts were not regular and consistent, the court found that customers were unlikely to be drawn to a competitor by the employee. *See id.; Klick v. Crosstown State, Inc.*, 372 N.W.2d 85, 87–89 (Minn. Ct. App. 1985) (finding a bank vice-president's eight-month employment too short to form close client relationships, even though the relationships might have been regular and exclusive).

11. Application of legitimate interest. For a discussion of applications, see Chapter 4, Part B.3.e.3. This memorandum includes the most complete citation. Many lawyers would choose not provide citation when applying the law to the client's facts. For a discussion of whether to include citation in the application, see Chapter 4, Part B.3.e.5.

A court would probably find that Mr. Long has a close relationship with Energy's customers because he met with them frequently and regularly over a long period. *See e.g., Davies,* 298 N.W.2d at 131; *Webb*, 426 N.W.2d at 450. While he was not the only contact with the customers, he had fairly exclusive contact with them as a member of a small team of four that had the only interaction the customers on behalf of Energy. *See e.g., Davies,* 298 N.W.2d at 131; *Webb*, 426 N.W.2d at 450. Furthermore, he was the sole representative responsible for working with the customers on equipment training. *See Webb*, 426 N.W.2d at 450. Thus, a court would probably find that his client relationships were close enough that they could draw those customers to his new employer. *See e.g., Davies*, 298 N.W.2d at 131; *Webb*, 426 N.W.2d at 450.

12. Example of case comparison. For a discussion of comparisons, see Chapter 4, Part B.3.e.3.

The court could consider the relationships in Mr. Long's case as similar to the close relationships found in *Webb*, where the employee worked for the business seven years, and during that time he developed regular, exclusive, and personal relationships with the clients, 426 N.W.2d at 447, 449. In that case, the totality of the relationships between the employee and the clients indicated that the relationships were sufficiently close that they could draw the clients to the departing employee's new employer. *See id.* The relationships in Mr. Long's case are similar in that he worked with his clients regularly and frequently for a period of six years. *See id.* Although the relationships are not exclusive or personal, the totality of Mr. Long's relationship with his clients is similar to the totality of the relationship in *Webb. See id.*

Furthermore, the client relationships in Mr. Long's case differ from those in *Menter*, where the employee had only infrequent, inconsistent, and brief contacts with clients. *See* 180 N.W. at 555. A court is likely to find that due to their relationships with Mr. Long, his customers are more likely to be drawn to his new employer than the customers in *Menter* because Mr. Long met with his customers regularly at least once a month for the past six years. *See id.*

If an employer has a legitimate interest in the departing employee's customer relationships, the court next requires that the clause reasonably protect those relationships in terms of time, subject matter, and territory. *See, e.g., Davies*, 298 N.W.2d at 131; *Overholt v. Bredeson*, 437 N.W.2d 698, 703–04 (Minn. Ct. App. 1989); *Dean Van Horn*

4

v. Wold, 395 N.W.2d 405, 409 (Minn. Ct. App. 1986). If the relationships are close but the clause is unreasonable, the court has the discretion to refuse to enforce the clause or modify it to make it reasonable with the "blue pencil" doctrine. *See, e.g., Davies*, 298 N.W.2d at 131; *Overholt*, 437 N.W.2d at 703–04; *Dean Van Horn*, 395 N.W.2d at 409.

To be enforceable, the courts require that the clause include a reasonable time limit. *See, e.g., Davies*, 298 N.W.2d at 131; *Overholt*, 437 N.W.2d at 703–04; *Dean Van Horn*, 395 N.W.2d at 409. To be reasonable, the clause cannot restrict the departing employee any longer than approximately the time that the employer trained the departing employee, with a maximum limit of about two years. *See, e.g., Davies*, 298 N.W.2d at 131; *Overholt*, 437 N.W.2d at 703–04; *Dean Van Horn*, 395 N.W.2d at 409. The departing employee's training time is a reasonable period because it is enough time for the employer to train a replacement and for the customers to adjust to the change in company representation. *Compare Overholt*, 437 N.W.2d at 703–04 (finding a two-year restraint reasonable because departing employee received about that much training), *with Davies*, 298 N.W.2d at 131 (finding a five-year restriction unreasonable and revising it to one year, the estimated time to train replacement); *Dean Van Horn*, 395 N.W.2d at 409 (finding a three–year restriction unreasonable and revising it to one year, about the departing employee's training period).

13. Example of case illustrations with parenthetical citations. For a discussion of such citations, see Chapter 4, Part B.3.e.2.

The courts also require that the clause include a reasonable subject matter restriction. *See, e.g., Davies*, 298 N.W.2d at 131–32; *Eutectic*, 160 N.W.2d at 570; *Overholt*, 437 N.W.2d at 703. Courts originally seemed to require that the subject matter be no broader than restricting employees from working for a competitor in a position that could put them in contact with the potential customers, usually the same position they held with the former employer. *See, e.g., Eutectic*, 160 N.W.2d at 570; *Overholt*, 437 N.W.2d at 703. This type of restriction protects employers' client relationships because it restricts departing employees from exploiting those relationships on behalf of competitors by prohibiting them from working in positions that could put them in contact with those customers. *See Eutectic*, 160 N.W.2d at 570 (finding subject matter unreasonable because it should have limited departing employee to similar position with competitor that he had with former employer).

More recently, courts seem to favor more limited subject matter restrictions that only prohibit departing employees from contacting their former customers on behalf of a competitor. *See, e.g., Davies*, 298 N.W.2d at 131–32; *Dean Van Horn*, 395 N.W.2d at 406; *Overholt*, 437 N.W.2d at 703. Such non-solicitation provisions more narrowly protect the client relationships than position-based restrictions. *See Dynamic Air v. Bloch*, 502 N.W.2d 796, 797–800 (Minn. Ct. App. 1993. When a job restriction is used, employees are restricted from taking a position that might put them in contact with former customers. *See, e.g., Davies*, 298 N.W.2d at 131–32; *Dynamic*, 502 N.W.2d, 502 N.W.2d at 797–800. Such a restriction effectively prevents employees for working with any potential customers, even though they may not have had any contact with many of those customers while working with the former employer. *See, e.g., Davies*, 298 N.W.2d at 131–32; *Dynamic*, 502 N.W.2d, 502 N.W.2d at 797–800. A non-solicitation restriction, on the other hand, only restricts employees from contacting former customers, which leaves them free to contact other potential customers that did not have a connection with the former employer through the departing employees. *Compare Dynamic*, 502 N.W.2d at 797–800 (finding subject matter reasonable because it only

5

restricted departing employee from contacting his former customers on behalf of competitor); *Overholt*, 437 N.W.2d at 703 (finding subject matter reasonable because it was interpreted to only restrict departing employee from contacting his former customers on behalf of competitor), *with Davies*, 298 N.W.2d at 131–32 (suggesting that appropriate revision to subject matter would be restrict departing employee from only contacting his former customers on behalf of competitor).

The court also requires that the territory of the clause be reasonable. *See, e.g., Walker v. Parkhurst*, 219 N.W.2d 437, 441 (Minn. 1974); *Eutectic*, 160 N.W.2d at 570; *Overholt*, 437 N.W.2d at 703. To be reasonable, courts generally require that the territory restriction be no broader than limiting departing employees from working in the same geographic area where they had worked for the employer. *See, e.g., Walker*, 219 N.W.2d at 441; *Eutectic*, 160 N.W.2d at 570; *Overholt*, 437 N.W.2d at 703. This type of restriction protects the employer's client relationships because it prohibits departing employees from working in areas where they could exploit their relationships with the former employer's customers to the benefit of the new employers. *Compare Walker*, 219 N.W.2d at 441 (finding territory reasonable because it limited departing employee from working in the county where he had worked for former employer); *Overholt*, 437 N.W.2d at 703 (finding territory reasonable because it limited departing employee from competing in his former sales territory), *with Eutectic*, 160 N.W.2d at 570 (finding territory unreasonable because it limited departing employee from competing in 50-mile radius of former territory, which included areas in which employee had not worked for former employer).

However, recently courts seem willing to allow employers to include an unlimited territory restriction if the subject matter provision only prohibits departing employees from contacting former customers, rather than restricting them from working in a particular position. *See Dynamic*, 502 N.W.2d at 797–800. Limiting employees from contacting former customers—wherever they are located—reasonably protects the employer's client relationships because it would still allow the former employees to contact other potential customers who had no previous connection with the former employer through the employees. *See id.* (finding territory restriction unnecessary because the subject matter limited departing employee from contacting all former customers).

If the non-compete clause is not reasonable, the court may refuse to enforce the clause entirely or modify it with the "blue pencil" doctrine to make it reasonable. *See, e.g., Davies*, 298 N.W.2d at 131; *Klick*, 372 N.W.2d at 88–89; *Dean Van Horn*, 395 N.W.2d at 409. Although the use of the doctrine is discretionary, the courts favor its application unless the clause suggests that the employer fashioned it to discourage competition generally, rather than tailoring an agreement that would reasonably protect its legitimate interest. *See Dynamic*, 502 N.W.2d at 800 (reminding trial court of the discretion to "blue pencil" a clause that it remanded for reconsideration). To make this determination, courts examine the terms of the clause as a whole to decide if they are so burdensome on the departing employee that the clause makes finding work elsewhere effectively impossible, even though much less burdensome restrictions would adequately protect the employer's legitimate interest. *See Davies*, 298 N.W.2d at 129–32 (revising clause even though all provisions were unreasonable because overall effect of the clause did not seem to suggest that employer was trying to make finding work effectively impossible for employee).

6

A Minnesota court probably would find that the Mr. Long's non-compete clause is unreasonable. *See, e.g., Davies*, 298 N.W.2d at 131; *Overholt*, 437 N.W.2d at 703–04; *Dean Van Horn at* 409. A court likely would determine the subject matter to be reasonable, but it probably would decide that the time and territory restrictions do not reasonably protect Mr. Long's relationships with Energy's customers *See, e.g., Davies*, 298 N.W.2d at 131; *Overholt*, 437 N.W.2d at 703–04; *Dean Van Horn* 395 N.W.2d at 409. Although a court likely would revise the clause with the "blue pencil" doctrine, the specific modifications a court would make are unclear. *See, e.g., Davies*, 298 N.W.2d at 131; *Klick*, 372 N.W.2d at 88–89; *Dean Van Horn*, 395 N.W.2d at 409.

A court probably would find the time restriction is unreasonable because it restricts Mr. Long for three years, even though his training period was only about a year. *See, e.g., Davies*, 298 N.W.2d at 131; *Overholt*, 437 N.W.2d at 703–04; *Dean Van Horn*, 395 N.W.2d at 409. The court likely would consider this three-year restriction overbroad like the unreasonable three–year restriction in *Dean Van Horn*, because they are both longer than the departing employees' training period of about a year. *See* 395 N.W.2d at 409.

A court probably would find that the subject matter restriction is reasonable because it restricts Mr. Long from working as "a service representative or salesperson with any Business that sells or markets Generator Equipment." *See Eutectic*, 160 N.W.2d at 570; *Dynamic*, 502 N.W.2d at 797–800. This provision is reasonable because it only restrict Mr. Long working for a competitor in a position that would put him in contact with his former customers on behalf of a competitor. *See Eutectic*, 160 N.W.2d at 570 (finding subject matter should have limited departing employee to similar position he held with former employer to be reasonable).

14. Comparison with facts of case using a parenthetical citation. For a discussion of parenthetical comparisons, see Chapter 4, Part B.3.e.3.

However, a court probably would find that the territory of the clause to be unreasonable because it restricts Mr. Long from working "in any state" where Energy does business. *See, e.g., Davies*, 298 N.W.2d at 131–32; *Walker*, 219 N.W.2d at 441 *Eutectic*, 160 N.W.2d at 570. This provision is not reasonable because it is not limited to restricting Mr. Long from working in the geographic area where he worked with Energy's clients. *See, e.g., Eutectic* 160 N.W.2d at 570; *Overholt*, 437 N.W.2d at 703. The territory restricts Mr. Long from working in any state where Energy sells its equipment, even though his customers were located in only part of Minnesota. *See, e.g., Eutectic*, 160 N.W.2d at 570; *Overholt*, 437 N.W.2d at 703. Therefore, a court likely would find this provision unreasonable because it restricts Mr. Long more than is necessary to protect Energy's interest in his relationships with its clients. *See, e.g., Eutectic*, 160 N.W.2d at 570; *Overholt*, 437 N.W.2d at 703.

Mr. Long's territorial restriction is similar to the unreasonable restriction in *Eutectic* because they both restrict the departing employee from geographic areas where the employees had not worked for the former employer. *See* 160 N.W.2d at 570. Thus, it is unlike the reasonable restriction in *Overholt*, which only limited the departing employee from working for a competitor in his former sales territory. *See* 437 N.W.2d at 703.

Even though a court likely would find the non-compete clause unreasonable, it would probably exercise its discretion to enforce the clause with modified terms, using the "blue pencil" doctrine. *See, e.g., Davies*, 298 N.W.2d at 131; *Klick*, 372 N.W.2d at 88–89; *Dean Van Horn*, 395 N.W.2d at 409. This result is likely because the provisions

7

of the clause are not so excessive to suggest that Energy was simply trying to prevent any possible competition rather than tailoring an agreement that would narrowly protect its interest. *See, e.g., Davies*, 298 N.W.2d at 131; *Klick*, 372 N.W.2d at 88–89; *Dean Van Horn*, 395 N.W.2d at 409. A court probably would decide that the overall impact of the clause is similar to the covenant that the court revised with the "blue pencil" doctrine in *Davies*, because even though both clauses had some unreasonable terms, they are not so broad as to suggest that the employer was trying to make finding work effectively impossible for the employees. *See* 298 N.W.2d at 131.

However, the modifications a court would make are unclear because the court would have several options. *See, e.g., id.* at 131; *Klick*, 372 N.W.2d at 88–89; *Dean Van Horn*, 395 N.W.2d at 409. A court probably would decrease the time restriction imposed upon Mr. Long from three years to 12 months because that is the amount of time it would take Energy to train Mr. Long's replacement. *See Davies*, 298 N.W.2d at 131; *Dean Van Horn*, 395 N.W.2d at 409. Any time restriction greater than 12 months would not be narrowly tailored to protect Energy's interest in effectively replacing Mr. Long and would merely serve to limit his personal freedom to pursue his preferred occupation for longer than necessary. *See Davies*, 298 N.W.2d at 131; *Dean Van Horn*, 395 N.W.2d at 409.

15. Counter prediction. For a discussion of counter predictions, See Chapter 4, Part B.3.e.4.

However, how a court would handle the subject matter and territory restrictions is uncertain. *See, e.g., Davies*, 298 N.W.2d at 131–32; *Eutectic*, 160 N.W.2d at 570; *Overholt*, 437 N.W.2d at 703. A court could decide that even though the subject matter alone seems reasonable, since the territory is more burdensome than necessary, the best way to improve the clause would be to make both the subject matter and territory narrower. *See, e.g., Davies*, 298 N.W.2d at 131–32; *Eutectic*, 160 N.W.2d at 570; *Overholt*, 437 N.W.2d at 703. In this situation, the court could modify the clause so it only restricts Mr. Long from contacting his former customers on behalf of a competitor in the northern region of Minnesota, his former sales territory. *See, e.g., Davies*, 298 N.W.2d at 131–32; *Eutectic*, 160 N.W.2d at 570; *Overholt*, 437 N.W.2d at 703. This change would make the clause similar to the reasonable clause in *Overholt* and the revised clause in *Davies* because they would all only limit the departing employee from contacting former customers on behalf of a competitor in the territory where they worked for the former employer. *See Overholt*, 437 N.W.2d at 703; *Davies*, 298 N.W.2d at 131–32.

However, a court could leave the subject matter alone, revising only the territory clause. *See, e.g., Eutectic*, 160 N.W.2d at 570; *Overholt*, 437 N.W.2d at 703. In this situation, the court would modify the agreement so it restricts Mr. Long from working as a sales representative for a competitor in his former territory, the northern part of Minnesota. *See, e.g., Eutectic*, 160 N.W.2d at 570; *Overholt*, 437 N.W.2d at 703. With this modification, the clause would be similar to the covenant the court suggested would have been reasonable in *Eutectic* because they would only be restricting the departing employees from working for a competitor in a similar position and territory as they had worked for the former employers. *See* 160 N.W.2d at 570; *see also Dynamic*, 502 N.W.2d at 797–800 (suggesting that non-compete clause can be reasonable if it includes reasonable job-based subject matter and territorial restrictions).

8

16. For a discussion of the Conclusion Section, see Chapter 4, Part B.3.f.

Conclusion

A Minnesota court probably would not enforce Mr. Long's non-compete clause as written. Although a court probably would find that Energy has a legitimate interest to restrict Mr. Long because of his close relationships with its customers, the clause itself is too broad to reasonably protect those relationships. While a court likely would find that the subject matter restriction is reasonable, it probably would decide that the time and territory provisions are not and revise them with the "blue pencil" doctrine. However, what modifications a court would make are unclear.

A court could revise the clause so that it restricts Mr. Long from contacting any of his former customers on behalf of a competitor in the northern part of Minnesota, his former territory with Energy, for one year. However, a court could modify the clause so it only restricts Mr. Long from working as a service or sales representative, his former position with Energy, for a competitor in the northern part of Minnesota for one year.

9

B. SAMPLE OF INFORMAL INTERNAL COMMUNICATION

1. For a discussion of informal internal office communications, including use of different formatting and style options, see Chapter 4, Part C.

To: Senior Colleague
From: Junior Colleague
Re: Long: Non-compete Clause—Potential Arguments

Attachments: Outline of Argument; Memo on Long Non-compete Clause

After our meeting about my memo on Mike's non-compete clause, I thought you might like a quick synopsis of the arguments we discussed to help prepare for your meeting with Mike and Barbara Trujillo, his new boss at Bright Lights. At the end of this message, I have included an outline of potential arguments we could use to support a petition for declaratory judgment or defend against a preliminary injunction action, as well as Energy's potential counter arguments.

I understand that Ms. Trujillo has told Mike that she is worried about his ability to continue working with Bright Lights because of the non-compete clause. Specifically, she is not sure if Bright Lights should invest in Mike's training if Energy will be able to use the clause to enjoin him from working for Bright Lights for the three-year limit. Based on my analysis and consideration of the various arguments, I do not think that a court would likely enforce the clause as written—in particular the three-year restriction—although it probably would enforce the clause with modified terms. Here are my bottom-line predictions if we challenged the clause in court:

- *Most likely result: Mike can work for Bright Lights anywhere, including northern Minnesota, but he will be restricted from contacting his former Energy customers for one year.* The court will revise the clause to restrict Mike for one year from contacting his former Energy customers on behalf of Bright Lights in northern Minnesota.

- *Worst-case scenario: Mike will be restricted from working for Bright Lights in northern Minnesota for one year.* The court could revise the clause to restrict Mike from working for one year as a service representative or salesperson for Bright Lights in northern Minnesota.

I also think we have a couple of arguments that might convince a court to throw out the clause entirely:

1. Energy has no legitimate reason to enforce a non-compete clause because Mike's contacts with Energy's customers were too weak; and

2. The terms of the clause are too onerous to modify.

Although these arguments may not completely sway a court, the ideas we use to support them would reinforce the arguments that the court is more likely to accept. Therefore, beginning with these best-case—though maybe less convincing—arguments could be a good organizational strategy for a brief. I have included more detail about these arguments in the outline below.

After your meeting, please let me know if you would like a memo supporting the different arguments or if you would like me to get started on a brief.

—Junior Colleague

P.S. I have attached the outline of the arguments below as separate document, as well as another copy of my original memo.

OUTLINE OF POTENTIAL ARGUMENTS

Mike's non-compete clause:

> [E]mployee will not, for a period of 36 months after Termination, enter into employment as a service representative or salesperson with any Business that sells or markets Generator Equipment in any state where Employer sells or markets Generator Equipment.

Court should refuse to enforce clause: Energy has no legitimate interest because client relationships are too weak:

- *Our argument: Insufficient customer relationships because they were not exclusive.* To decide if an employer has a legitimate interest in the departing employee's client contacts, the court determines if the customers would be drawn to a competitor because the relationships are so strong that the customers see the employee as the face of the company. The court considers a variety of factors together, including exclusivity, regularity, duration, and level of personal friendship. Although none of these is required, in almost all of the cases where the court found sufficient relationships, the employee was the only contact between the employer and the customers. Mike was one of four team members who contacted the customers. Thus, we would argue that he had not become the face of Energy because he was one of four employees who have about the same amount of contact.

- *Energy's possible counter arguments: Exclusive contact is not required.* Energy would counter that the court has consistently used a variety of factors, including—but not requiring—exclusivity. Energy would focus on the regularity and length of time of Mike's contacts to argue that customers would likely follow him to a competitor because of those relationships.

- *Likely outcome*: *Energy has a legitimate interest.* Although the analysis gives us an opening with this argument, if I were a judge deciding this issue, I probably would agree with Energy. Mike met with customers regularly for a long time. Although he was not the exclusive contact, he was a primary contact as one of only four of the employer's representatives who met with his customers. Furthermore, the pattern of cases seems to favor Energy: The court almost always finds the contacts to be sufficient when the employee meets customers regularly for over a year or so.

- *Strategy: Weaken the court's impression of the strength of the legitimate interest.* Even if the court decides that the customer contacts were sufficient to give Energy a reason to enforce some type of non-compete clause, our argument should help persuade the court that that interest is not very strong. This idea should sway the court to our point of view in the next arguments.

<u>Court should refuse to enforce clause: The terms are too onerous to "blue pencil":</u>

- *Our argument: Overbroad terms demonstrate Energy's lack of good faith.* The courts have said that they will not enforce a non-compete clause if the employer's intent seemed to be to prevent competition generally, rather than to restrict the employee in a manner that protects the employer's legitimate interest. Using this idea, we could argue that the terms of this particular clause were much broader than necessary to protect Energy's interest in Mike's customer contacts, and thus indicate that Energy was trying to protect itself from Mike competing against it, even in situations where his former customer contacts would not benefit his new employer. This idea, along with the weak customer contacts from our legitimate interest argument, suggest that Energy did not act in good faith by including the clause in Mike's employment agreement.

- *Energy's possible counter arguments: Broad clause was necessary at the time of hiring.* Energy could argue that tailoring a clause at the time of hiring that narrowly protects the employer's interests based on unknown facts is difficult. Energy could argue that the terms—although possibly broad now that the facts of Mike's employment are clear—were not overly restrictive at the time they hired him. The terms limited his future employment only as much as they thought could be necessary, depending on his potential future job responsibilities.

- *Likely outcome: Court will use the "blue pencil" doctrine.* Although this outcome is less clear than the legitimate interest question, a trial court likely would "blue pencil" the clause rather than throw it out entirely. While the policy is on our side, the weight of authority supports Energy's arguments. In almost every case since the court adopted use of the "blue pencil," the court had modified unreasonable agreements. Furthermore, in remanding one case back to the trial court, the Court of Appeals encouraged the trial court to use the doctrine, even though it is discretionary.

- *Strategy: Convince the court to make the clause as narrow as possible.* Using this argument to demonstrate that Energy overreached with this non-compete clause, combined with the idea that the client contacts are weak in the legitimate interest argument, should help us convince the court to modify the clause to Mike's benefit in the next arguments.

<u>Court should "blue pencil" clause so it only restricts Long for one year:</u>

- *Our argument: One year was Mike's training period.* The cases are fairly clear that the best time restriction is the amount of training the employer provided the departing employee. One year is the amount of training Energy provided Mike, so that is all the time Energy needs to train a replacement.

- *Energy's possible counter arguments: Time must be time for new employee to establish sufficient contacts.* The cases include language that the appropriate standard for the time restriction is enough time for a replacement to develop sufficient contacts with the customers to become the face of the employer.

- *Likely outcome: Court modifies time to one year.* While Energy does have some language from the opinions to support its argument, the courts seem to have settled on using the departing employee's training period, suggesting that this is enough time to replace the departing employee as the face of the employer.

- *Strategy: Create Catch-22 for Energy.* Energy will either have to concede on the time restriction or create a dilemma that could weaken its argument regarding legitimate interest, which could help us win that point. If Energy argues that it needs three years for a replacement to develop sufficient contacts, it will be arguing that the contacts are hard to establish. That point would strengthen our position that Mike's contacts were insufficient to create a legitimate interest. The harder it is to establish the relationships, the more likely we are to win the legitimate interest argument.

<u>Court should "blue pencil" the clause so it only restricts Long from northern Minnesota:</u>

- *Our argument: Mike's former territory was limited to northern Minnesota.* The cases are clear that an employer should restrict a departing employee only from competing in the geographic area where the employee could take advantage of the relationships with former customers, generally the employee's former trade area. Mike's territory was limited to northern Minnesota.

- *Energy's possible counter argument: Not much.* The cases do not provide Energy with much to convince the court that the area should be broader than Mike's former trade area.

- *Likely Outcome: Court modifies area to northern Minnesota.*

- *Strategy: Forcing Energy to concede the unreasonableness of another part of the clause strengthens Long's arguments about how the court should use the "blue pencil" doctrine.* Demonstrating that Energy cannot counter our arguments regarding the territory strengthens our position that the court should refuse to "blue pencil" the clause or use it to make the clause as narrow as possible.

<u>Court should "blue pencil" the clause so it only restricts Long from soliciting former customers instead of working as sales or service representative:</u>

- *Our argument: The subject matter must be revised to narrowly protect Energy's interest in Mike's customer relationships.* The court has consistently said that the goal when using the "blue pencil" doctrine is to modify unreasonable non-compete clauses so they narrowly protect the employer's legitimate interest. If the court is going to "blue pencil" this clause, rather than throwing it out entirely, the court should revise it holistically and revise the entire clause, including the subject matter, so it narrowly protects Energy's client relationships. Therefore, the subject matter restriction should be revised to be in line with most of the cases: Rather than restricting Mike from working as a sales or service representative for a competitor, he should only be restricting from contacting his former Energy customers on a competitor's behalf. This restriction is the most Energy would need to protect its customers from Mike's influence.

- *Energy's possible counter arguments: Subject matter is already reasonable and policing non-solicitation restrictions is too cumbersome.* Energy could argue that the court does not need to modify the subject matter restriction as written because it is reasonable, based on the cases that seem to allow a job-based restriction. Energy might also use persuasive authority to argue that verifying that a former employer is not violating a non-solicitation restriction is too cumbersome.

- *Likely outcome: Court modifies clause to only restrict Mike from contacting his former customers.* If Energy convinces the court to use the "blue pencil" doctrine to revise the time and territory portions of the clause, the court is likely to reconsider the clause in its entirety and change the job-based restriction to our proposed non-solicitation restriction. The cases consistently explain that the most reasonable manner to protect an employer's interest in its customer relationships is to simply restrict departing employees from contacting those customers.

- *Strategy: Convince court to revise subject matter so Mike is able to continue to work for Bright Lights.* While the court might not revise the subject matter restriction if the other portions of the clause were reasonable, the court likely will modify the job-based restriction to a non-solicitation restriction because the cases strongly support this revision. If the court is going to use the "blue pencil" doctrine, it should modify the entire clause so it narrowly protects the employer's interest. Our argument about Mike's weak customer relationships, as well as our claim that the onerous nature of the clause should preclude Energy from taking advantage the "blue pencil" doctrine, should reinforce our position that the entire clause must be reconsidered. Although we might not convince the court that it should refuse to enforce the clause entirely, all of our arguments combined should help convince the court that revising the clause to make it as narrow as possible, including the subject matter restriction, would be a good compromise.

C. SAMPLE OF CLIENT LETTER

1. For a discussion of client letters, see Chapter 4, Part D.

Mr. Mike Long
333 Lake View Avenue
Robbinsdale, MN 55422

Re: Non-compete Clause in Employment Agreement with Energy Resources, Inc.

Dear Mr. Long,

2. Introduction to letter. For a discussion of introductions to client letters, see Chapter 4, Part D.3.a.

Thank you for returning the signed retainer agreement to me so quickly. As you requested, we have researched the question about whether Energy Resources, Inc. will be able to enforce the non-compete clause in your employment agreement through an injunction. You also wanted to know if you would have a strategic advantage by asking the court to review the clause yourself through a declaratory judgment petition, rather than waiting for Energy to file an action against you.

Based on your explanation of the situation, I do not think a court would enforce the clause that you signed, but it probably would impose a modified version. I do not believe that you would gain any advantage by requesting a declaratory judgment rather than waiting to oppose an action by Energy. In either case, until this matter is settled, I would advise you not contact your former customers at Energy.

Factual Background

The following summary is based on the information you have provided us. If any of this information is incorrect or incomplete, please let me know right away.

Energy hired you to work as part of its sales force about six years ago. Energy markets large energy generators to commercial businesses throughout the Midwest. Energy uses a team approach to sell and service its equipment, assigning a team of four representatives for each region. Although all team members are competent to handle all the customers' servicing needs, each member is mainly responsible for one of four areas: mechanical upkeep of generators, ongoing customer training, maintenance of computer equipment, and updating the computer software. On your team, you were responsible for customer training. Your team was assigned to the northern half of Minnesota.

1

Before a sale, your teams typically met with customers as a group several times a week for about six moths. After a sale, each team member met with the customers equally, which usually included at least a monthly meeting. Although you were not friends with your customers, you met with many of them for the six years you were employed with Energy.

Your training at Energy lasted for about a year. Although Energy familiarized you with the equipment and technical information, Energy did not disclose to you any of its confidential information.

At the time you were hired, you signed an employment agreement that included the following clause:

> [E]mployee will not, for a period of 36 months after Termination, enter into employment as a service representative or salesperson with any Business that sells or markets Generator Equipment in any state where Employer sells or markets Generator Equipment.

Several months ago, you left Energy to accept a position as a salesperson for a competitor, Bright Lights Unlimited, Inc. Your territory with Bright Lights is the entire state of Minnesota. Since leaving Energy, you have not contacted any of Energy's customers.

Analysis and Evaluation

3. Evaluation of client's legal question. For a discussion of presentation of the evaluation of legal question in client letters, see Chapter 4, Part D.3.b.

To enforce a non-compete clause in an employment agreement, Minnesota courts first require that the employer have a genuine need to restrict the employee. An employer has such a need if the employee has acquired its confidential information or developed close relationships with its customers.

In your situation, a court probably would find that Energy has a genuine need to restrict you from competing against it. Although you did not obtain Energy's confidential information, you probably did have close relationships with its customers. You met with them frequently and regularly for a fairly long period. Furthermore, you were one person of a team of only four Energy representatives who met with the customers. Additionally, the court would find that Energy's need to restrict you would be even greater if any of your former Energy customers moved their business to Bright Lights after you contacted them.

If the employer has a genuine need to restrict the employee because the employee has close relationships with its customers, the non-compete clause itself must be narrowly written to guard those relationships. In your situation, a court probably would find that the clause is too broad because it restricts you from competing for three years in any state where Energy does business.

2

Generally, courts only allow employers to restrict departing employees from competing in the geographical area where they worked for the employer. The amount of time employers can restrict former employees is usually limited to the amount of time the employer spent training the departing employee.

When an employer has a need to protect the employee's client relationships, but the clause is too broad, the court has the option of throwing it out entirely or enforcing a modified version. In your situation, I think a court would likely modify the clause to change the time to one year and the area to northern Minnesota. However, what activities the court would restrict you from doing are uncertain.

I think a court could revise the clause to prohibit you from only contacting your former Energy customers on behalf of a competitor, rather than restricting you from working as a sales or service representative for a competitor. Thus, you could work for Bright Lights in your current capacity, but you could not contact your former Energy customers for a year after the date you left Energy.

However, a court could leave unchanged your restriction of working for a competitor as a sales or service representative. In this situation, you could not work in your current capacity for Bright Lights in northern Minnesota for one year.

On the other hand—although unlikely—I think we have arguments that might convince the court to throw out the clause entirely. Specifically, we could argue that your relationships with Energy's customers were too attenuated to create a need for Energy to restrict you because you were not the only representative to contact the customers. In addition, even if Energy had some need to protect itself because of your relationships with its customers, we might be able to convince the court that the clause itself was so onerous—with the very long time limit and far-reaching territory restriction—that the court should throw it out entirely rather than modify it for Energy.

Recommendations and Options

At this point, I think you should wait until Energy attempts to enforce the clause before doing anything more. I do not believe that you gain any advantage by requesting a declaratory judgment rather than waiting to oppose an action by Energy. If Energy decides to enforce the clause, we can respond.

4. For a discussion of concluding client letters, see Chapter 4, Part D.3.c.

If Energy attempts to enforce the clause (or you do decide to request a declaratory judgment), I think we should consider negotiating with Energy to avoid the time and cost of litigation. In negotiations, I would suggest that you offer to abide by a clause that is broader than the clause a court is likely to enforce for Energy, but still allows you to work in your current capacity

3

at Bright Lights. For example, you could agree not to contact any of your former Energy customers on behalf of a competitor for two years. I think this offer would be a good deal for you and Energy. These terms are broader than restricting you from contacting your former customers in northern Minnesota for one year, the terms that a court would probably enforce. Energy would obtain a more comprehensive clause, and you both would avoid the cost of litigation. We can explore other options, too.

Finally, I advise you not to communicate with your Energy clients until this situation is settled, or for at least a year. Any contact you have with Energy's customers could strengthen Energy's position if this matter goes to court.

If you have any questions or you would like to discuss this situation in more detail, please give me a call.

Sincerely,

Senior Lawyer

4

APPENDIX 4

Sample of Persuasive Writing

STATE OF MINNESOTA DISTRICT COURT
COUNTY OF ST. LOUIS - DULUTH
SIXTH JUDICIAL DISTRICT

1. For a discussion of Court Briefs, see Chapter 5, Part B.

Michael Long, Plaintiff, v. Energy Resources, Inc. Defendant.	Court File Number: _________ Case Type: Declaratory Judgment

2. Caption. For a discussion of captions, see Chapter 5, Part B.3.a.

MEMORANDUM OF LAW IN SUPPORT OF
PLAINTIFF'S PETITION FOR DECLARATORY JUDGMENT

<u>Statement of Undisputed Facts</u>

3. Statement of Facts. For a discussion of the Statement of Facts, see Chapter 5, Part B.3.b.

The parties filed with the Court a Stipulation of Facts that sets forth the undisputed facts necessary to resolve the Plaintiff's Petition for Declaratory Judgment. Three months ago, plaintiff, Michael Long, left Energy Resources, Inc. ("Energy"), to accept a sales position with a competing company, Bright Lights, Inc. ("Bright Lights"). Stipulation of Facts ("Stip.") at ¶¶ 6, 7. Energy and Bright Lights sell and service large generator equipment for commercial enterprises. Stip. ¶¶ 1, 7. Energy markets its equipment and services throughout the Midwest; Bright Lights' business is limited to the state of Minnesota. Stip. ¶¶ 1, 7. Mr. Long's new sales territory with Bright Lights includes all of Minnesota. Stip. ¶ 7.

While employed at Energy, Mr. Long did not acquire any of Energy's confidential information. Stip. ¶ 8. He worked as one member of a sales team of four employees assigned to the northern part of Minnesota. Stip. ¶ 5. Mr. Long worked at Energy for six years. Stip. ¶¶ 2, 5.

The sales team met with potential customers in its territory as a group. Stip. ¶ 2. The team only met a fraction of the potential generator customers in that territory. Stip. ¶ 5. About six months before a sale, the team met with the customers a few times per week to discuss equipment selection, installation, and long-term servicing options. Stip. ¶ 2. After a sale, the team members worked as a group and individually with customers to plan and perform regular upkeep and servicing of the equipment. Stip. ¶ 3. During that period, each team member spent about the same amount of time with a given customer; customer contact usually included a quarterly regular meeting with customers and some kind of additional meeting about once a month. Stip. ¶ 3. Although each team member is competent to deal with all the servicing needs of the customers, Mr. Long typically handled customer training. Stip. ¶ 4.

Since leaving his employment with Energy, Mr. Long has not solicited or contacted any of Energy's customers. Stip. ¶ 9. Mr. Long is a not friend with any of Energy's customers. Stip. ¶ 9. Energy provided approximately one year of training to Mr. Long, which is the time it trains most of its sales team employees. Stip. ¶ 10.

Mr. Long is concerned that Energy may attempt to prevent his continued employment at Bright Lights by seeking to enforce the following clause that Energy included in his employment agreement:

> [[E]mployee will not, for a period of 36 months after Termination, enter into employment as a service representative or salesperson with any Business that sells or markets Generator Equipment in any state where Employer sells or markets Generator Equipment.

Stip. ¶ 11.

Accordingly, Mr. Long filed a petition against Energy Resources, Inc. seeking judgment declaring the non-competition clause unenforceable. This memorandum is filed in support of that petition.

4. Heading. For a discussion of headings, see Chapter 5, Part B.3.c.2.

5. Argument Section. For a discussion of the Argument Section, see Chapter 5, Part B.3.c.

Argument

ENERGY'S NON-COMPETITION RESTRAINT SHOULD NOT BE ENFORCED BECAUSE ENERGY DOES NOT HAVE A LEGITIMATE NEED TO RESTRICT MR. LONG AND THE RESTRAINT EXCESSIVELY BURDENS HIS RIGHT TO WORK

The Court should declare Energy's non-competition clause unenforceable because it is unnecessary for the protection of Energy's legitimate business interests and its terms are excessively burdensome on Mr. Long's ability to earn a living. See Bennett v. Storz Broad. Co., 134 N.W.2d 892, 899 (Minn. 1965); see also Davies & Davies Agency, Inc. v. Davies, 298 N.W.2d 127, 131 (Minn. 1980); Webb Publ'g Co. v. Fosshage, 426 N.W.2d 445, 450 (Minn. Ct. App. 1988). Energy's restraint prevents Mr. Long from working in his occupation in all the states in the Mid-

2

west for three years. If enforced as written, Energy's restrictions would leave Mr. Long with two equally burdensome options—move out of the Midwest entirely or choose a different career path.

Courts are reluctant to validate non-employment restrictions because they severely restrict employees' ability to earn a living. See, e.g., Davies, 298 N.W.2d at 131; Bennett, 134 N.W.2d at 898; Webb, 426 N.W.2d at 450. Therefore, courts only enforce such restraints when the employer has conveyed to the employee a competitive advantage that creates a legitimate interest in restricting the employee, and the restraint narrowly protects that specific interest. See, e.g., Davies, 298 N.W.2d at 131; Bennett, 134 N.W.2d at 898; Webb, 426 N.W.2d at 450. If the employer is unable to make this showing, restricting an employee is unjustified because the employer would be able to use the non-competition clause to shield itself from normal competition of the marketplace, rather than to narrowly protect its business from the employee unfairly competing against it. See, e.g., Davies, 298 N.W.2d at 131; Bennett, 134 N.W.2d at 898; Webb, 426 N.W.2d at 450.

Energy cannot justify the restraints in the case because Energy does not have a legitimate interest in restricting Mr. Long's right to work. See, e.g., Davies, 298 N.W.2d at 131; Bennett, 134 N.W.2d at 898; Menter, 180 N.W.2d at 555. Furthermore, the excessiveness of Energy's restraint demonstrates that Energy is attempting to simply shield its business from regular competition rather than narrowly tailoring the clause to protect its purported legitimate interest. See, e.g., Davies, 298 N.W.2d at 131; Bennett, 134 N.W.2d at 898; Menter, 180 N.W.2d at 555. Even if the Court decides that Mr. Long's ability to work should be restricted to some degree, the Court should modify the clause with the "Blue Pencil Doctrine" to narrowly protect Energy's purported legitimate interest, rather allowing Energy to use the clause to buffer its business form normal competition by limiting Mr. Long's ability to earn a living. See, e.g., Davies, 298 N.W.2d at 131–32; Dean Van Horn v. Wold, 395 N.W.2d 405, 409 (Minn. Ct. App. 1986).

A. Energy has no legitimate interest in restricting Mr. Long because he did not acquire confidential information or develop close relationships with Energy's customers.

Energy does not have a legitimate interest in restricting Mr. Long's ability to work and earn a living through a non-competition restraint. See, e.g., Davies, 298 N.W.2d at 131; Bennett, 134 N.W.2d at 898; Webb, 426 N.W.2d at 450. Mr. Long poses no threat of using any advantages that he gained from Energy to compete against it. See, e.g., Davies, 298 N.W.2d at 131; Webb, 426 N.W.2d at 450. The stipulated facts reveal that Mr. Long cannot claim a legitimate interest in protected information because Mr. Long did receive any confidential information from Energy. Thus, the only interest that Energy can purport to protect with a non-competition clause is Mr. Long's relationships with its customers. See, e.g., Davies, 298 N.W.2d at 131; Webb, 426 N.W.2d at 450. Energy does not have a legitimate interest in

6. Example of an argument using basic construction techniques. For a discussion of basic argument construction, see Chapter 5, Part A.2.

3

protecting these relationships because the totality of Mr. Long's contact with his clients shows that he did not form the type of close relationships that would likely influence his customers to follow him to a new employer. See, e.g., Davies, 298 N.W.2d at 131; Webb, 426 N.W.2d at 450.

Courts are only willing to allow an employer to restrict an employee's right to work because of client relationships if the employer can show that the departing employee is likely to draw the employer's customers to a competitor. See, e.g., Davies, 298 N.W.2d at 131; Webb, 426 N.W.2d at 450. Yet the facts of this case demonstrate that Mr. Long's customers will be inclined to stay with Energy rather than follow Mr. Long to the competition: Mr. Long was not the exclusive or primary contact between his clients and Energy; he did not develop personal friendships with his clients; and, he has not solicited any of his former Energy customers since leaving the company for a competitor.

As a member of a team of four, Mr. Long lacked one of the most important elements courts consider when determining whether an employee has developed close client relationships—exclusivity of contact. See Davies, 298 N.W.2d at 129; Webb 426 N.W.2d at 449. Exclusive or primary contact between an employee and client is essential to foster the type of personal relationship that would cause a client to follow the employee to a competitor. See, e.g., Davies, 298 N.W.2d at 129; Webb, 426 N.W.2d at 449. With exclusive contact, the employee becomes more than just a representative for the business to the customers; the employee becomes the face of the company to them. See, e.g., Davies, 298 N.W.2d at 129; Webb, 426 N.W.2d at 449.

For example, in Webb, the court found an employer was entitled to protect its client relationships mainly because the employee was the primary contact between the company and its clients. See 426 N.W.2d at 449–50. The primary nature of the relationships meant that the customers' total association with the business was through the departing employee, and thus they would likely follow that employee to a competitor. See id. Similarly, the court in Davies found the exclusive nature of the contact between the employee and his clients led to the personal hold the employee had over his clients because the customers considered the departing employee to be the face of the business. See 298 N.W.2d at 129–31.

In contrast, Mr. Long's contact with his clients was less intimate than that of the employees in Davies or Webb because it was not exclusive, but shared evenly between four team members. See Davies, 298 N.W.2d at 129–31; Webb 426 N.W.2d at 449–50. As one of a group of several company representatives, Mr. Long's customers may have considered him one of many ambassadors for Energy, but he did not become the face of Energy to those customers. See Davies, 298 N.W.2d at 129–31; Webb 426 N.W.2d at 449–50. The customers likely choose to do business with Energy because of several representatives, rather than just because of their relationships with

4

Mr. Long. See Davies, 298 N.W.2d at 129–31; Webb 426 N.W.2d at 449–50. Therefore, those customers are likely to keep their business with Energy and the other representatives instead of following just one member of a group of four to a new employer. See Davies, 298 N.W.2d at 129–31; Webb 426 N.W.2d at 449–50.

Moreover, although Mr. Long worked for Energy for six years, he never developed any friendships with his clients that created loyalty on the part of customers. See Davies, 298 N.W.2d at 130; Webb, 426 N.W.2d at 449. Thus, this case is different from Webb, where the court was swayed by the fact that the employee had worked closely with clients for seven years and considered them friends when determining that the employer had a protectable interest in the client relationships developed by him. See 426 N.W.2d at 449. Unlike the employee in Webb, Mr. Long's relationship with his clients was solely professional, thus making it less likely that a client would leave Energy if Mr. Long left the company for a competitor. See id.

A final indication that Mr. Long developed no close client relationships while employed with Energy is the absence of any contact with or solicitation of his former Energy clients since assuming his current position with a competing company. See Overholt Crop Ins. Serv. Co. v. Bredeson, 437 N.W.2d 698, 701 (Minn. Ct. App. 1989); Webb, 426 N.W.2d at 450. The courts have been especially likely to protect an employer's interest in its client relationships if the former employee already has been able to successfully solicit the employer's clientele. See Overholt, 437 N.W.2d at 701; Webb, 426 N.W.2d at 450. In Webb, the court held that a publishing company had a legitimate interest in protecting itself from deflection of clients where the success of the employee in soliciting two out of four of his former clients demonstrated the personal hold he had over them. 426 N.W.2d at 450. In contrast, Mr. Long's lack of contact with or attempted solicitation of Energy's clients suggests that his former clients would be unlikely to follow him to the competition, and therefore Mr. Long poses no threat to Energy's customer base that would give Energy the right to restrict his ability to work. See id.

B. Energy's restrictions are unjustified because they impose restraints on Mr. Long's ability to earn a living that do not narrowly protect Energy's customer relationships.

Even if the Court finds that Energy has some legitimate interest in Mr. Long's client relationships, the Court should not enforce Energy's restraint because every aspect of the clause restricts Mr. Long considerably more than Energy needs to protect itself from his purported close relationship with its clients. See, e.g., Davies, 298 N.W.2d at 131; Eutectic, 160 N.W.2d at 570–71. Furthermore, the Court should decline to modify the unreasonable clause with the "Blue Pencil Doctrine" because the burdensome terms demonstrate that Energy was not attempting to safeguard its possible legitimate interest, but trying shield itself from as much regular market-

5

place competition as possible. See, e.g., Davies, 298 N.W.2d at 131; Eutectic, 160 N.W.2d at 570–71. If the Court decides to restrict Mr. Long's right to work to some extent, it should "blue pencil" the restraint to ensure that it only allows Energy to narrowly protect the relationships Mr. Long might have developed with a few of its customers. See e.g., Davies, 298 N.W.2d at 131–32; Dean Van Horn, 395 N.W.2d at 409.

1. Energy's restraint is excessive because the time, territory, and subject matter are broader than necessary to protect Energy's customer relationships.

The Court should refuse to enforce Energy's restrictive clause because it effectively prevents Mr. Long from working in his occupation in every state in the Midwest for three years. Courts only allow an employer to restrict an employee's right to work when the time, territory, and subject matter of the restriction narrowly protect the employer's specific legitimate interest. See, e.g., Davies, 298 N.W.2d at 131; Eutectic, 160 N.W.2d at 570–71. None of Energy's restrictions was narrowly tailored to safeguard its purported interest in Mr. Long's customer relationships: The time was too long; the territory was too broad; and the subject matter was excessive. See, e.g., Davies, 298 N.W.2d at 131; Eutectic, 160 N.W.2d at 570–71.

The three-year temporal restriction imposed upon Mr. Long is unreasonable because it exceeds the amount of time necessary for Energy to train a replacement for Mr. Long. See, e.g., Davies, 298 N.W.2d at 131; Dean Van Horn, 395 N.W.2d at 409. When an employer has an interest in protecting its client relationships, the employer may only restrict the employee for the same amount of time that the employer trained the departing employee. See, e.g., Davies, 298 N.W.2d at 131; Dean Van Horn, 395 N.W.2d at 409. That period is sufficient time for the employer to find and train a replacement and for customers to adjust to the change in company representation. See, e.g., Davies, 298 N.W.2d at 131; Dean Van Horn, 395 N.W.2d at 409. Mr. Long was trained for one year and therefore Energy should only have restricted his right to work for that amount of time. See, e.g., Davies, 298 N.W.2d at 131; Dean Van Horn, 395 N.W.2d at 409. Anything longer is not necessary for Energy to effectively train a new employee to take his place with its customers. See, e.g., Davies, 298 N.W.2d at 131 (finding five-year restriction unreasonable and modifying it to one year, enough time for employer to train replacement for departing employee); Dean Van Horn, 395 N.W.2d at 409 (finding three-year restraint unreasonable when departing employee's training period was one year).

7. Example of fact-focused argument. For a discussion of such arguments, see Chapter 5, Part A.3.b.2.

Energy's territorial restraint placed on Mr. Long also is excessive because it far exceeds the geographic area where Mr. Long had contact with Energy's customers. See, e.g., Walker 219 N.W.2d at 441; Eutectic, 160 N.W.2d at 570; Overholt, 437 N.W.2d at 703. Energy's restraint restricts him from every state where it does business—all states in the Midwest—even though

6

Mr. Long had limited contacts with Energy's customers in one region of only one of those states. Restrictions that extend beyond the area in which an employee had contact with the employer's clients are never warranted to protect an employer's customers. Compare Eutectic, 160 N.W.2d at 570 (finding territory unreasonable because it limited departing employee from competing in 50-mile radius of former territory, which included areas where employee had not worked), with Walker, 219 N.W.2d at 441 (finding territory reasonable because it limited departing employee from working in the county where he had worked for former employer); Overholt, 437 N.W.2d at 703 (finding territory reasonable because it limited departing employee from competing in his former sales territory).

Prohibiting Mr. Long from competing in areas in which he had no contact with Energy's clients imposes a severe limit on his ability to work and unreasonably shields Energy from competition that would not be based on Mr. Long's actual relationships with customers. See Davies, 298 N.W.2d at 131–32; Webb, 426 N.W.2d at 450; see also Dynamic Air, Inc. v. Bloch, 502 N.W.2d 796, 799-800 (Minn. Ct. App. 1993). Instead of a blanket geographical restriction, Energy should have restricted Mr. Long only from northern Minnesota, the only area where he could have developed any relationships with its customers. See, e.g., Walker 219 N.W.2d at 441; Eutectic, 160 N.W.2d at 570. Using a more excessive restriction on Mr. Long's right to earn a living demonstrates that Energy was trying to shield itself from more competition than just Mr. Long's purported ability to use his relationships with its customers. See, e.g., Walker 219 N.W.2d at 441; Eutectic, 160 N.W.2d at 570; Overholt, 437 N.W.2d at 703.

The subject matter of Energy's restraint also is excessively broad, especially in light of the unreasonable time and territorial restraints. See, e.g., Davies, 298 N.W.2d at 131–32; Dean Van Horn, 395 N.W.2d at 406; Overholt, 437 N.W.2d at 703. Energy's restraint effectively precludes Mr. Long from working in his chosen field anywhere in the Midwestern region of the country by restricting him from working as a sales or service representative for any of Energy's competitors in that area. Minnesota courts have consistently held that when an employer claims a legitimate interest in client relationships, the employer should only restrain the employee from contacting the specific customers with whom the employee developed close relationships. See, e.g., Davies, 298 N.W.2d at 131–32; Dean Van Horn, 395 N.W.2d at 406; Overholt, 437 N.W.2d at 703. Broader job-based restrictions—like Energy's restriction—unfairly restrict employees by effectively preventing them from working with any potential customers, even customers who had no connection with the former employers because of the departing employees. See, e.g., Davies, 298 N.W.2d at 131–32; Dean Van Horn, 395 N.W.2d at 406; Overholt, 437 N.W.2d at 703.

7

As part of the sales team at Energy, Mr. Long did not contact all potential commercial generator customers in his territory, let alone develop close relationships with all those customers. He only could have developed any type of relationship with the small group of customers his team contacted while he worked with Energy. See, e.g., Davies, 298 N.W.2d at 131–32; Dean Van Horn, 395 N.W.2d at 406. Therefore, Energy does not need to prevent him from working as a sales or service representative for competitors to protect its purported interest in his relationships with its customers. See, e.g., Davies, 298 N.W.2d at 131–32; Dean Van Horn, 395 N.W.2d at 406; Overholt, 437 N.W.2d at 703. If Energy had desired to narrowly protect those relationships—as the courts require—it should have only restricted him from contacting his former customers on behalf of a competitor, rather than effectively precluding him from working in his occupation. Compare Dynamic, 502 N.W.2d at 797–800 (finding subject matter reasonable because it only restricted departing employee from contacting his former customers on behalf of competitor); Overholt, 437 N.W.2d at 703 (finding subject matter reasonable because it was interpreted to only restrict departing employee from contacting his former customers on behalf of competitor), with Davies, 298 N.W.2d at 131–32 (suggesting that appropriate revision to subject matter would be to only restrict departing employee from contacting his former customers on behalf of competitor).

2. The Court should not "blue-pencil" the restraint because its excessive terms demonstrate that Energy did not draft it in good faith.

8. Example of policy-focused argument. For a discussion of such arguments, see Chapter 5, Part A.3.b.3.

The Court should not exercise its discretion to use the "Blue Pencil Doctrine" to modify Energy's clause because the excessive terms demonstrate that Energy was not trying to narrowly safeguard Mr. Long's relationships with its clients, but rather was attempting to shield itself from as much competition as possible, at the expense of Mr. Long's right to earn a living. See, e.g., Bennett, 134 N.W.2d at 898; Davies, 298 N.W.2d at 131; Klick, 372 N.W.2d at 88–89; Dean Van Horn, 395 N.W.2d at 409. The courts did not adopt the "Blue Pencil Doctrine" to encourage employers to impose oppressive agreements, hoping a court will simply rewrite an unreasonable clause in the rare situation that an employee has the resources to challenge its enforcement. See, e.g., Davies, 298 N.W.2d at 131; Klick, 372 N.W.2d at 88–89; Dean Van Horn, 395 N.W.2d at 409. Rather, the doctrine is designed to protect both parties by motivating employers to draft fair agreements from the outset. See, e.g., Davies, 298 N.W.2d at 131; Dean Van Horn, 395 N.W.2d at 409. Therefore, courts only use the doctrine to make minor adjustments and only if the employer made a good faith attempt to prepare an agreement that narrowly protects its specific legitimate interest. See Davies, 298 N.W.2d at 131; Klick, 372 N.W.2d at 88–89; Dean Van Horn, 395 N.W.2d at 409.

8

Every term of Energy's clause was much more restrictive that necessary to protect Mr. Long's relationships with Energy's customers. See, e.g., Davies, 298 N.W.2d at 131; Dean Van Horn, 395 N.W.2d at 409. The clause restricts Mr. Long for two years longer than reasonable; it prohibits Mr. Long from working in several entire states in which he had no relationships with any of Energy's customers; and the clause effectively precludes Mr. Long from working in his chosen occupation, even though Energy's only purported need was to restrict him from contacting his former Energy customers.

The spirit of these oppressive restraints demonstrates that Energy did not attempt to tailor a clause that would narrowly protect its purported interest in Mr. Long's contacts with its customers. See, e.g., Bennett, 134 N.W.2d at 898; Davies, 298 N.W.2d at 131; Klick, 372 N.W.2d at 88–89; Dean Van Horn, 395 N.W.2d at 409. If Energy's goal was to protect Mr. Long's relationships with the customers he had contacted, it should have drafted a much narrower agreement that restricted his contact with those customers in northern Minnesota, rather than precluding Mr. Long from working in his occupation in an entire region of the country for three years. See Davies, 298 N.W.2d at 131; Klick, 372 N.W.2d at 88–89; Dean Van Horn, 395 N.W.2d at 409.

This is not a situation in which the Court would able to use the "Blue Pencil Doctrine" to make minor adjustments to protect both parties. See, e.g., Davies, 298 N.W.2d at 131; Dean Van Horn, 395 N.W.2d at 409. To make the restrictions reasonable, the Court would have to completely redraft all the terms of the clause. See, e.g., Davies, 298 N.W.2d at 131; Dean Van Horn, 395 N.W.2d at 409. Refusing to rewrite such an oppressive agreement will encourage other employers to carefully tailor agreements to protect only their legitimate interests. See, e.g., Davies, 298 N.W.2d at 131; Dean Van Horn, 395 N.W.2d at 409.

3. If the Court applies the "Blue Pencil Doctrine," it should only restrict Mr. Long from contacting his former customers in northern Minnesota for one year.

If the Court decides to "blue pencil" Energy's unreasonable restrictions, it should revise the clause to narrowly protect Energy's claimed interest in Mr. Long's contacts with its customer so that it does not overburden Mr. Long's right to work. See, e.g., Davies, 298 N.W.2d at 131–32; Dean Van Horn, 395 N.W.2d at 406; Overholt, 437 N.W.2d at 703. To narrowly protect those relationships, the Court should modify the restraint so that it only restricts Mr. Long from contacting his former Energy customers in northern Minnesota for one year. See Davies, 298 N.W.3d at 131; Webb, 426 N.W.2d at 450.

The Court should restrict Mr. Long only from contacting his former Energy customers in northern Minnesota on behalf of a competitor, rather allowing Energy to broadly restrict him from working a sales or service representative in every state in which Energy does business.

9

See, e.g., Davies, 298 N.W.2d at 131–32; Dean Van Horn, 395 N.W.2d at 406. As written, the broad job-based and territorial restrictions effectively preclude Mr. Long from working for any competitor in several states, even though there are many potential customers who had no connection with Energy in those states, through Mr. Long or otherwise. See, e.g., Davies, 298 N.W.2d at 131–32; Dean Van Horn, 395 N.W.2d at 406; Webb, 426 N.W.2d at 450. Restricting Mr. Long only from contacting his former customers in northern Minnesota will fully protect Energy's purported interest in Mr. Long's relationships with its customers. Compare Davies, 298 N.W.2d at 131–32 (finding appropriate "blue pencil" revision to change clause to only restrict departing employee from contacting his former customers on behalf of competitor in former territory) with Dynamic, 502 N.W.2d at 797–800 (finding no "blue pencil" revision necessary because clause only restricted departing employee from contacting his former customers on behalf of competitor); Overholt, 437 N.W.2d at 703 (finding no "blue pencil" revision necessary because clause was interpreted to only restrict departing employee from contacting his former customers on behalf of competitor in former territory).

Furthermore, the Court should decrease the time restriction imposed upon Mr. Long from three years to twelve months. See, e.g., Davies, 298 N.W.2d at 131; Dean Van Horn, 395 N.W.2d at 409. Twelve months is the amount of time Energy trained Mr. Long, and therefore it is enough time for Energy to train his replacement. See, e.g., Davies, 298 N.W.2d at 131 (modifying five-year restriction to one year, enough time for employer to train replacement for departing employee); Dean Van Horn, 395 N.W.2d at 409. Any time restriction greater than twelve months would not be narrowly tailored to protect Energy's interest in effectively replacing Mr. Long and would merely serve to limit Mr. Long's freedom to pursue his preferred occupation for longer than necessary. See Davies, 298 N.W.2d at 131; Dean Van Horn, 395 N.W.2d at 409 (finding three-year restraint unreasonable when departing employee's training period was one year).

9. Example of legal standard-focused argument. For a discussion of such arguments, see Chapter 5, Part A.3.b.2.

Conclusion

10. Conclusion. For a discussion of the Conclusion section, see Chapter 5, Part B.3.d.

For the reasons discussed above, the Plaintiff respectfully requests that the Court grant the Petition for Declaratory Judgment that the non-competition clause is unenforceable.

Respectfully submitted,

Signed: ______________________________

Attorney for Plaintiff

Address: 12345 Thousand Lakes Way,
Duluth, MN 98765

10

APPENDIX 5

Sample Agreement

AGREEMENT TO SETTLE CLAIMS AND TRANSFER PROPERTY

1. For a discussion of agreement drafting, see Chapter 6.

This Agreement to Settle Claims and Transfer Property (this "Agreement") is made and entered into as of the 17th day of December, 2013, by and between the Benson Hospitality Group, LLC ("Benson"), a Delaware limited liability corporation, Tritown Bay Investors, Inc. ("Tritown Bay"), a Florida corporation, and TBI Golf & Resorts, LLC, ("TBI") a Delaware limited liability company wholly owned by Tritown Bay. Tritown Bay and TBI may hereinafter be referred to jointly as the "Tritown Parties." Each of Benson, Tritown Bay, and TBI may hereinafter be referred to as a "Party" or together as the "Parties."

RECITALS

2. Introductory recitals. For a discussion of introductory sections in agreements, see Chapter 6, Part B.1.a.

A. Benson and TBI previously entered into certain Project Agreements (as defined below) relating to the potential development of a hotel and golf resort operation (the "Project") to be owned by Benson.

B. At various times, the Tritown Parties advanced funds under the terms of the Project Agreements in furtherance of the development of the Project.

C. Principals of TBI acquired three parcels of land in Sonoma County, California, in anticipation of the development of the Project.

D. Title to two of the three acquired parcels of land (the "Benson Parcels") was transferred to Benson, subject to the lien of separate promissory notes and deeds of trust with principals of TBI as the beneficiaries.

E. All rights of the principals of TBI in and to the notes and deeds of trust relating to the Benson Parcels were subsequently transferred and assigned to TBI.

F. In 2012, Benson satisfied its obligation to TBI under a promissory note relating to one of the Benson Parcels, and the related deed of trust was released.

G. The Parties have agreed that they are no longer interested in jointly pursuing the Project or any business relationship, and therefore they desire to terminate any contractual relationship that may exist between them and to completely settle any existing or future claims or disputes; provided, however, the lien of the deed of trust on the Forty-Acre Parcel (as defined below), shall remain in full force and effect until such time as the 2010 Promissory Note (as defined below) is paid in full.

H. Benson desires to purchase all rights of TBI in and to the Real Property (as defined below) and to obtain a release and settlement of any and all claims the Tritown Parties may have against Benson arising out of the Project Agreements.

I. The Tritown Parties desire to obtain a release and settlement of any and all claims Benson may have against them under the Project Agreements.

J. This Agreement is given and accepted by each Party for the purposes of i) compromising any disputed claims under the Project Agreements and avoiding the expense, inconvenience, and uncertainty of litigation; and ii) establishing the terms and conditions for the sale and transfer of the Real Property by TBI to Benson.

K. The Parties agree that this mutual release of claims and final settlement of their disputes is in the best interest of each Party.

ARTICLE I
DEFINITIONS

3. Definition Section. For a discussion of definitions in agreements, see Chapter 6, Part B.1.c.

Section 1.1. Definitions. In addition to terms defined in this section, terms may be defined at other places in this Agreement. The terms set forth below shall have the following definitions:

a) "Benson Deed of Trust" means that certain Deed of Trust secured by the Forty-Acre Parcel, dated November 15, 2009, executed by Benson (Trustor), to Trujillo Escrow, a California corporation (Trustee), and recorded as Instrument No. 2010-345-9 of the Official Records of Sonoma County, California, with TBI as the beneficial owner under the Deed of Trust.

b) "Closing Date" shall be the actual date on which all of the closing obligations of the Parties are satisfied and the sale and transfer of the Twenty-Acre Parcel is completed, which date may or may not be the Designated Closing Date.

c) "Designated Closing Date" shall mean the anticipated date for closing the transactions contemplated under this Agreement, which date is anticipated by the Parties to be a 90-day escrow, or sooner if possible.

d) "Effective Date" shall mean the date on which the settlement and mutual releases of claims set forth in this Agreement become effective, which date shall coincide with the Closing Date.

2

e) "Escrow Agent" shall mean an officer of Sonoma Lakes Title Company located in Sonoma, California.

f) "Forty-Acre Parcel" shall mean the 40.72 +/- acres of real property located in Sonoma County, California, Assessor's Parcel Number XXX-XXX-XXX, which parcel is owned by Benson and subject to the 2009 Promissory Note and the Benson Deed of Trust.

g) "Project Agreements" means all contracts, whether written or oral, entered into between the Tritown Parties or any principals or authorized representatives of the Tritown Parties and Benson or any authorized representatives of Benson relating to the Project, including, without limitation, all Management Agreements, Development Agreements, Loan Agreements, and Promissory Notes, but excluding from such definition the Deed of Trust, dated November 15, 2009, executed by the Redwood Development, Inc., a California (Trustor), to Tahoe View Escrow, a California corporation (Trustee), and recorded as Instrument No. XXXX-XX, of the Official Records of Sonoma County, California, together with the 2009 Promissory Note.

h) "2009 Promissory Note" shall mean the promissory note of Benson in the principal amount of $1,250,000, which is secured by the Benson Deed of Trust.

i) "2010 Promissory Note" shall mean the Promissory Note in the principal amount of $1,000,000 evidencing the payment obligation of Benson to TBI, as described in detail in Section 3.6 of this Agreement.

j) "Real Property" shall mean, together, the Twenty-Acre Parcel and the Forty-Acre Parcel.

k) "Settlement Payment" shall mean that $2,500,000 portion of the Total Consideration representing Benson's cash payment for settlement of the matters described in this Agreement.

l) "Total Consideration" shall mean the amount of $5,000,000, the total amount of monetary consideration to be paid under the terms of this Agreement.

m) "Twenty-Acre Parcel" shall mean the 20.47 +/- acres of real property located in Sonoma County California, Assessor's Parcel Number XXX-XXX-XXX, which parcel TBI owns in fee simple.

ARTICLE II
SETTLEMENT OF CLAIMS

Section 2.1. Nature and Effect of Agreement. This Agreement consists of a compromise and settlement by each Party with respect to such Party's claims against the other Party and a release given by each Party relinquishing all claims against the

3

4. Terms explaining the rights and responsibilities of the parties and related consequences are included in Articles II-V. For a discussion of explaining the right and responsibilities of the parties and related consequences in agreements, see Chapter 6, part B.1. a.

other Party. By executing this Agreement, each of the Parties intends to and does hereby extinguish the obligations presently existing between them, and all obligations or claims that may arise in the future, except for the obligations created under this Agreement and the lien of the Benson Deed of Trust pertaining to the Forty-Acre Parcel. This Agreement is not, and shall not be treated as, an admission of fault or liability by any Party for any purpose.

Section 2.2. Mutual Release and Covenant.

a) As of the Effective Date, each Party, on behalf of itself and its officers, directors, members, employees, principals, agents, contractors, attorneys and successors then and forever releases and discharges the other Parties to this Agreement, and their officers, directors, members, employees, principals, agents, contractors, attorneys and successors, from any and all claims, demands, losses, expenses, damages, liabilities, action and causes of action of any nature, that in any manner arise from or relate to the formation, existence, performance, or breach of the Project Agreements.

5. Example of repeating in-text definition in two places rather than including the definition in the definitional section. For a discussion of using such in-text definitions, see Chapter 6, Part B.1.c.1.

b) Each Party on behalf of itself and its officers, directors, members, employees, principals, agents, contractors, attorneys and successors covenants and agrees that it will not make, assert, or maintain any claim, demand, action, or cause of action that is discharged by this Agreement against the other Parties, and their officers, directors, members, employees, principals, agents, contractors, attorneys and successors.

c) Each Party represents and covenants that it owns all claims that are within the scope of this release or that pertain in any way to the Project Agreements, that it has not assigned, conveyed or transferred any such claims to any other person or entity, and that it will not do so.

Section 2.3. Release of Unknown Claims. As of the Effective Date, this Agreement extends to and includes any and all claims, liabilities, injuries, damages, and causes of action that the Parties do not presently anticipate, know, or suspect to exist, but that may develop, accrue, or be discovered following the Effective Date. EACH PARTY EXPRESSLY WAIVES ALL RIGHTS UNDER CALIFORNIA CIVIL CODE SECTION 1542, WHICH PROVIDES: "A general release does not extend to claims which the creditor does not know or suspect to exist in his favor at the time of executing the release, which if known by him must have materially affected his settlement with the debtor." Each Party represents and warrants that it has considered the possibility that claims, liabilities, injuries, damages, and causes of action that it does not presently know or suspect to exist in its favor may develop, accrue, or be discovered in the future, and that it voluntarily assumes the risk as part of the consideration for this Agreement.

Section 2.4. Exception to Release. Each Party covenants and agrees that the obligations under the 2010 Promissory Note and the terms and obligations under the Deed of Trust, as amended by the First Amendment to Deed of Trust, a copy of which is attached to this

4

Agreement as Exhibit B, shall remain in full force and effect and shall not be subject to the releases and covenants set forth above.

ARTICLE III
TOTAL CONSIDERATION AND
PURCHASE AND SALE OF REAL PROPERTY

3.1. Total Consideration. The total amount of consideration to be paid under this Agreement is $5,000,000. Of such total consideration, $4,000,000 shall be paid to TBI on the Closing Date in readily available funds via wire transfer to TBI's account in accordance with wire transfer instructions that TBI will provide to the Escrow Agent. The remaining $1,000,000 shall be paid in accordance with the terms of the 2010 Promissory Note, which Benson will deliver on the Closing Date, as described in Section 3.6, below.

3.2 Agreement to Sell Twenty-Acre Parcel. On the Closing Date, TBI agrees to sell, transfer, and convey all of its right, title, and interest in and to the Twenty-Acre Parcel to Benson.

Section 3.3 Purchase Price for Real Property. The Purchase Price for the Twenty-Acre $1,500,000).

Section 3.4. Agreement to Release Lien. On the Closing Date, the 2009 Promissory Note relating to the Benson Deed of Trust shall be nullified and replaced in its entirety by the 2010 Promissory Note. The Benson Deed of Trust, as amended by the First Amendment to Deed of Trust (a copy of which is attached to this Agreement as Exhibit B) shall remain in full force and effect until such time as the 2010 Promissory Note is paid in full. Upon payment in full of the 2010 Promissory Note, TBI agrees to release all of its right, title, and interest in and to the Forty-Acre Parcel.

Section 3.5. Allocation of Payments. For purposes of the transactions contemplated in this Agreement, the Parties agree that the following allocation of the Total Consideration shall apply:

a) The Purchase Price for Twenty-Acre Parcel shall be $1,500,000;

b) The payment for lien release of the Forty-Acre Parcel shall be $1,000,000 in the form of the 2010 Promissory Note; and

c) The Settlement Payment by Benson to settle all outstanding claims of TBI and Tritown Bay shall be $2,500,000, which amount represents a portion of the actual amounts expended by the Tritown Parties for development of the Project.

Section 3.6. Terms of Promissory Note. The 2010 Promissory Note (the "Note") shall be due and payable in full on a date which is 48 months from the Closing Date (the "Due

5

Date"). Installment payments in the amount of $250,000 each shall be due and payable to TBI on the first, second, and third anniversaries of the Closing Date. The Note shall not bear interest, and it shall be secured by the existing Benson Deed of Trust, as amended, on the Forty-Acre Parcel. The Note shall be in the form attached to this Agreement as Exhibit A.

ARTICLE IV
CLOSING OBLIGATIONS

Section 4.1. Establishment of Escrow Account. To facilitate the sale and transfer of the Real Property interests and to manage other matters governed by this Agreement, Benson and TBI shall work cooperatively to establish an escrow account (the "Escrow Account") with Sonoma Lakes Title Company located in Sonoma, California (the "Title Company").

Section 4.2. Closing Obligations of Benson. On or prior to the Designated Closing Date, Benson shall complete the following:

a) Execution and delivery to the Escrow Agent of Escrow Instructions acceptable to Benson and the Tritown Parties;

b) Delivery to the Escrow Agent of an executed original copy of this Agreement;

c) Deposit of readily available funds into the Escrow Account in the amount of $4,000,000, representing the sum of the purchase price for the Real Property and the Settlement Payment;

d) Delivery of the executed 2010 Promissory Note to Escrow Agent; and

e) Execution and delivery to the Escrow Agent a copy of the First Amendment to Deed of Trust, a form of which is attached to this Agreement as Exhibit B.

Section 4.3. Closing Obligations of TBI. On or prior to the Designated Closing Date, Benson shall complete the following:

a) Execution and delivery to the Escrow Agent of Escrow Instructions acceptable to Benson and the Tritown Parties;

b) Delivery to the Escrow Agent of an executed original copy of this Agreement;

c) Delivery to Escrow Agent of a fully executed deed transferring ownership of the Twenty-Acre Parcel to Benson;

d) Execution and delivery to the Escrow Agent a copy of the First Amendment to Deed of Trust, a form of which is attached to this Agreement as Exhibit B; and

6

e) Cancellation of the 2009 Promissory Note.

Section 4.4. Closing Obligations of Tritown Bay. On or prior to the Designated Closing Date, Benson shall complete the following:

a) Execution and delivery to the Escrow Agent of Escrow Instructions acceptable to Benson and the Tritown Parties; and

b) Delivery to the Escrow Agent of an executed original copy of this Agreement.

Section 4.5. Payment of Closing Costs and Taxes. All costs of closing, including without limitation the fees of the Escrow Agent, filing fees, the cost of any title report, and title insurance, shall be born equally by the Parties and paid on the Closing Date. TBI shall be responsible for its allocable share of property taxes for 2013 due and payable on the Twenty-Acre Parcel up to and including the Closing Date. Benson shall be responsible for its allocable share of 2013 real property taxes relating to the Twenty-Acre Parcel following the Closing Date. Benson shall pay all real property transfer fees. Each Party shall be solely responsible for payment of their own attorney's fees.

Section 4.6. Closing Date. The Closing Date shall occur on a mutually agreed upon date promptly following the date on which all of the obligations of the Parties set forth in Sections 4.2, 4.3 and 4.4 above have been fully satisfied.

ARTICLE V
MISCELLANEOUS PROVISIONS

Section 6.3. Authority. Each Party represents and warrants:

a) That it has taken all necessary governmental or company action, as applicable, to execute and obligate itself to this Agreement and performance of the obligations hereunder; and

b) The persons executing this Agreement on its behalf are duly authorized to act on its behalf and to legally obligate such Party.

Section 6.4. Indemnification. Each Party agrees to indemnify, defend, and hold the other Party harmless from and against any and all claims, demands, liabilities, expenses, losses, or damages, including attorney fees, which may arise from the falsity or breach of any representation, covenant or warranty contained in this Agreement.

Section 6.5. Legal Representation. Each Party represents and warrants that it has consulted with and relied upon legal counsel of its own choosing concerning such Party's settlement and the execution of this Agreement. Each Party further represents and warrants that it is relying solely upon its own investigation, knowledge, information, belief, and judgment, and the advice of its own attorney in settling its claims and executing this Agreement.

7

Section 6.6. Counterpart Signatures. This Agreement may be executed in any number of multiple counterparts with the same effect as if the signatures thereto and hereto were upon the same instrument. Each such counterpart shall be deemed an original, but all of which together shall constitute one and the same instrument.

Section 6.7. Governing Law. This Agreement shall be governed by and interpreted in accordance with the laws of the State of California.

Section 6.8. Severability. If any provision of this Agreement is held invalid or unenforceable by any court of competent jurisdiction, the other provisions of this Agreement will remain in full force and effect. Any provision of this Agreement held invalid or unenforceable only in part or degree will remain in full force and effect to the extent not held invalid or unenforceable.

Section 6.9. Entire Agreement. This Agreement contains the entire agreement between the Parties with respect to the subject matter contained in this Agreement and supersedes all prior agreements and understandings, oral or written, between the Parties with respect to the subject matter contained in this Agreement.

Section 6.10. Successors and Assigns. This Agreement shall be binding upon and shall inure to the benefit of Benson, Tritown Bay, and TBI and their respective successors and assigns.

SIGNATURE PAGE FOLLOWS

8

IN WITNESS WHEREOF, each of Benson, Tritown Bay, and TBI has executed this Agreement to Settle Claims and Transfer Property, through its duly authorized representatives, as of the respective dates set forth below.

Benson Hospitality Group, LLC

BY: ______________________________
ITS:

Tritown Bay Investors, Inc.

BY: ______________________________
ITS:

TBI Golf & Resorts, LLC

BY: ______________________________
ITS:

9

SCHEDULE OF EXHIBITS

Exhibit A	2010 Promissory Note
Exhibit B	First Amendment to Deed of Trust

10

INDEX